Digital Storytelling and Ethics

Digital Storytelling and Ethics: Collaborative Creation and Facilitation provides a method for analyzing digital storytelling practices that focuses on the rhetorical, dialogic, co-productive, creative storymaking space rather than the finished stories or the technologies.

Looking through a new media lens, Amanda Hill situates the digital storytelling genre and writing practice as a co-creative media process created between writers, storytellers, educators/facilitators, institutions, and the audience, and discusses the inter-relationships within the collaborative writing workshop as well as in those found in the dissemination of the final digital stories. *Digital Storytelling and Ethics* provides a reflexive look at the responsibility of the facilitator in co-creative digital storytelling writing spaces and makes use of diverse international case studies as examples.

Hill shows that writing educators/facilitators should interpret their roles within the collaborative creation process. This will ensure that responsible facilitation practices based in witnessing guide the storytelling process and create an environment that treats participants as subjects with the ability to respond to the world. This innovative book is an essential read for collaborative digital writers and facilitators.

Amanda Hill is an Associate Professor of Communication Studies at St. Mary's University specializing in storytelling and media production. She holds a PhD in Texts and Technology from the University of Central Florida.

Routledge Studies in Creative Writing
Series Editors: Graeme Harper (Oakland University, USA) and Dianne Donnelly (University of South Florida, USA)

Strategies of Silence
Reflections on the Practice and Pedagogy of Creative Writing
Edited by Moy McCrory and Simon Heywood

Theories and Strategies for Teaching Creative Writing Online
Edited by Tamara Girardi and Abigail G. Scheg

Creative Writing Scholars on the Publishing Trade
Practice, Praxis, Print
Edited by Sam Meekings and Marshall Moore

The Rise of Creative Writing in Asia
Edited by Darryl Whetter

Depersonalization and Creative Writing
Unreal City
Matthew Francis

Digital Storytelling and Ethics
Collaborative Creation and Facilitation
Amanda Hill

For more information about this series, please visit: https://www.routledge.com/Routledge-Studies-in-Creative-Writing/book-series/RSCW

Digital Storytelling and Ethics
Collaborative Creation and Facilitation

Amanda Hill

LONDON AND NEW YORK

First published 2023

by Routledge
4 Park Square, Milton Park, Abingdon, Oxon OX14 4RN

and by Routledge
605 Third Avenue, New York, NY 10158

Routledge is an imprint of the Taylor & Francis Group, an informa business

© 2023 Amanda Hill

The right of Amanda Hill to be identified as author of this work has been asserted in accordance with sections 77 and 78 of the Copyright, Designs and Patents Act 1988.

All rights reserved. No part of this book may be reprinted or reproduced or utilised in any form or by any electronic, mechanical, or other means, now known or hereafter invented, including photocopying and recording, or in any information storage or retrieval system, without permission in writing from the publishers.

Trademark notice: Product or corporate names may be trademarks or registered trademarks, and are used only for identification and explanation without intent to infringe.

British Library Cataloguing-in-Publication Data
A catalogue record for this book is available from the British Library

Library of Congress Cataloging-in-Publication Data
Names: Hill, Amanda, 1988-author.
Title: Digital storytelling and ethics: collaborative creation and facilitation/ Amanda Hill.
Description: Abingdon, Oxon; New York, NY: Routledge, 2023. |
Series: Routledge studies in creative writing | Includes bibliographical references and index. |
Identifiers: LCCN 2022056653 (print) | LCCN 2022056654 (ebook) | ISBN 9781032061238 (hardback) | ISBN 9781032061252 (paperback) | ISBN 9781003200826 (ebook)
Subjects: LCSH: Authorship–Collaboration. | Creative writing. | Digital storytelling. | Writers' workshops.
Classification: LCC PN171.C65 H55 2023 (print) | LCC PN171.C65 (ebook) | DDC 808.042071–dc23/eng/20231119
LC record available at https://lccn.loc.gov/2022056653
LC ebook record available at https://lccn.loc.gov/2022056654

ISBN: 978-1-032-06123-8 (hbk)
ISBN: 978-1-032-06125-2 (pbk)
ISBN: 978-1-003-20082-6 (ebk)

DOI: 10.4324/9781003200826

Typeset in Sabon
by Deanta Global Publishing Services, Chennai, India

To R. C. H. who taught me to love stories and for his unwavering belief in me.

And to the storymakers working to bring diverse narratives to the forefront of our society. May we continue to find new perspectives and implications in unheard narratives and think responsibly about how best to share and analyze such stories to enrich the narrative tapestry of this world.

Contents

Foreword		viii
Acknowledgments		x
1	Introduction: Collaborative Storymaking and Ethical Facilitation	1
2	Contextualizing Personal Narratives: The Digital Storytelling Process	15
3	The Politics of Storytelling: Stakeholders in Collaborative Media Creation	43
4	Navigating Authenticity: Challenges and Considerations in Writing Personal Narratives	63
5	Who's Listening? The Audience as Stakeholder	78
6	Ethical Collaboration: The Responsible Facilitator in Theory	99
7	Ethical Collaboration: The Responsible Facilitator in Practice	119
8	Epilogue: Where Do We Go from Here?	143
	Index	153

Foreword

Every story matters. Every person is the expert on their own story; the story is theirs to tell. These are bedrock principles for digital storytelling facilitators in communities and campuses around the world. But those principles are complicated to sustain in practice. In intensive workshops or classes, where the story is the most visible product or outcome (because it may be publicly shared, because it receives an academic grade, and so on) it can be hard to remember we are facilitating, foremost, interpersonal relationships – witnessing, caring, listening – not just the making of narratives or videos. *Digital Storytelling and Ethics* helps us observe the various factors influencing the storyteller and the story they develop within a co-creative process, and it offers generative questions and practices to help us support the person as well as the story. Above all, this book asks us to interrogate our own assumptions – about teaching, about storytelling, and about those who join us for this process – because so often we are the influencer, intentionally or not.

Amanda Hill's Framework for Response-able Facilitation connects the dots between our understanding of the responsible facilitator in theory and the responsible facilitator in practice and it invites us to observe whether those two roles align in our own praxis. Responsible facilitation begins with our reflections and preparations long before the storytellers first enter the room (or screen) and it continues after the group shares their finished stories, as we maintain our commitments regarding informed consent and publication. For every phase on this continuum, *Digital Storytelling and Ethics* can be a touchstone for developing a more critically reflective practice.

Building upon the author's carefully curated collection of interdisciplinary scholarship, each chapter offers a deep dive into a dimension of storytelling that has more to teach us. We are challenged to recognize that "authenticity" is co-created, and to view even unknown viewers as stakeholders. We are reminded of Indigenous story work methodologies that train the researcher to be ready to listen, and we are introduced to critique processes that prioritize the storyteller-as-artist's ability to respond immediately to their audience. Students and professional researchers will appreciate the bibliographical foundation as much as the author's syntheses.

As this book goes to press, our community of practice is gearing up for the 11th International Digital Storytelling Conference in Washington, D.C., in 2023. This year will also mark the 30th anniversary of the first public digital storytelling workshop, which was facilitated at the American Film Institute in Los Angeles by the founders of the Center for Digital Storytelling, now called StoryCenter. My work on the conference committee includes an ongoing discussion about how to acknowledge the histories and legacies of digital storytelling while highlighting partnerships and practices that can inspire and equip our next generation of story workers. Whatever lies ahead, we know that a just future depends on the ethical, equitable, and inclusive exchange of stories – and the skill and courage to bring them to light. *Digital Storytelling and Ethics* is an invaluable resource for those who are new to the field, as well as for experienced practitioners who are ready to pause and let Professor Hill lead us to examine how and why we facilitate storytelling as we do, and then how we may do better. It is an essential guide to co-creativity through story.

Brooke Hessler
California College of the Arts
Scholar in Residence, StoryCenter

Acknowledgments

This book is about the creation of work in dialogic spaces, and I have felt a tremendous amount of gratitude to have spent time with people who are willing to enter such spaces with me. To the many people who helped bring this book to life, I am indebted, first and foremost, to all of the storytellers and community partners in the myriad digital storytelling (and other) projects I've conducted who have inspired me and made me curious about how I can constantly strive to better my facilitation techniques; to the digital storytelling community, who has continued to question how we continue to grow and has invited me into conversations about ethics, storymaking, and facilitation.

This work grew from my doctoral dissertation at the University of Central Florida. I will be forever grateful to Melody Bowdon, my dissertation adviser, who brought form and focus to my research, and who stood by my side from day one, willing to persevere with me through to the end; Shelley Park and Blake Scott who helped me craft theory; and countless others at UCF, including Rudy McDaniel, Natalie Underberg-Goode, Joey Fanfarelli, Patty Hurter, Anastasia Salter, and Mel Stanfill who problem solved writing and ideas with me over the years; I am so grateful for you all. At UCF, I was surrounded by inspiring intellectual conversations both in and out of the classroom, and I am equally grateful for the friendship and support of Mark Kretzschmar, Sara Raffel, and Eric Murnane while writing this dissertation.

Much of this work stems from work I conducted in the theatre world, I am also grateful for the many, many people who helped me hone my craft and skills to devise and create with others. First, the incomparable Wendy Harms, who took me under her wing at an early age and taught me to guide. I am so grateful for the decades of mentorship and friendship that continue to inspire how I interact with others and work in spaces of creation. I am grateful to those who gave me early opportunities to create new and exciting things with youth, especially Wendy Fay, Birgitta De Pree, and Jim Jackson, who helped me grow as a facilitator before I knew to call it that. I am equally grateful for the friendship and thoughtfulness of my colleagues

Rebecca Pate, Lilly Hastings, and Courtney Helen Grile who continue to push for community arts and the importance of coming together. Thank you for your unending willingness to talk through complicated ideas and for your commitment to bringing justice and art to the lives of many.

I came to digital storytelling through the luck of the powerful Diane Messina at Orlando Repertory Theatre who said to me one day, "you do computer stuff, right?" For opening that door, and countless others, I will be forever grateful. I was privileged to work with an incredible education team The REP, Gary Cadwallader, Stacey Perez, Emily Killian, and Emily Freeman who helped me evaluate and reflect on my work as a facilitator. I am also grateful for the opportunity to work with thoughtful theatre practitioners during this time, including, Elizabeth Brendel Horn, Vandy Wood, Julia Listengarten, Jonathan Jackson, Jenn Adams, Lucy Lynn Bryson, and Brandon Yagel, who worked with me onstage and off to find the best ways to engage with a community, to ask questions, and to devise new works.

I am been honored to become part of a robust international digital storytelling community. I am deeply grateful for the collegiality and friendship of Brooke Hessler who continues to inspire this work and who saw me through early versions of this work on my dissertation committee; for the dedication of Joe Lambert who has been so generous in sharing his story with me and for his unending commitment to community arts, civic engagement, and story work; and for the many others who have worked to help me understand the challenges and opportunities of digital storytelling including Amy Hill, Parul Wadhwa, Rob Kershaw, Marie Lovejoy, Janet Ferguson, Mark Silver, Xanthe Golenko, Dagmar Wallenstorfer, and countless others too numerous to mention. I am grateful to have a community so dedicated to story and who champions stories and storytellers around the world.

I have been lucky to walk many different trails in my life and I have been grateful to find teams of people who have supported and bolstered my work in this field along the way; from sparking new ideas about how best to work with others, the power of stories, and the importance of dialogue to harboring a furious writer who needed a quiet place to work. Much gratitude is given for my Youth Documentary Academy team, especially Tom Shepard, Eric Risher, Mona Adelgren, Karen Walldorf, Kathy Stults, and Mari Moxley, who have given me the respect of response-ability and provided me a home and a place to tell stories with youth that challenge my own, and I hope, others' preconceived notions. I am equally grateful for the unending support, friendship, and deep commitment to care and strength of my Girl Scouts of Alaska family, especially Amanda Block, Kelly FitzGerald, and Marnie Stewart; working here has helped me hone the ability to develop safe spaces no matter the location, endeared in me the importance of intentionality and character, and prepared me to problem solve and adapt in any task I undertake.

This book was finished at St. Mary's University, who has welcomed me into the fold and entrusted me to be an ethical facilitator of their students.

I would not be where I am today, or who I am today, without the support and mentorship of Bill Israel and Eileen Breslin, who took me in, sight unseen, and have continued to push me to be and do the best I can. Your kindness and generosity mean the world to me. I entered into a thoughtful, intellectual community at St. Mary's and I am grateful for my colleagues in the Communication Studies department, Camille Langston, Kathe Lehman-Meyer, Katherine Hampsten, Dennis Bautista, and Jeff Schomburg, as well as Lindsey Wieck, Sue Nash, Betsy Smith, Allison Gray, Sara Ronis, and Juan O'Campo who helped me grow into my role and continue to champion anti-racist, ethical pedagogy, which continues to inspire me. My research at St. Mary's has been supported by an Internal Faculty Research Grant and an Edward and Linda Speed Faculty Development and Research Grant. For these, and the myriad other ways the university and its family have supported me, I will be forever grateful.

I am further grateful to Heather Lundine who helped me strengthen and develop the tone of this work and my friends and family who have stood alongside me since the beginning of this journey and who made themselves available to talk through opportunities and challenges of my research and writing. I am especially grateful for my father, Bob Hill, who has always pushed me to find optimism, curiosity, and responsibility in all my endeavors and whose continued support has propelled me to where I am today. Thank you for reading every version of every chapter, editing every article, and watching every play and film. I would not be who I am without you. To all of you, I am deeply grateful for your words of encouragement, reflection, and advice, for helping me continue to move forward with grit, gratitude, and self-control. I would not be where I am today if it were not for the resilience, zest, and optimism you have brought into my life. My sincerest gratitude.

1 Introduction
Collaborative Storymaking and Ethical Facilitation

Introduction

In a seminal work on digital storytelling, Jean Burgess wrote that digital storytelling workshops fashioned in the StoryCenter style enable "the production of elegant, high-impact stories by people with little or no experience, *with minimal direct intervention by the workshop facilitator*" (207) (emphasis mine). In the years since I have begun developing and conducting digital storytelling workshops, I have come to question what "minimal direct intervention" means and what it looks like in the workshop. I have spent so much time questioning it, in fact, that I've come to write this book about the ways in which the facilitator can affect the personal narratives created through digital storytelling workshops. Specifically, this book examines the co-productive relationship that exists in digital storytelling writing spaces and the communicative interactions that take place therein. Unlike many of the existing works that examine digital storytelling practices, this book will provide a method for analyzing these practices that focuses on the rhetorical, dialogic, co-productive, creative storymaking space rather than the finished stories or technologies. By analyzing the collaborative relationships within these writing spaces in connection with concepts of politics and authenticity, we can inform future digital storytelling and other collaborative writing research and practices.

This book is set up to address the different political aspects of collaboration within a digital storytelling workshop. It contends with the relationships of the individual to society, the individual to audience, the individual to other workshop participants, and the individual to the facilitator. Each chapter takes on a different concern about the ways in which such social relationships impact individual decision making. Digital storytelling, as an overarching term, can encompass a range of meanings beginning with a broad understanding where all "mediatized" stories, those stories told using digital media and media-based storytelling methods and practices, are included. Understood in this way, the term can encompass diverse storytelling platforms including video games, video essays, and social media posts, all of which can make use of the tenets of storytelling

DOI: 10.4324/9781003200826-1

in digital spaces using digital tools. Inside this large umbrella of digital storytelling is a genre and movement of storytelling stemming from the work of StoryCenter, formerly the Center for Digital Storytelling, also identified as "digital storytelling." StoryCenter, headquartered in Berkley, California, is the originator of both the genre and storymaking methodology. The genre is noted for its use of accessible software to tell short autobiographical narratives through video. As the root of digital storytelling focuses on stories only the participants can tell, or stories that are personal to them, my research centers on the idea of personal narratives created collaboratively, especially addressing practices and instances of digital storytelling. A personal narrative is a story told by the person who lived the events and experiences described within the story. For the purposes of this work, the terms story and narrative will be used interchangeably, and their understanding need not be any more complicated than would be expected in their everyday use. When used in this work, "digital storytelling" will specifically refer to the genre and storymaking process defined by StoryCenter.

This book is part research monograph and part practical guide. It takes an active look at the practices conducted by a digital storytelling facilitator. A digital storytelling facilitator will wear many hats throughout a program. They are part teaching-artist and part guide, and are often viewed as the experts in the workshop space. At different moments in time, they may serve as an educator, audience, community builder, artist, scholar, and researcher. They will support quality assurance, manage technical difficulties, and guide the learning of genre and technologies. Digital storytelling facilitators come to the practice from all walks of life. Several of us arrived through the theatre and through education; many others arrived through writing, visual arts, and community engagement. More have found their way to digital storytelling through myriad other means. This book will understand the term facilitator as someone who wears many hats and utilizes different approaches within the digital storytelling space. It will also understand the facilitator as the person guiding the creative path for digital storytellers. That is, the facilitator, for the purposes of this book, is examined only when they are in the digital storytelling workshop. While it is true that many facilitators will also host or fund digital storytelling workshops, these practices will be considered as separate entities, for even if they are conducted by a single person, that person is wearing many more hats than just those worn by the facilitator within the digital storytelling workshop. Throughout this work, I will use the terms educator, facilitator, expert, and researcher interchangeably to identify the facilitator and to best understand what hat that person might be wearing at the time. The terms participant and storyteller will also be used interchangeably to identify the people creating digital stories within the workshops.

The practices employed by digital storytelling facilitators are political and reflexive, connecting aspects of both the private (individual) and the public (social) with objective as subjective characteristics. As Stephen Kemmis and Mervyn Wilkinson write, this perspective

> understand[s] practice as enacted by individuals who act in the context of history and in ways constituted by a vast, historical web of social interactions between people ... [and] as having both objective (externally given) and subjective (internally understood and interpreted) aspects, both of which are necessary to understand how any practice is really practised, and how it is constituted historically and socially, and how it can be transformed if people critically transform what they do to enact the practice, transform the way it is understood and transform the situations in which they practice.
>
> (31)

By contextualizing practice as something that happens in a social context, we can understand practice as political, and by understanding how practice is complicated by objective and subjective components, we can understand a need for reflexivity within practice. By considering how our work as digital storytelling facilitators is political and collaborative, we can craft a reflexive approach to create more response-able facilitation practices.

My Personal Connection to This Book

I am drawn to digital storytelling because it privileges the everyday voices and perspectives of those involved in co-productive, participatory writing practices. I come to this work from a long history of working in the creative arts, especially creative writing, performing arts, and digital media. A through-line in my research, however, has always been the telling of everyday stories by ordinary people, what Jean Burgess calls "vernacular creativity" (205). The initial attraction to vernacular creativity stems from my interests in storytelling, performance, personal narratives, authorship, the arts, community education, cultural and historical memory, and social change as well as my experience writing, devising, and facilitating the creation of original works in a variety of multimodal media.

I also come to this research from a continuing interest in digital storytelling as a space for everyday community voices to be heard and valued. Over the past several years I have facilitated numerous digital storytelling workshops as well as other community arts programs, and in that time have learned to reflect on the importance of my presence in the workshop space. Often, I have been an outsider to the communities in which I've worked, which has impacted the ways in which I related and spoke to the people within the workshop. I have become increasingly cognizant of how my actions and words influence the stories shared and created in these workshops and continuously strive to ensure the participants' voices are heard above my own in these projects.

I was introduced to digital storytelling in 2010, when the Orlando Repertory Theatre (The REP), a professional theatre company in Orlando, Florida, approached me about connecting ideas of performing arts to video narratives. Since that time, I have worked with many populations in Florida and Texas to create digital storytelling projects with people of all ages, predominately within systems of education and community engagement. My facilitation skills are based on applied theatre practices where I learned to approach collaborative storymaking with a consideration for the collective company, individual members, institutional stakeholders, and the audience. My skills in facilitating the tools and technologies needed to edit the digital narratives come from personal interest and scholarship in digital media narratives such as film and games. Additional facilitation skills have come from training work done in partnership with Essential Partners and through experience training staff for, and running, summer camp programs. I have received professional training in the art of digital storytelling facilitation through StoryCenter and have additionally taken other digital storytelling workshops with the company. As such, my understanding of the genre and underlying ideologies about the benefits of digital storytelling are rooted in their work. I have further acquired relevant skills through experiential learning, reading, and watching the media ecology of other digital stories, and I recognize that holding graduate degrees and teaching and researching within an academic setting have influenced the ways in which I approach my facilitation practices and my approach to writing this book.

This text is informed by a foundation in community engagement specifically through work with youth and adults in extracurricular activities including afterschool and summer programming including arts programs such as digital storytelling and theatre and camp. I come to this work after several years of conducting digital storytelling work based on the format and genre outlined by StoryCenter. In all my community and institutional practices, I foremost work to honor the person as an individual and attempt to meet individuals where they are, rather than assume an individual's knowledge and experience match my own or that there is a singular collective group knowledge or experience. I recognize that individuals come from a variety of backgrounds – be they racial or ethnic, social, political, economic, religious, or otherwise. Recognizing and including diverse individuals is a key to any work within any community, as is recognizing my place within or outside of the same community. A facilitator's interaction within such a community is wholly dependent on their own background and experience and those of the individuals within that community.

I identify as an artist, scholar, and educator, and move between and combine these roles. These monikers suit me well within the digital storytelling workshop space. I believe that a digital storytelling facilitator embraces both the artist and the educator (and depending on the specific project, can also embrace the scholar). Artist and educator are key practices at the heart of digital storytelling facilitation. As I work to navigate how to wear both of these hats under the guise of a larger one (that of facilitator), I arrive at tensions in the way in which I practice as a facilitator, which leads me to question what the balance is between arts and instruction in my workshop setting, and what constitutes as "minimal direct involvement."

My experiences led to the formation of the research questions that inform this work:

- How does the role of the facilitator affect the creative practices of the participants?
- How can we understand the practices of a facilitator as both arts- and education-based and embrace these qualities to engage participants responsibly?
- How can we value diverse perspectives and experiences within the workshop space?
- How does a facilitator guide digital storytellers through the process of story creation in ways that embrace and activate the storyteller's own artistic aesthetic and voice?
- How might a facilitator impact this guidance so that it opens storytellers' subjectivity rather than limit it?
- How do facilitators contend with entering spaces mired in previously developed systems and hierarchies of power that affect the participants, facilitator, and the relationship between the two?
- How is digital storytelling situated as a collaborative art, and how do we reflect as a group and as facilitators on this collaboration throughout the workshop experience?

Facilitators are one influence on the storymaking process, yet they are not the only influence on storytellers. Three main situations in which interaction occurs within the digital storytelling process shape the ways in which storytellers define and share their narratives: The digital storytelling creation workshop, the end-of-workshop screening of the short films, and the dissemination of the stories in online platforms and public venues. The relationships among the storytellers, the facilitators, the other workshop participants, and the viewing audience are all critical spaces of engagement and are, therefore, similarly impacted by the context in which they were created. Examining diverse co-productive media endeavors, reveals breakdowns in the digital storytelling model within the creation space.

By thinking about the storymaking space in terms of communicative interactions and relationships and thereby in terms of the processes enabled and formed in the contexts of these relationships, we begin to see how co-creative media necessitates a space of responsible facilitation. Individuals involved in digital storytelling or other co-creative media practices geared toward social change and aiming to renegotiate the power of everyday voices should address how to make responsible, collaborative storymaking practices. The time has come to understand co-creative storymaking spaces as collaborative practices where everyday storytellers with specific and diverse perspectives and stories work in relationship with workshop facilitators in a process of deconstructing, reconstructing, and constructing power structures with an eye toward eliminating oppression and marginalization, fostering agency, and creating more equitable and just power dynamics. For this reason, a framework is needed to analyze the collaborative process of such storymaking experiences, especially as personal narratives are creative dialogically. I propose facilitators use a Framework for Response-able Facilitation.

A Framework of Response-able Facilitation

Response-able facilitation is asset- and experience-based to affirm the culture, values, and perspectives of all participants. It works to decrease the effects of those hierarchical pedagogical practices focused on the expertise of the leader to bring a greater power to the collaboration that occurs in the digital storytelling workshop, and derives its name from Kelly Oliver's "response-ability" – the ability to respond to and to be responded by others. This framework recognizes and names the ways in which digital storytelling is co-constructed as a way to empower, first and foremost, the voice of the storyteller.

The goal of response-able facilitation is ultimately that future digital storytelling practices can develop from within, rather than continuing to require the oversight of an outside facilitator. While this may not happen overnight, it is important that the framework teaches sustainability. Yes, this means that in one sense, those of us leading digital storytelling workshops are eliminating the need for our own jobs. What the growth of StoryCenter has shown us over the last 30 years is the flexibility of multimodal storytelling. Their organization has become increasingly relevant and necessary, even as they teach others to support their own digital storytelling workshops. They amplify voices across the world through digital storytelling and more and more in practices like podcasting and virtual/augmented reality, and they continue to find more people with whom to work. Your own journey as a facilitator will depend on your own values, goals, and experiences. A commitment to providing the tools and techniques for sustainability in a community should not hinder this journey for you. Rather, a commitment to sustainability values the growth of the community in the same way it values a growth in your own career. It prioritizes the act of change, moving us past a mere recognition that change is needed for a system that privileges expertise and hegemony.

A framework of response-able facilitation asks us to first interrogate and name our own assumptions and values about facilitation, and to pay particular attention to those ideals that we have come to believe are beyond dispute. It asks us to question our previous practices as well as the belief systems that guided them. We should examine these for the ways in which the practices have reinforced and succeeded because of hegemonic privilege and the benefits they provide those who prosper from such privilege. Then, we can work to dismantle such privileges and hierarchy within collaborative creation spaces like digital storytelling workshops. Examining, naming, and changing these practices are difficult tasks for those of us who have benefited from the hegemonic narratives and narrative structure of mainstream media as well as the pedagogy practices that prioritize teaching those with privilege. Furthermore, it can be difficult to call into question the values, assumptions, and structures that have formulated our sense of who we are as artists, writers, and facilitators. It can be especially difficult if it feels like our facilitation practices are the "way it's always been done." To truly create a systemic change in facilitation, we should be open and selfless in our ability to call out and cast out any and all practices that operate within a system of power and privilege. This isn't an easy task. We have to approach this work with a willingness and bravery.

How do we begin to deconstruct our own beliefs around facilitation? The answer is twofold. We should interrogate our beliefs about what makes a narrative and how we approach pedagogy. We first need to stretch and diversify our understanding of narrative structures and storytelling approaches as well as the way in which we choose to value storytellers' voices. Then we should contend with the pedagogical practices we saw in our own educational experiences as well as those (if any) that we have been formally taught. We should recognize the assumptions and values that underlie and are embedded within these pedagogical practices and interrogate these practices to consider whom they privilege. Thus, we are charged with acknowledging and enlarging our world view as they directly relate to these two areas. For instance, when we start thinking about narrative we might begin by asking questions such as: What have I learned to be a "good" storytelling structure? What have I learned to be the "correct" use of language? What have I learned to be "correct" composition practices for multimodal media? What makes a narrative "standard"? What narratives do I believe are appropriate to share in the workshop? What narratives do I believe are atypical or divergent? How does this affect my attitude toward such narratives? Likewise, we might begin to question our uncontested notions of pedagogy (whether formal or otherwise) by asking ourselves: What pedagogical practices have I normalized? How do I engage and communicate (verbally and non-verbally) with my workshop participants? How do I care for participants and keep them "safe" within the workshop and what does safety mean to me? What do I do to ensure participants feel like they are free to take risks, express themselves, and share with others? How do I "correct" participants' behavior, narratives, and techniques? What do I believe is appropriate communication practice amongst participants? What are my assumptions about the participants' assets, composition experiences, and media backgrounds? How do my values about narrative come through in my pedagogy?

These questions are just an appetizer. There are myriad additional questions we could ask ourselves as we reflect, name, and interrogate our previously conceived notions about narrative and pedagogy. And asking ourselves these questions is just a start of the process. We should follow this reflection with another reflection focused on considering our answers in a new light. How might my typical practices be seen as problematic? How might my beliefs and practices alienate participants from fully participating? Who is privileged? Who is hurt? What would happen if I broaden my definitions of "good," "correct," and "successful"? In what ways am I trying to "improve" my participants and what/who does this "improvement" privilege and benefit? What happens when I implicate narrative strategies that go beyond Western hierarchies? What values, principles, and practices did I previously believe to be universal? How can I embrace voices, perspectives, and experiences with which I am less familiar or those with which I don't agree? Why do I value and give import to how my pedagogical approaches inhibit or advance participants' agency? Can I eliminate any rules, values, or beliefs to promote and amplify participants' voice and creativity? What can I do "better" and what values inform my understanding of better? Interrogating our values and practices will help us move our facilitation processes beyond those that privilege the things that we hold as sacred, traditional, and correct. It allows us to invest in narratives and practices that go beyond that to which we are accustomed to see those things that might otherwise remain unseen.

Understanding the Principles behind a Framework of Response-ability

Digital storytelling is a multimedia compositional practice wherein storytellers create narratives using filmic techniques. Its origin "was informed by the traditions of community arts and community-based media practices representing a half-century of social activist, grassroots arts making" (Hessler and Lambert 23). Even at its inception, digital storytelling operated as a political medium. It sought to engage the individual as a critical practitioner of their own political landscape. As Brooke Hessler and Joe Lambert write,

> A central aspect of these perspectives was conscientization, the ability of the learner/storyteller to grasp their own metacognitive process within the context of their social situation (Freire 1970). This underscores why digital storytelling has always been, at heart, an approach that is potentially transformative rather than narrowly instrumental.
>
> (ibid.)

The practice originated with five principles. These principles are outlined by Lambert, one of the founders of the Center for Digital Storytelling (now StoryCenter) in his reflection of the genre, "Where It All Started" (86–87):

1. "Everyone has a story to tell"
2. People will share stories when they have the opportunity
3. "There is no formula for making a great story"
4. Anyone can tell a story creatively
5. Learning digital literacy can promote growth and opportunity for the individual

From these beginnings, we can see that digital storytelling has a long tradition of operating with the goal of helping individuals understand their public and social connections to the world.

Over the last several decades, the literature on digital storytelling is significant and expanding rapidly. The seminal text, *Digital Storytelling: Capturing Lives, Creating Community*, now in its sixth edition with a new title *Digital Storytelling: Story Work for Urgent Times*, addresses the emergence and growth of the digital storytelling genre and its application. It additionally guides readers through the workshop facilitation process. Additional works and anthologies augment this text by successfully showcasing the benefits, areas of opportunity, and practices of digital storytelling in different cultural contexts for diverse purposes such as education, empowerment, health, and anthropology. These texts present an international scope of digital storytelling residencies and practice, yet recently, scholars have critiqued digital storytelling literature as not taking into consideration the systematic and structural forces that can impact the stories that get told through digital storytelling workshops and the ways in which the stories get told and shared (Hill; Rice and Mündel). This work aims to remedy this disconnect from the literature. As a movement, digital storytelling has further been criticized for an increased focus of hyperindividualism (Freund), as well as their assumed ability to reach large audience (Hartley; Hartley and McWilliam), and their assumed potential to make a political difference (Dreher). It has further been critiqued for its dependence on significant funding and technological resources (Jenkins) and its often "one-and-done" community interventions (Jenkins; Clarke). To some extent, this work will address each of these critiques, although it will focus more on the systematic and structural forces impacting the workshops. Rather, this book will utilize theoretical and practical frameworks from many of the previously written texts, and will expand these theories to include an educator/facilitator perspective that has been largely absent in the majority of the books on digital storytelling.

This book examines the process of writing, creating, and sharing digital stories in spaces of media-driven performance and products created from those story sharing experiences, with specific focus on the personal narratives created in the digital storytelling genre. A variety of variables influence the workshop such as the physical space; the project's hosting institutions; additional stakeholder institutions (including, often, the ones funding the project); the activities facilitators use to encourage creativity, collaboration, and communication; the community within which facilitators work; the location in which the workshop is held; and the principles and requirements of storytelling in the "traditional" sense. At the heart of this book is a consideration of the ways in which personal narratives are told through the genre and how others in the creation process complicate understandings of what it means to be "personal." It approaches personal narratives with the theory that the personal is public (Arendt) and because of this, those involved in the creation process of personal narratives need to contend with the ethical implications of their involvement in the creative writing process. This book begins with an examination of these politics, then delves into how these politics work to complicate our understandings of authentic personal narratives. It then appraises the ways in which those involved in the telling of personal narratives, especially digital storytelling facilitators, can operate with an awareness of the ways in which their communication and actions can influence the finished narrative.

In this work, I emphasize certain principles that inform any successful creative writing endeavor. These principles include collaboration, "response-ability" (Oliver), communication, space and place, and reflexivity. The book addresses each of these principles and considers how they work individually and interrelatedly to enhance and support the success of digital storytelling work. Above all, this work considers how these principles play into constructions of power and expertise when producing creative writing collaboratively through media production and, often, between strangers. What can we gain by working with others to tell stories through digital storytelling? Who has the right to tell stories? What can we learn from others? Where is it appropriate to step back and where do we need to step forward? These questions, and many more, advise the ways we each step into collaborative writing spaces, and how we do so ethically and responsibly so as to enhance the path for the writers' voices to reach larger audiences.

The themes addressed in this book provide a combination of ethics, personal narratives, facilitation, and creative writing to support the creation of personal narratives through digital storytelling. These themes include:

- Surveying the complexity of responsibility in collaborative creative writing practices
- Considering the relationship between ourselves as artists/scholars/educators/facilitators and as artistic collaborators
- Weighing the interaction of the past and present of our lives with those of our students and of the communities in which we interact
- Appraising our theories and practices as community practitioners and as facilitators with reflexivity and an openness to change

I base my research in an understanding of both facilitation and storytelling as political entities, shaped and framed culturally and socially on and in large and small scales and contexts. These factors are of great importance because digital storytelling is a creative writing practice that serves as sites of co-production between writers and facilitators, all of which are couched in larger cultural and institutional practices. My interest in collaborative storytelling work as a political site, stems from my personal experiences. The role and importance of the facilitator in the co-collaborative environment of digital storytelling is the critical reason why I am interested in the creative process. While I want storytellers' unique voices to shine, it's important not to disown the collaborative process entirely. If we understand that all stories are created in dialogue, in communicative practices among diverse people, then we can see that guidelines are needed to work within the process of creative writing for digital storytelling and the rhetorical, dialogic activities that happen within that space for the purpose of ensuring that storytellers guide and/or are thoughtful participants of the creative process.

Engaging facilitators in an approach to co-creative writing practices built on a responsibility of ethics is important to the future of the digital storytelling genre and creative writing practices as a whole. A thorough review of each facet of media ethics is outside the scope of this work. I focus here on addressing the ways co-creative writing, especially the co-creative forces inherent in the relationship between the digital storytelling facilitator and the storyteller, operate in an ethics of responsibility. Still, this is a wide and expanding conversation, and this work will not address the entire scope of ethics involved in this relationship. Further research could be conducted, for instance, on the ethics of responsibility in co-creative storytelling practices with a specific focus on survivors of trauma and vulnerable populations. While I hope that much of the groundwork I lay in this work will prove useful for this subsequent research, I additionally recognize that there are special considerations that will need to be included in that specific ethical structure to account for the potential re-traumatizing or creating secondary trauma for participants. Ultimately, I believe the questions with which I engage in this work and the concerns I raise go beyond digital storytelling and can be expanded to include any space where writers create narratives in the presence of, or in conjunction with, others.

By interpreting their roles within the collaborative creation process, digital storytelling facilitators can ensure that responsible practices guide the storytelling process and can create an environment that treats participants as subjects with the ability to respond to the world. In so doing, facilitators can challenge the power dynamics of authorship and the expert paradigm commonly found in teacher/student and researcher/participant relationships to include citizen-storytellers as meaning-makers and change-agents within digital storytelling initiatives.

Conclusion

As someone who takes the time to examine story through both artistic and scholarly endeavors, it is important to me that I identify as both an artist and an educator, and that both of these perspectives on narrative work come into my work within the learning and collaboration space. I know I still have a lot to learn and recognize that my perspectives on narrative and story creation have been formulated through a strongly Caucasian, Western lens. I often return to Aristotle's beginning, middle, and end – a three-act structure – to situate story within my workshops and often ask my participants to do the same. While this is not a hard and fast rule, and I remain open to other narrative structures and other storytelling methods, I have found that the populations with whom I have worked have been able to easily recognize and comprehend the three-act structure due to their own consumption of Western media. I find that students also often recognize the structure of Joseph Campbell's Hero's Journey within their media consumption. The brevity of a digital story easily lends itself to the need for a highly structured and narrowly framed narrative. This genre is designed to allow the audience to enter into a person's experience and understand something about that experience within a three-to-five-minute time frame. Often, digital storytelling facilitators, especially those who have had guidance from StoryCenter, will ask participants to focus their story on a single moment of a past experience. Following a specific moment creates the spine for a comprehensive, cohesive, and efficient narrative. Yet, these moments are still often couched within the Aristotelian three-act structure and to some degree, within the idea of the hero's journey. That is, personal digital stories often mark a noticeable change within the protagonist's journey. The moments chosen to expand upon within the narrative are tied to the growth of that person. Such growth, in the perspective of the hero's journey and in the tradition of Western narratives, offers the audience a narrative to which they can relate and easily recognize. It makes the story more "tellable," an idea we will discuss further in Chapter 3. Yet, as a facilitator, I struggle to find the balance between my own ideas about what makes a story "tellable," and it is this very struggle that leads me to write this book.

I do not mean to imply in this work that the facilitator should completely remove themselves from the storymaking process in order to ensure that the participant has total control over the telling of her narrative. Rather, facilitators' experience with creative writing and using multimedia tools and technologies frequently serves as a useful guide for participants. However, concerns arise when facilitators do not allow participants to shape the stories as the storytellers' desire. If a digital storytelling facilitator intends to facilitate responsibly, they should reflect on their own goals and agendas as a researcher and consider how their dialogic practices within the digital storytelling workshop space affect the participants. Ultimately, I find that it is impractical and perhaps unethical to study digital storytelling or any co-creative writing practice without consideration for the active presence of the facilitator, the institution, the other participants, and the audience in the finished texts.

Additionally, many of us, myself included, should contend with our privilege as facilitators, especially when it manifests in ways that look like White knight syndrome, that is, when it manifests in a way that presupposes we are capable of saving others because they *need* to be saved. In digital storytelling, I sometimes see that as a presumption that we can "give voice" to others or that our projects are the only way for their stories to be heard. Rather, by contending with our unique privileges, perspectives, and subject-position, we create the opportunity to enable response-ability and meet our storytellers where they are as individuals and as members of diverse communities. Therefore, this work is not meant to provide a single process that will work with every community. Presuming that each community is waiting for someone to save them presupposes that this community would not, all things being equal, be able to conduct this same work on their own. While I feel that my principles can inform the work we conduct in diverse communities, it is impossible to prescribe a one-size-fits-all application for people to take forward into every engagement. Rather, these principles should be adapted to meet the needs of each community and should be considered in every circumstance in which a media production facilitator goes in to meet with a community member.

My hope is that this book will invite dialogue on the practices and communicative interactions of the digital storytelling facilitator to consider how we might best conduct ourselves within co-creative, compositional settings through a Framework of Response-able Facilitation.

References

Arendt, Hannah. *The Human Condition*. 2nd ed., University of Chicago Press, 1998.

Burgess, Jean. "Hearing Ordinary Voices: Cultural Studies, Vernacular Creativity and Digital Storytelling." *Continuum: Journal of Media and Cultural Studies*, vol. 20, no. 2, 2006, pp. 201–214.

Dreher, Tanja. "A Partial Promise of Voice: Digital Storytelling and the Limits of Listening." *Media International Australia*, vol. 142, no. 1, 2012, pp. 157–166.

Freund, Alexander. "Under Storytelling's Spell? Oral History in a Neoliberal Age." *Oral History Review*, vol. 42, no. 1, 2015, pp. 96–132.

Hartley, John. "Problems of Expertise and Scalability in Self Made Media." *Digital Storytelling, Mediatized Stories: Self-Representations in New Media*, edited by Knut Lundby, Peter Lang, 2009, pp. 197–212.

Hartley, John, and Kelly McWilliam, editors. *Story Circle: Digital Storytelling around the World*. Wiley-Blackwell, 2009.

Hessler, Brooke, and Joe Lambert. "Threshold Concepts in Digital Storytelling: Naming What We Know about Storywork." *Digital Storytelling in Higher Education: International Perspectives*, edited by Grete Jamissen, Pip Hardy, Yngve Nordkvelle, and Heather Pleasants, Palgrave Macmillan, 2017, pp. 19–36.

Hill, Amy. "Digital Storytelling and the Politics of Doing Good: Exploring the Ethics of Bringing Personal Narratives into Public Spheres." *Community-Based Multiliteracies and Digital Media Projects: Questioning Assumptions and*

Exploring Realities, edited by Heather M. Pleasants and Dana E. Salter, Peter Lang, 2014, pp. 21–43.

Jenkins, Tricia. "Ageing Narratives: Embedding Digital Storytelling Within the Higher Education Curriculum of Health and Social Care with Older People." *Digital Storytelling in Higher Education: International Perspectives*, edited by Grete Jamissen, Pip Hardy, Yngve Nordkvelle, and Heather Pleasants, Palgrave Macmillan, 2017, pp. 261–277.

Kemmis, Stephen, and Mervyn Wilkinson. "Participatory Action Research and the Study of Practice." *Action Research in Practice: Partnership for Social Justice in Education*, edited by Bill Atweh, Stephen Kemmis, and Patricia Weeks, Taylor Francis, 1998, pp. 21–36.

Lambert, Joe. "Where It All Started." *Story Circle: Digital Storytelling around the World*, edited by John Hartley, and Kelly McWilliam, Wiley-Blackwell, 2009, pp. 79–90.

Lambert, Joe, and H. Brooke Hessler. *Digital Storytelling: Story Work for Urgent Times*. 6th ed., Digital Diner Press, 2020.

Oliver, Kelly. *Witnessing: Beyond Recognition*. University of Minnesota Press, 2001.

Rice, Carla, and Ingrid Mündel. "Multimedia Storytelling Methodology: Notes on Access and Inclusion in Neoliberal Times." *Canadian Journal of Disability Studies*, vol. 8, no. 1, 2019, pp. 118–148.

2 Contextualizing Personal Narratives
The Digital Storytelling Process

Introduction to Digital Storytelling

There are many ways people can and do share stories: In their everyday conversations and oral storytelling practices, through social media, and within other familial or global and local community contexts. Digital storytelling emerged as a genre in the early 1990s "from a diverse lineage of cultural production, among which we could include home video, photoessays, [etc.]" (Fletcher and Cambre 114). This lineage allows digital storytelling to have a broad range of meaning, encompassing a wide variety of frameworks ranging from small-scale narratives to large video game productions, yet within this work, the terms refer distinctly to the short personal videos created using readily available tools that require no special authority to access. Digital stories of this nature are often very short, only three to five minutes in length, and frequently depict personal narratives. The genre is attributed to the founders of California's San Francisco Digital Media Center, which became a well-established entity under the name The Center for Digital Storytelling, and is known today as StoryCenter. The concise writing and audio/visual style of the narrative format that makes up the StoryCenter genre of digital storytelling is the product of a collaborative workshop experience based in empowering citizen voices through a combination of artistic practices and computer literacy and digital media training.

Creating digital stories in a workshop setting strengthened by a collaborative process and often far-reaching institutional support impacts the development and potential reach of a narrative. Additionally, the highly developed and structured compactness of the digital story makes it a popular and easily produced genre that can be shared individually or as a collection. The genre is recognized for its concise narrative format that highlights a singular event, typically told in two to three minutes, and makes use of easy-to-use, off-the-shelf software like iMovie, WeVideo, or Windows Movie Maker, which allow storytellers to create short, personal narratives by "creatively using and recombining easy-to-access elements of 'traditional' or common media such as photographs, films, music, or text" from found digital objects and personal archives (Helff and Woletz 135). An author can make meaning

DOI: 10.4324/9781003200826-2

through the composition of their chosen assets within and between these audio and visual layers. Renowned digital storytelling practitioner Daniel Meadows notes the genre and method of digital storytelling has "roots in community arts and oral history" and "stretches from pre-literacy cultural traditions" (191). Because this stylized genre can be created with a variety of different technologies and software, facilitators can bring portable devices such as iPads to communities or make use of existing technologies within the community to facilitate story creation. One power of the digital story is the potential for circulation. The videos created within these workshops are short and digital, two key factors that allow for an easier spread across digital networks.

Digital storytelling workshops often begin with a process called story circles to elicit stories authors may want to tell. Then participants write their narratives, gather and choose audio-visual assets, create a storyboard, and assemble their digital stories. Often, stories will be shared among participants and facilitators several times in follow-up story circles as works in progress, allowing authors to reflect on the ways in which audiences hear their stories. Feedback can then be incorporated into the editing process. After the editing process is complete, many digital storytelling workshops end in a final celebration to share their created stories with participants' communities. In certain circumstances, the stories are then shared or published digitally and/or in physical galleries to broaden their reach.

The Emergence of Digital Storytelling

The genre and workshop process evolved out of a collaboration between StoryCenter founders Joe Lambert and Dana Atchley while at work on Atchley's theatrical and multimedia work called *Next Exit* and draws on Atchley's work in visual and video arts over the previous three decades. Digital storytelling scholar John Hartley links the process of digital storytelling to Atchley's original film work in the 1970s and 1980s, arguing that digital storytelling extends from these works and is

> based loosely on independent film practice, in a tradition going back to Lenny Lipton in the 1970s and to the film workshop movement in British independent cinema ... where individuals produce work for distribution via festivals or cultural institutions. This is an artist+festival model, often with a radically democratized notion of 'artist.'
> (Hartley 200)

Coming from a theatre background myself, I draw inspiration from the ways in which the genre itself grew out of Atchley's theatrical and video work.

Atchley began his career as a printmaker and visual artist before moving to "assemblings" (artist magazines) and finally to digital storytelling (Fimrite; Saper 139). He earned his bachelor's degree from Dartmouth

College in 1962 and his master's from Yale University in 1965 (Ibid.). Upon graduating, he taught at the Maryland Institute of Art and later at the University of Victoria. In 1969, the same year he moved to the University of Victoria, Atchley began a new art project, ushering in what was to become the mail art[1] movement. He invited people across the world to contribute a mimeograph-able work of up to ten pages for a collective artwork he was "assembling" (Saper). Harden notes, "Participants were asked to make 250 copies of each contribution and in return each of the contributors received two copies of everyone's work, assembled in a three-ring notebook binder." Atchley's "Space Atlas" took two years to complete and included material from 120 different contributors.[2] He created the works in binders so "if people didn't like it they could turn the page, open up the ring binder and get rid of it or change the order for themselves" (Harden). In this way, Atchley created a physical, interactive, and networked work of art assembling the ideas of diverse folk from around the world.

Atchley is perhaps best known, however, as Ace, the Colorado Spaceman, a performance persona he created in the 1970s to share the stories he collected on his travels of ordinary folk around the United States. What started as a trip to hand deliver copies of the "Space Atlas," soon became a larger performance endeavor: "I started out with a VW bus, doing what I called 'Trunk Stops', where I took out this big Space Trunk. It was filled with slides, videotapes, books and all kinds of stuff" (qtd. in Harden). Atchley incorporated the photographs and audio recordings he took on his journey with the "Trunk Stops" to create the *Ace Space Show*, a multimedia theatre work, which Atchley performed throughout North America. He maintained this persona until Lorimar Productions obtained the rights to Ace Space, although nothing came of the purchase (Saper 138; Daniel Pink). Atchley's work on the "Space Atlas" and the *Ace Space Show* shows an invested interest in individuals, diverse communities, and vernacular creativity (Burgess). Craig Saper notes Atchley's early works "worked to 'develop structures capable of creating gestalt communities whose members reflect technically and conceptually diverse points of view'" (138). Placing value in these collaborative works would continue to be important to Atchley's work, both in his performance piece, *Next Exit*, and in digital storytelling.

After Atchley stopped performing the *Ace Space Show*, he began experimenting with new digital media that would help him create more polished video materials for use in future performances: "Over the two decades that I have been performing, I have felt constrained by available technologies. Too slow! Too complicated! Too expensive! Too fragile! The solution: TA DA! ... Interactive multimedia!" (Harden). Atchley felt the capabilities of the new digital technologies were finally capable of doing what he envisioned artistically and at a price he could afford. The result was his performance, *Next Exit*, which premiered in 1991 and which he toured around the world. Using a similar devising technique as the *Ace Space Show*, Atchley created his one-man show, *Next Exit*. Inspired by his interest for family history,

Atchley created "an interactive monologue woven through with images from family scrapbooks, music, voices of family members and text" (Fimrite). The performance encompassed 70 different stories and spans 150 years of family history and makes use of "more than two dozen image formats from the daguerreotype to digital video," which were assembled by some of the most sophisticated technologies of the time into a multimodal collage of storytelling:

> Images are processed on a Macintosh G3 using Adobe Photoshop, Adobe Premiere and AfterEffects. Video is captured on using [sic] a Targa RTX system direct to StreamLogic Arrays. The performance combines Quicktime stories along with original words and music via Macromedia Director. Although Next Exit [sic] takes advantage of digital technologies to be transparently interactive, there are nearly one hundred pages of code written by Patrick Milligan, that facilitate the show's interactive capabilities including the use of a wireless mouse from the stage.
>
> ("Dana Atchley Gives Benefit")

Atchley used an infrared mouse to control the program from stage and, with the help of the audience, created a virtual road map of the approximately 12 stories he would tell in each performance. Each story was represented by a different pictorial icon:

> The icons would be dragged to a double yellow line running horizontally across the bottom of the screen. That line represented a highway. Atchley's father would pile the family into a car and take a Sunday drive. He would randomly take an exit just to explore what was there—hence the name of Atchley's show Next Exit. The sequence of the icons from left to right on the highway was the sequence of the show. Atchley sat at the side of the stage and provided bridge narration between the stories and sometimes commentary within them.
>
> (Brown)

The digital and networked capabilities of the computer programming allowed Atchley the freedom he desired to create this personal and interactive narrative. He acknowledged that the combination of the media made "the medium and the message inseparably one," and gave him greater control over the authorship in each show:

> I am able, on stage, to control the sequence of stories and the pacing of the show. I can seamlessly move from one story to another and have

my lighting, keyboard and machine control cues and sets automatically follow. I can pause and continue. I can even offer the audience choices.

(Atchley, qtd. in Harden)

The audience participation in the performance created an improvisational and networked digital experience. Atchley loosely scripted the 70 stories into a changeable, one-man show modeled on the oral storytelling tradition of telling stories around a campfire: "he would sit on a tree stump on stage and blow on a television encased in logs to bring forth video flames" (Woo). This obvious metaphor caused many journalists to remark on the ways in which storytellers like Atchley were able to remix the ancient art of storytelling (Silberman; Pink).

Next Exit reframed the age-old practice of oral storytelling with the new media practices of the late 20th Century. In so doing, Atchley's work reconnected the listener with the humanity of oral storytelling traditions. The novelty of this new performance technique was widely popular. Atchley performed his work in Canada and throughout the United States and later created Dana Atchley Productions to help corporations build brand identities using these new storytelling techniques and what Atchley termed "Emotional Storytelling"[3] (Fimrite; Pink; Max). He found that digital media was capable of reshaping oral storytelling traditions in ways that at once mirror and expand the structures of oral storytelling. Atchley's diverse digital storytelling practices over the years mimic various structures of storytelling like the long-form storytelling (both fiction and non-fiction) of online journalism, film, and television and conversational narratives like those later seen in spaces like Twitter, Facebook. While storytelling using digital technologies share similar properties to oral storytelling traditions, it expands on the multimodal practices and structures of these traditions, as the composition capabilities of digital technologies create a space for their constant overlap.

Even Atchley's earlier works show an interest in multimodality as a defining feature. Atchley's works across media show an interest in the way visual images and the arrangement of visual images tell stories.[4] Atchley notes this fascination dates back to childhood:

My uncle gave me my first camera at age seven,[5] a Brownie Twin Lens Reflex and I have every image I have taken since that age, on an increasingly sophisticated and expensive variety of formats. And I never just kept them in boxes. Ever since I was a little kid I made displays, and put them out and shared them ... for me, they define the way I remember things.

(qtd. in Harden)

In addition to his fascination with visual memory, Atchley's collected works also seem to privilege the collecting of diverse stories and histories of diverse people.[6] Atchley's background with visual and video arts in the decades leading to his work in digital storytelling certainly reflect the idea of the "independent" filmmaker and in watching his works, it is clear he has a greater expertise with the art of video and multimodal video editing. Although multimodal storytelling has become an "everyman" practice with the introduction of easy-to-use and easy-to-access technology, Atchley's early digital storytelling work was more complex than that of the average user. Atchley's Digital Stories, some of which have been uploaded to YouTube, show a remarkable understanding of the ways in which digital technologies can be used to collage together images, video, and audio. His works, "Redheads," "Home Movie" or "Turn," "Shipwreck," and "Horse/Cow," make use of audio and video footage as well as photographs and computer animation to create multimodal works of video art. Unlike stories created by users new to the genre, Atchley's work showcases technical expertise and an interest in the avant-garde and the assemblage of found objects at the same time on screen.

Lambert also comes from a theatre arts background, and earned a bachelor's degree in dramatic arts from the University of California, Berkeley. He was especially interested in studying the scholarship and process-work of artists and companies engaged in radical theatre (Lambert, Personal Interview). He drew inspiration from groups who were really invested in radical engagement like Los Angeles Poverty Department and At the Foot of the Mountain and the radical theatre scenes in California and New York. After graduating from college, Lambert spent a decade working in theatre in the San Francisco Bay Area, including time at The Peoples Theatre Coalition in the 1980s and Life on the Water, a theatre he co-founded in 1986 with Ellen Sebastian Chang, Leonard Pitt, and Bill Talen and focused on developing contemporary theatre with diverse voices. His work in theatre was grounded in process-work, a factor which he mirrored in the digital storytelling methodology.

Lambert's background in radical theatre significantly informed his approach in crafting the genre and method of digital storytelling as a community-engaged practice (Lambert, Personal Interview). The subtitle for his 1997 article, written a mere four years after the start of digital storytelling, reads "The Role Of A Community Arts Aesthetic In The Information Technology Revolution" (Lambert, "The Memory Box"). The line reads like an epigraph for Lambert's framework of digital storytelling, pairing community arts with information technology and announces it as a movement that is part of a larger revolution. A decade later, Lambert wrote that this article was an "early [effort] in self-definition" (Lambert, "Where it all Started," 80). Still, a community-arts lens persists in digital storytelling and influences the growth and development of the movement. As Lambert wrote in 2007, community-arts and his approach to digital storytelling can be seen as political: "we understand that the choices we make in sharing stories as examples, in how we guide the considerations of meaning, of making connections to the social construct, are not meant to be balanced" (Ibid. 82). Such an awareness of the dialogic nature that shapes the digital storytelling process is important, as it speaks to the agenda and personal politics of any facilitator, and it greatly influenced the approach and methodology Lambert built around digital storytelling in the following decades.

With his focus on community-arts, Lambert was responsible for shaping the methodology of digital storytelling as a practice, including the adopting and adaptation of story circles in the digital storytelling process. Lambert first heard of the story circle process while studying at UC Berkeley. There, he learned about John O'Neal and the process he used at the Free Southern Theatre and later Junebug Productions (Lambert, Personal Interview). O'Neal's story circle process was intentionally ambiguous, to allow for a variety of stories, voices, perspectives, and experiences to come forward. In an undated essay called "The Story Circle Process Discussion Paper," O'Neal writes,

> I hesitate to present these suggestions for the operation of the Story Circle process in writing because the process, like the stories that people use it to share, is essentially oral in nature. When things are written down we have a tendency to treat them as more final than they need to be.

Still, O'Neal wrote down three specific laws in his treatise: You have to listen actively, you have the right to pass when it is your turn to share, and you have to respect every storyteller's right to tell their story. O'Neal additionally lists further advice on guiding the story circle process including letting each group member describe their goals for the discussion, have only a few rules, have a planned trajectory of speakers (such as moving clockwise through the circle), shared responsibility among participants to keep track of time, don't participate in power struggles with a storyteller, give a summation of the circle at the end, leave space between stories to let them marinate with listeners, provide time for conversation, and design a follow-up activity for the group.

O'Neal's process has been adapted for a variety of arts and community-engaged processes that privileged the voices and narratives of individuals in the community. While some practices use the story circle to open discussions centered on specific topics, the process Lambert adapted for digital storytelling focuses on developing the story itself. A digital storytelling story circle takes the story a teller comes in with and moves it to a different place, that is, moves it to fit within the genre. The key to this kind of work is to ensure the storyteller controls what that movement looks like. Digital storytelling facilitators are not there to talk about their version of the storyteller's story. Rather, they're there to hold storytellers accountable for visioning, moving, and editing their story forward, and to guide conversations so they are story-focused as opposed to psychology- or perspective-focused. In all, the story circle is designed as an equitable space for all storytellers. One notable guideline O'Neal omitted is a time frame, now often a staple defined by the circumstances surrounding the programs in which story circles live, including Lambert's. Time frames for the process and for individual talking time allows a better sense of equity to inform the process; setting an allotted time for each speaker ensures no one voice is privileged over another. Facilitators can further a commitment to such equity by asking for feedback from story circle members who remain silent or don't speak up as often in the discussion section.

Lambert's digital storytelling methodology is further influenced by his training as an organizer in the 1970s and 1980s (Lambert, Personal Interview). Working from a leftist perspective, organizing became a key influence in his development as a community-arts practitioner and gave him the skills he needed to establish himself as a facilitator of story work. In a conversation in March 2022, Lambert said that integral story circle ideas like stepping up, stepping back, which leaves room for participants who speak too little or too much an opportunity to self-modify, came from his work in organizing. As did some principles, such as, the understanding that you will speak only for yourself and not on behalf of or for others ("Personal Interview").

With his community-arts based focus, it is easy to see how Lambert influenced the issue of access of the digital storytelling genre. He intentionally developed a civic resource (Lambert, Zoom Interview). As Lambert writes,

> The ability to express oneself in digital media, in our case using digital video editing, has become a central literacy for full participation in society. And as we started this work, we recognized that unlike some other forms of community arts activity, there would be barriers of access; the penetration of digital culture to virtually all sectors of society has mitigated this critique.
>
> (Lambert, "Where it all Started," 85)

Lambert worked to make digital storytelling a methodology and a movement rather than solely a genre and product. This distinction and the creation of free support materials like the *Digital Storytelling Cookbook* allowed digital storytelling to spread widely across the nation and internationally.

Lambert met Atchley at a Life on the Water production, and bonded over the possibilities of new technologies, creating works the length of a song, and the importance of championing diverse, everyday stories (Lambert, Zoom Interview). Together with Nina Mullen, Atchley and Lambert founded the San Francisco Digital Media Center in 1994. The founders wanted to bring together writers, media producers, visual artists, performers, and designers to empower the telling of community narratives through digital technologies. In 1998 the center moved to Berkeley where it honed the practice of digital storytelling as an educational co-productive and workshop-based practice and took the name The Center for Digital Storytelling. A later shift in 2005 brought the organization into closer work with non-governmental organizations and human services agencies that focused on the use of storytelling as a means to help people facing challenging and traumatic circumstances (Lambert and Hessler 35). The Center for Digital Storytelling renamed itself StoryCenter in 2015 and continues to focus on storytelling as a way to empower citizens and communities. Despite the years and re-brandings, the organization's mantra – "Listen deeply. Tell stories." – remains unchanged, reflecting the original roots of the organization that engages ordinary people in the creation and sharing of their personal narratives.

StoryCenter offers consulting and workshops for institutions and groups that wish to promote their images through storytelling, put forth narratives, and/or tell personal stories of those involved. As the genre of digital storytelling solidified, they started to teach workshops on the genre and creation process to people around the world. Originally these workshops began as in-person residencies in Berkeley, California. These residencies expanded throughout the United States as satellite campuses of the organization opened following the growing popularity of the movement. Additionally, workshop facilitators went abroad to conduct residencies with interested parties in various countries. With the growth of cloud-based video editing software such as WeVideo, the company expanded its residencies to include online workshops.

In all of these workshops, the company trains participants to create personal narratives in the genre of digital storytelling. These narratives are characterized by their use of their authors' personal archives and are voiced and edited by those same authors. At the third annual Digital Storytelling Festival in 1997, Lambert, who is currently the director of StoryCenter, emphasized,

> What we're talking about is a system of values about the importance of memory – an intergenerational dialogue about storytelling and remembrance. We're trying to inculcate the importance of taking the time to tell the story of yourself or the people you love.
> (qtd. in Rosenberg)

The focus on personal narratives solidified digital storytelling as a genre dedicated to archiving and sharing diverse and under-heard narratives.

Digital Storytelling Comes of Age

At present, the genre of digital storytelling envisioned by StoryCenter in California is 30 years old and StoryCenter today is one of several institutions leading digital storytelling workshops and projects around the world. What began as a specific storytelling practice gradually became a movement and a stylized genre that began to be used as a research methodology in various public sectors including public health,[7] anthropology,[8] Indigenous studies,[9] disability studies,[10] marketing and brand identities,[11] education,[12] social change,[13] history,[14] archeology,[15] and public culture.[16] Since its conception, the genre, which includes an intensive workshop process, has grown into what the genre's co-founder Joe Lambert describes as a "successful international movement" (Lambert and Hessler 35). Spurgeon suggests this growth is due to the organizations "codified 'procedural knowledge' (Hartley et al. 2008, pp. 128–129) of their first-person digital storytelling method" as a systematic practice that helped spread and evolve the genre and methodology over the past several decades:

> This made it accessible and easily transferable to independent producers and a range of professionals (media, education, health, arts and culture) and government and non-government public cultural and service institutions with an interest in expanding their repertoire of skills for community development and engagement. Researchers from a range of disciplinary contexts were also captivated by the criticality of the method as well as the variety of contexts in which it could be applied.
>
> ("The Ethics" 121)

Lambert codified the StoryCenter approach with his definitive theoretical guidebook for the genre that has been published and revised six times[17] and two detailed anthologies dedicated to the genre appeared in the late 2000s.[18] Interest in digital storytelling theory has only grown in the following decade with several new and revised texts and anthologies published.[19] These books suggest a wide desire to study the expansion of the field. These works successfully showcase the benefits, areas of opportunity, and practices of digital storytelling in different cultural contexts for diverse purposes such as education, empowerment, health, and anthropology.

Digital Storytelling has also grown to be international in scope. Digital projects exist in many countries, such as the United States (Freidus; Li), Ireland (Alexandra), United Kingdom (Hardy and Sumner), Wales (Meadows), Turkey (Şimşek), Greece (Meimaris), South Africa (Kannengießler; Reed and Hill), Kenya (Rainbird), Brazil (Clarke), Southeast Asia (Tacchi), Singapore (Koh), and Australia (Spurgeon et al.; Klaebe et al.). Beyond these digital storytelling practices, many others are additionally engaging in practices using participatory photography and video and other methods of media production as community-engaged practices. However, most authors who discuss digital storytelling projects around the world continue to point to the principles Lambert outlines, which situates the digital narratives as a source of empowerment and agency for the storytellers. In defining this guiding principle, Lambert writes, "Everyone has a story to tell ... [but] most people do not feel that their story has meaning or significance" (Lambert, "Where It All Started" 86). Lambert hoped digital storytelling would even empower those who didn't feel their stories were worthy of telling. The deep connection to the political nature of storytelling Lambert alludes to here, grounds my in-depth research into digital storytelling and the importance of facilitating responsibly in the collaborative workshop.

Digital Storytelling: The Genre and Writing Process

The genre of Digital Storytelling is developed from a process of story work. StoryCenter defines story work as

> encompasses[ing] a range of activities rooted in two fundamental approaches: the sharing and development of first person narratives, through group or collaborative process; and the production of an accompanying media artifact, resulting in a text, a photograph, a video, or an audio recording.
>
> (Lambert and Hessler 245)

This definition focuses on the process of the story's development, but genre is also understood from the side of the audience. As literary theorist Steven Earnshaw writes, "genre isn't just about what we are writing, it is about how we are reading and what we are expecting when we do pick up a poem or novel, or sit down to watch a film or play" (3). This is no less true of digital storytelling. To truly understand the genre, one should consider how these short films are *produced* and *read*. As a multimodal technology, the composition practice of digital storytelling is unique in traditional creative writing practices. Creative writing today is changing with the growth of digital technologies, as writers and "readers" need to take in complex media literacy practices to comprehend the genre and discipline. Different individual layers combine to create a multimodal digital story as part of a unique composition practice. Yet, like other narratives, digital storytelling focuses on a plot, which generally centers around a specific moment in a person's life, especially those dramatic moments which facilitate growth; is contained within a structure that typically includes clear delineation between the beginning, middle, and end; and, finally, is moved forward by the personal storytelling and narrator who serves as the narrative's main character.

Familiar structures of narratives are compounded by the structures of the digital. Not only will a digital project outcome depend on the resources available, the programs the authors chose to use, and their proficiency with these tools, but the digital medium additionally imposes its own set of codes and expectations that are different from previous media and oral traditions. As media theorist Nick Couldry writes:

> These features stem in various ways from the oversaturation of the online information environment: first, a pressure to mix text with other materials (sound, video, still image) and more generally to make a visual presentation out of narrative, over and above its textual content; second,

26   *Contextualizing Personal Narratives*

> a pressure to limit the length of narrative, whether to take account of the limits of people's attention when reading text online, or to limit the file size of videos or sound tracks; third, a pressure towards standardization because of the sheer volume of material online and people's limited tolerance for formats, layouts or sequences whose intent they have difficulty interpreting; fourth, a pressure to take account of the possibility that any narrative when posted online may have unintended and undesired audiences.
>
> (49)

In short, even the narrative structures themselves exhibit some sort of prescription that dictates the ways in which the authors structure and code their Digital Stories. This should not only make us question whether or not it is possible to structure a narrative authentically, but also question whose story structures we are privileging when creating a "good" story.

As a multimodal narrative, numerous ligaments hold a digital story together. These connect layers of semiotic and contextual meaning, juxtaposing literacy modes and creating new meaning in the process. Lambert and Hessler define multiple layers that are used to create a single story:

> Digital stories contain multiple visual and audio layers. The visual layers are:
>
> - The composition of a single image
> - The combination of multiple images within a single frame, either through collage or fading over time
> - The juxtaposition of a series of images over time
> - Movement applied to a single image, either by panning or zooming or the juxtaposition of a series of cropped details from the whole image
> - The use of text on screen in relation to visuals, spoken narration, or sound
>
> The audio layers are:
>
> - Recorded voice-over
> - Recorded voice-over in relation to sound, either music or ambient sound
> - Music alone or in contrast to another piece of music.
>
> (67–68)

The writing and composition process for a digital story is thus a layering process, and a period of "construction" (Lundby 5). This construction process happens over a series of creative steps, beginning with a process of creative writing. This is followed by the creation of a storyboard utilizing the written narrative and anticipated audio and visuals that will accompany the narrative. These audio and visual assets are then collected from personal archives, copyright-free resource databases, or created specifically for use in the digital story. Once the audio and visual assets have been gathered, writers construct their narrative following their storyboard making use of digital audio and video editors such as iMovie, Windows Movie Maker, or WeVideo. While any video editor will do, the accessibility of these three (both financial and in terms of user-friendliness) make them strong favorites of the digital storytelling community. Indeed, the collaborative nature of WeVideo has been a favorite of StoryCenter for the past several years.

Writing

In a footnote to his work, "The Value of Narrativity in the Representation of Reality," Hayden White sets forth the etymological roots of the word narrative: "The words 'narrative,' 'narration,' 'to narrate,' and so on derive via the Latin *gnārus* ('knowing,' 'acquainted with,' 'expert,' 'skilful,' and so forth) and *narrō* ('relate,' 'tell') from the Sanskrit root gnâ ('know')" (5). Through narrative, then, authors, as experts, tell what they know based on their lived experience; that is, they write what they know. This is an especially useful tracing for digital storytelling, a genre focused on the personal narrative. When I help storytellers consider their creative works, I ask them to look for stories only *they* can tell. By framing the task for storytellers in this way, I am asking them to put themselves at the center of their stories and to develop a narrative from their own experience, perception, and reflection.

To maintain their concise telling, the narratives told within digital stories need to be written in only a few hundred words. A general rule I tell storytellers I am working with is to consider writing at most 300 words for their final script. This will help keep their works within a two-to-three-minute time frame. Often, however, stories can span this time frame with significantly less words by placing focus on other layers of the digital story or by valuing pauses within their voice-over delivery. Writing in such a short number of words proves challenging for many writers, who want to place extra details and context to elongate their narratives. While these details may work in another genre, the digital story is meant to engage viewers for only a few minutes. Brevity and conciseness are part of what has come to define the genre of digital storytelling. As such, significant time is spent with storytellers revising their works during the writing phase to encourage clarity and focus within the narrative so that it is propelled forward in a timely manner. Once the storytellers are satisfied with their work, they move into the process of considering audiovisual layers that can enhance their work.

Storyboarding

The storyboard is the first place where storytellers are able to envision the overall appearance of their digital story after they finish writing their narratives. The storyboard is a process of two-dimensional pre-planning, where storytellers layer the text of their writing with their envisioned visuals, audio, and cinematic effects and transitions onto paper in order to discover and shape the flow of their story. Edward Tufte, a noted professor who researches information design, sums up the challenges of information design on a two-dimensional space, what he calls "flatland":

> Effective layering of information is often difficult; for every excellent performance, a hundred clunky spectacles arise. An omnipresent, yet subtle, design issue is involved: the various elements collected together on flatland interact, creating non-information patterns and texture simply through their combined presence.
>
> (53)

This is a perfect example of the compositional layering process that takes place within a storyboard. The final technological interaction of layers, while still ultimately two-dimensional, looks and sounds fundamentally different from the two-dimensional planning the storytellers might create on their storyboards.

Storyboards range in the amount of content they ask storytellers to consider. At their most basic, storyboards ask storytellers to write their text line by line and include a descriptive, sketches, or image they want to put with that specific line of text. This often looks like Figure 2.1:

Storyboards can also include significantly more information and ask a writer to consider all layers that can be contained within a digital story (Figure 2.2).

While the majority of the revision of the narrative's plot may have taken place during the writing process, it is likely that storytellers may find additional places to revise their narratives as they consider the additional media layers, as storyboards provide storytellers with another way to visualize the overall arc of the story. As Edward Tufte notes, "visual displays of information encourage a diversity of viewer styles and rates of editing, personalizing, reasoning, and understanding" (31). By using the storyboard to organize their thoughts, storytellers have to structure their written text (understood during this process as their voice-over), as well as their anticipated or desired visuals, and the flow of visual and aural information.

Audio Assets

Generally speaking, there are four types of audio elements that can be found in digital stories: Voice-over, music, sound effects, and sound from video.

Contextualizing Personal Narratives 29

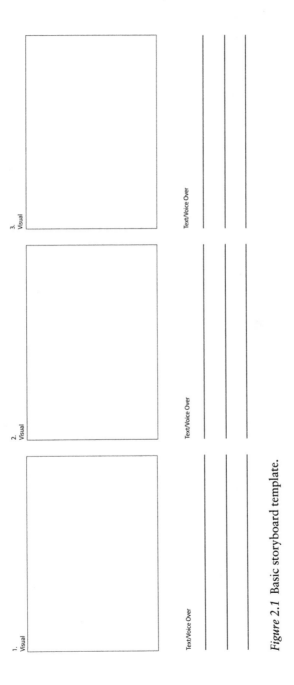

Figure 2.1 Basic storyboard template.

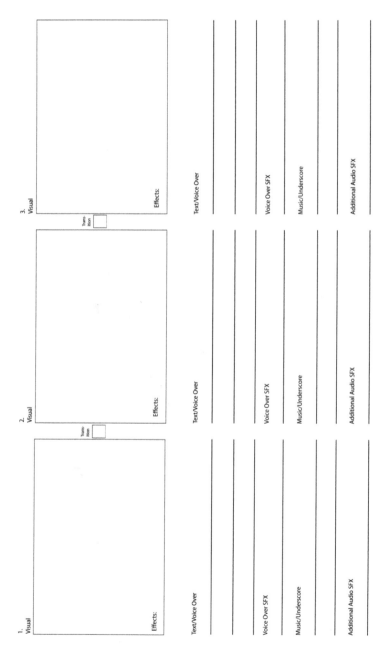

Figure 2.2 Advanced storyboard template.

Because the human brain can only process so much information aurally, it is especially important to consider how these elements layer together. Too many different audio lines can confuse the listener. As such, it is important to ensure that the volume level of each audio line works to enhance the main audio, which is most often, the voice-over. This means that while the voice-over might play at a higher audio level, any background music has its volume turned down to ensure the voice-over can be heard. For some writers, the audio portion of their digital stories will end with the recording and placement of their voice-overs. Others will use all four types of audio. Still others will use no audio whatsoever, preferring instead to tell their stories through visual text.

Another aspect of the voice-over is the recording process itself, where the writer's voice becomes an integral part of composing a digital story. To create the most effective voice-overs, it is important to consider the voice as an instrument with vocalics that influence the meaning and affect that reaches audiences. Specifically, it is important to consider these elements of vocalics: Pitch, tone, prosody, enunciation, pronunciation, modulation, volume, tempo, stress, rhythm, and timbre or vocal quality. Combining these factors can help create aural affect displays for listeners and help them to comprehend the meaning of the narrative as well as the narrative's structure. By using these tools and understanding the voice as an instrument, storytellers are able to give richness to their narratives through their unique voices, thereby "[capturing] the essence of the narrator, their unique character, and their connection to the lived experience" (Lambert and Hessler 64). In these vocal performances of the texts, writers can emphasize certain moments, phrases, or words to further enhance the semantic nature of their writing and showcase more of their person within their writing.

Visual Elements

Visuals in digital stories could include photographs, video, illustrations, animation, and the written word among others. These visuals can come from the writer's personal archives, from collective databases of others' works, or be created specifically for the digital story by the writer. Each of these elements can influence the tone and ambiance of a digital story, and storytellers should use the same consideration and deliberation when selecting or creating visuals that they do when they write the text of their narrative. Lambert and Hessler note, "Well-chosen images act as mediators between the narrative and the audience ... images have the power to reveal something to the audience that words just can't say" (63).

The conversation about which visuals to add will likely occur during the process of storyboarding, if not before so writers can easily find or make the visuals they require before moving to the construction phase of story development. Often, when storytellers do not have a good grasp of the visual elements they want to include, browsing the Internet for inspiration or visuals can be a significant time commitment. It is easy to get sucked down the Internet rabbit hole. Asking writers to consider instead their visual assets without the assistance of computers or other archives can help them think more specifically about which visuals would best suit their text, rather than selecting an image because it has made itself known through a non-specific search. These latter visuals may not fit as well with the text, but may make their way into writers' digital stories because they are the first visuals they find. The difference here is finding a more *perfect* image versus finding an image that merely *works*.

Additionally, it is important to consider how the visuals relate to the text and what meaning the writer wants to add on top of their already written narrative. Visuals can be either explicitly or implicitly related to the narrative. An explicit visual "mirrors each of the different points throughout their entire narrative," while implicit visuals "[convey] another layer of meaning" to the narrative (Lambert and Hessler 62). Explicit visuals give literal representations designed to give the audience additional understanding by connecting the spoken text to an associated image, while implicit visuals add new directions in the meaning-making process.

Combination and Construction

The construction process of the different media layers occurs through editing software like WeVideo, iMovie, or Windows Movie Maker to combine elements into a cohesive digital story. The ways in which individual elements combine to create a digital story is just as important as the individual assets. Glynda Hull and her colleague, Mark Evan Nelson, observe, "images, written text, music, and so forth each respectively impart certain kinds of meanings more easily and naturally than others" (6), but together, these assets create new, more complex meanings. While the storyboard process gives writers the opportunity to examine how disparate elements might come together, it is often only in the digital editing and replay process where the cacophony of narrative elements makes itself known. It is important for the writer to keep in mind that spectacle is not the goal of the project and can muddy the story's clarity. Therefore, it is important to have a solid written and storyboard base to work from. This helps limit the influence of "cool tech," or creating elements just because it produces a "cool" effect. While these effects can and do have purposes and will work to enhance some digital stories, the technology should always follow and speak to the narrative. The focus then stays on the narrative itself rather than the technology.

Additionally, creating effective narratives in the construction process means combining elements and layers in ways that produce greater meaning rather than enhancing confusion. As such, the elements and layers that go into a digital story should be considered in connection with one another. This includes the individual lines of connection from one element to another as well as the overall effect that these connections produce. A viewer needs time to fully and clearly comprehend the meaning of each element in order to begin to make meaning from the whole. Tufte suggests, "The point is to find design strategies that reveal detail and complexity – rather than to fault the data for an excess of complication" (53). Effective storytelling is an essential part of a digital composition. This is especially important when considering a story's audience. Helping writers comprehend how the audience might view their work can help bring about clarity in the writing, organization, and construction of digital stories.

Literacy and Multimodality in Digital Storytelling

From his early print and video work, we can see how Atchley's fascination with multimedia and personal narrative influenced his work in digital media and led to the devising of digital storytelling as a new structure for traditional oral storytelling practices. Multimodality, however, should not be thought of as a new process that only embeds itself in the storytelling process with the invention of digital technologies. Digital technology introduced a wave of modalities that can be considered as literary modes given that they provide a symbol and context for meaning-making. While the use of image and sound are not new modes of meaning-making, technology allows for a wider span of literacy understanding as it redefines our ability to "see" and "read" these literacy modes and the possible combination therein. Both aural and visual literacies have the ability to convey meaning to an audience without the addition of text-based language. This plays a major role in digital storytelling where aural and visual modalities often convey the majority of the work. Glynda Hull acknowledges, "Ours is an age in which technologies for multi-media, multi-modal authorship proliferate" ("At Last" 230). These authorship practices make significant use of their available digital technologies to help storytellers shape and mold their narratives and create meaning in new ways:

> It is possible now to easily integrate words with images, sound, music, and movement to create digital artifacts that do not necessarily privilege linguistic forms of signification but rather that draw on a variety of modalities—speech, writing, image, gesture, and sound—to create different forms of meaning.
>
> (Hull and Nelson 1–2)

A digital story exists within artistic combination of such layers, assets, and modalities and work together to influence the viewers' meaning-making process of the film as a whole.

Even though recent technological developments have created more avenues by which to use multimodal composition and create multimodally, media scholar Knut Lundby notes, "Composition across modes is nothing new. Even oral storytelling may apply a range of modes in a complex whole, as a composition of tale, ballad, melody and text" (8). Lundby, citing Gunther Kress, further suggests "through digital technologies multimodality is made 'easy, usual, [and] natural,'" suggesting that while both oral and digital storytelling practices make use of multimodality, it is one of the key evidentiary features of digital storytelling's growth from oral traditions (8). Storytelling is the practice of communicating events and ideas using a variety of different methods including, but not limited to, words and text, language patterns, visual signifiers like gesture, image or film, and sound, which can include concepts of vocal tone and tambour as well as the incorporation of music. Stories do not need to include all of the layers described above, nor must they be multimodal. In some cases, authors may only use one medium through which to tell a story.

Both oral and digital storytelling practices should be considered to some extent multimodal. Communicating and telling stories using digital technologies "should not be understood as a phenomenon equivalent to either oral storytelling or to written narratives" (Hertzberg Kaare and Lundby 107). It is a process that intermixes these forms of storytelling and moves them into the digital realm. The process of multimodal digital composition does not privilege one media over another, but rather succeeds through the explicit and thoughtful amalgamation that "integrate words with images, sound, music, and movement to create digital artifacts that ... draw on a variety of modalities—speech, writing, image, gesture, and sound—to create different forms of meaning" (Hull and Nelson 1–2). As a communication tool, multimodality is essentially the layering of different semiotic modes present in the creation and telling of a "communicative artifact or event" (Nelson and Hull 126). New-media scholars Glynda A. Hull and Mark Evan Nelson identify the importance of multimodality as used in digital storytelling practices outlined by StoryCenter, and suggest multimodal composition, especially digital composition, can "increase the meaning-making potential of a text" as it has the ability to "create a different system of signification, one that transcends the collective contribution of its constituent parts" (Hull and Nelson 2).

Digital storytelling expands oral storytelling practices by creating the potential for further combinations of media in new ways, making these processes easier to employ, and using easily gatherable or readily available multimodal materials to increase the sensory performance. Yet assuming all digital stories are multimodal is problematic. David Herman contends that simply because a story uses digital technologies, the story does not necessarily engage with the same multimodalities that can be found within the digital stories. In his assessment of the remediation of oral storytelling in technologies, Herman points to multimodality in oral storytelling where he asserts storytellers "typically use two semiotic modes to design verbal as well as visual (gestural) representations in narratively organized discourse" (197). However, he argues that when digital technologies record an oral storytelling performance, the technologies determine whether the multimodality of the original oral storytelling performance remains. For instance, audio recordings represent a lived experience as monomodal, whereas video captures multiple modalities (198). For digital storytelling, the use of audio and video recording in this way becomes one piece of the ultimate multimodal work, as digital storytelling practices typically combine the audio and/or video performances with other media such as music and text. Ultimately, the process of composing multimodal digital stories allows writers to author short personal narratives through a process of layering and construction, giving them the opportunity to think deeply about how text, visuals, and sounds create the overall look, feel, and sound of their digital story.

Contemplating Authorship in the Construction of Texts

Today's authors are continually embracing audio/visual technologies as a method of composition through which to reach the audience. In the age of secondary orality, writing is no longer associated only with alphabetic text. Today's authors use a combination of media through which to communicate. Digital storytelling makes use of a combination of such elements to share narratives with the audience. In digital storytelling, participants author short personal narratives that stem from personal lived experiences. They are responsible for the creation, perspective, and telling of the story in text, and the choosing of images, film, and other visuals used in their pieces, sounds to incorporate, and ultimately creating the overall look, feel, and sound of their Digital Story. This comprehensive authorship gives unprecedented agency to the authors. Digital storytelling scholar Megan Alrutz notes that, in this way, authors become "both the subject and object of their representations, performing often hidden/invisible stories" (39). She is speaking specifically of youth of color who live in urban environments in the United States, but I posit this view of authorship could be expanded to all creators of autobiographical digital narratives, though with specific regard to traditionally marginalized communities who have previously seen their stories represented for them by outside authors. Daniel Meadows strongly agrees with the power of telling one's own story and says of digital storytelling:

> No longer must we [the public] tolerate media being done to us. No longer must we put up with professional documentarists recording us for hours and then throwing away most of what we tell them, keeping only those bits that tell our stories their own way and, more than likely, at our expense. If we will only learn the skills of Digital Storytelling then we can, quite literally, "take the power back."
>
> (192)

This is perhaps the crucial difference between authorship practices in digital storytelling and, say, documentary filmmaking. Filmmaking at worst runs the risk of doing media *to* people, where, as Meadows implies, the filmmaker takes ownership of the narrative in a way that re-tells someone's story in "their own way." However, digital storytelling still operates in a collaborative production process.

What then does authorship mean in a collaborative, digital writing process? To begin to contextualize this question, it is important to understand what "texts" mean within a digital landscape. The word "text" comes from the Latin *textus* meaning to weave; thus, texts are created by the interweaving of thoughts and ideas. Text as weaving is an apt metaphor for the videos created through digital storytelling as these texts organize and structure thoughts and ideas in a way that is meant to effectively communicate a message. Often, and certainly in the case of the digital storytelling practices I am discussing here, this happens through narrative and argument. As such, digital storytelling is designed to create films that give context, meaning, and direction to threads of thought so they are combined in a comprehensible and engaging way to reach potential audience members. Contextualizing understandings of texts and authorship reveals how the interchange of ideas from a wide range of collaborative creators weave through the final product.

Today, we operate in a largely digital world where elements of oral and print culture are apparent in the dissemination and consumption of texts. And where print publication methods generally distanced the author from the reader (Ong, Vandendorpe), digital publication has greatly reduced the distance between author and audience. In *From Papyrus to Hypertext Toward the Universal Digital Library*, scholar Christian Vandendorpe discusses how digital technologies have affected peoples' reading and writing processes. Of interest in this section is his discussion about the distance between author and audience. Vandendorpe suggests the Internet closes the gap between author and reader and encourages dialogue between the two parties. This bringing together of the author and audience returns to the sense of orality. Vandendorpe argues that where print culture separated the author from the reader, in the Internet era authors are expected to continue a dialogue with readers about their subject and works even after publishing a work. This is true regardless of where that text is published – the Internet, television, books, etc. He writes about blogs as an example of a site of discussion between author and reader where authors are expected to read and respond to comments and questions from their readers. As Vandendorpe writes about authors who use blogs as texts:

> the distance between author and reader is substantially reduced. More than a personal journal, the blog has given rise to a kind of writing in several voices, or more precisely, a kind of public writing with integrated feedback and applause meter.

(153)

Vandendorpe understands the audience as impactful components in a dialogic meaning-making process. He writes, "Far from being given, meaning is the product of our activity of comprehension or expression and exists only in the process through which it was born" (40–41). Thus, the comprehension of a work involves the pairing of information together, that is, information interpreted in light of contextual elements and other information such as memory, experiences, previously conceived notions, etc. Vandendorpe goes as far to say that the author just by writing a work is engaging in a dialogic response with an imagined audience: It is "possible to see in writing a form of interactivity anticipated by the author, who constructs the text in view of the encounter with the reader" (64).

Although not every digital story created will be displayed with comments enabled in a digital landscape, the return to orality and the removal of distance between author and audience is an important aspect of the digital storytelling creation process. Specifically, this action takes place in every digital storytelling workshop that makes use of story circles or other peer-to-peer constructive criticism practices. The story circle is the key collaborative event in digital storytelling workshops, actively inviting feedback from the facilitator and other workshop participants about a storyteller's narrative. In the practice, the storyteller gains new ideas and perspectives about how their story comes across, what strikes others, and what feelings it produces in a limited audience. This can be an invaluable tool for story development, yet it can also develop a hierarchical pretense for the facilitator to be seen as the primary or only storytelling expert in the room. This is especially true within classroom settings where grades may be dependent on the story's outcome. In order to develop a practice that reduces this impact of expertise, the facilitator should critically examine their practices and communication during story circles and adopt a method of "minimal direct intervention" (Burgess) and a Framework of Response-able Facilitation.

Notes

1. Also identified as Correspondence Art (Harden).
2. Atchley's *Space Atlas*, published in 1971, was preceded in the creation of the mail art movement by the *Ace Space Notebook*, also published by Atchley (under Ace Space Company), in 1970: "A compilation of correspondence items redistributed to artists on the network, Ace Space Notebook included contributions from Ray Johnson, General Idea, Image Bank, Michael Morris (Marcel Dot), Vincent Trasov (Mr Peanut), Eric Metcalfe (Dr Brute), Terry Reid, Gary Lee Nova, and others" (Luis Jacob).
3. Dana Atchley Productions additionally hosted many early digital storytelling workshops.
4. See for example Atchley's 1977 piece on Eric Metcalfe, *Spots Before Your Eyes*.
5. His artist profile for the Dartmouth '63 Art Show lists his age as ten. https://web.archive.org/web/20170226202145/www.dartmouth63artshow.org/danaatchleyprofile1.pdf
6. See his 1982 interview on KPIX, "Travelling With Ace."
7. See: Hardy and Sumner; Lenette et al.; Gubrium et al.; Gubrium "Digital Storytelling: An Emergent Media."

8 See: Gubrium "Digital Storytelling as Method;" Nuñez-Janes et al.
9 See: Cunsolo Willox et al.; Iseke and Moore; Manuelita; Poitras Pratt.
10 See: Rice and Mündel; Bliss.
11 See: Wu; Pink; Max.
12 See: Hull; Hull and Katz; Erstad and Silseth; Alrutz.
13 See: Kannengießler; Şimşek; Freidus.
14 See: Klaebe; González-Tennant; Klaebe et al.; Fisanick and Stakeley.
15 See: Earley-Spadoni.
16 See: Meadows; Argo et al.
17 The majority of this work makes use of the 5th edition of *Digital Storytelling: Capturing Lives, Creating Community*. However, due to rewrites, this work may occasionally reference other editions of this text. The newer editions additionally includes Brooke Hessler as a co-author. Citations for the 5th and 6th editions will be identified as "Lambert and Hessler."
18 Knut Lundby's 2008 edited collection, *Digital Storytelling, Mediatized Stories*, and John Hartley and Kelly McWilliam's 2009 edited collection, *Story Circle: Digital Storytelling around the World*.
19 Megan Altrutz's 2014 *Digital Storytelling, Applied Theatre, & Youth: Performing Possibility*; three anthologies published in 2017: *Deep Stories: Practicing, Teaching, and Learning Anthropology with Digital Storytelling* edited by Mariela Nuñez-Janes, Aaron Thornburg, and Angela Booker; *Digital Storytelling: Form and Content* edited by Mark Dunford and Tricia Jenkins; and *Digital Storytelling in Higher Education: International Perspectives* edited by Grete Jamissen, Pip Hardy, Yngve Nordkvelle, and Heather Pleasants; a 2018 revised edition of *Digital Storytelling: Capturing Lives, Creating Community* by Joe Lambert and Brooke Hessler; and a revised edition of the same book re-titled, *Digital Storytelling: Story Work for Urgent Times* published in 2020; the 2018 anthology *Cultivating Compassion: How Digital Storytelling is Transforming Healthcare* edited by Pip Hardy and Tony Sumner; Yvonne Poitras Pratt's 2020 *Digital Storytelling in Indigenous Education: A Decolonizing Journey for a Métis Community*; and Christina Fisanick and Robert O. Stakeley's 2021 *Digital Storytelling as Public History: A Guidebook for Educators*.

References

Alrutz, Megan. *Digital Storytelling, Applied Theatre, & Youth: Performing Possibility*. Routledge, 2014.

Argo, Bartley, et al. "The Way It Used to Be: Exploring Cultural Heritage through the Augmented Reality Story of a Neighborhood Soul Food Restaurant." *Visual Ethnography*, vol. 5, no. 2, 2016, pp. 55–78.

Atchley, Dana, and Metcalfe, Eric. "Spots Before Your Eyes." *YouTube*, uploaded by Bart Friedman, 20 Feb. 2017, https://www.youtube.com/watch?v=sMt4Dh6IgyI. Accessed 4 July 2017.

Bliss, Elaine. "Engaged Scholarship and Engaging Communities: Navigating Emotion, Affect and Disability through Digital Storytelling." *Digital Storytelling in Higher Education: International Perspectives*, edited by Grete Jamissen, Pip Hardy, Yngve Nordkvelle, and Heather Pleasants, Palgrave Macmillan, 2017, pp. 321–334.

Brown, Jim. "Reaching Through Time." *Storytelling* Online, https://www.storytellingonline.info/essays/reaching-through-time/. Accessed 4 July 2017.

Burgess, Jean. "Hearing Ordinary Voices: Cultural Studies, Vernacular Creativity and Digital Storytelling." *Continuum: Journal of Media & Cultural Studies*, vol. 20, no. 2, 2006, pp. 201–214.

Clarke, Margaret Anne. "Developing Digital Storytelling in Brazil." *Story Circle: Digital Storytelling around the World*, edited by John Hartley, and Kelly McWilliam, Wiley-Blackwell, 2009, pp. 144–154.

Couldry, Nick. "Digital Storytelling, Media Research, and Democracy: Conceptual Choices and Alternative Futures." *Digital Storytelling, Mediatized Stories*, edited by Knut Lundby, Peter Lang, 2008, pp. 41–60.

Cunsolo Willox, Ashley, et al. "Storytelling in a Digital Age: Digital Storytelling as an Emerging Narrative Method for Preserving and Promoting Indigenous Oral Wisdom." *Qualitative Research*, vol. 13 no. 2, 2012, pp. 127–147.

"Dana Atchley Gives Benefit Performance for ASCI @ Kitchen." *Art & Science Collaborations, Inc.*, 20 May 1999. http://amsterdam.nettime.org/Lists-Archives/nettime-l-9905/msg00188.html. Press Release.

Dunford, Mark, and Tricia Jenkins, editors. *Digital Storytelling: Form and Content*. Palgrave MacMillan, 2017.

Earley-Spadoni, Tiffany. "Spatial History, Deep Mapping and Digital Storytelling: Archeology's Future Imagined through an Engagement with the Digital Humanities." *Journal of Archaeological Science*, vol. 84, 2017, pp.95–102.

Earnshaw, Steve. *The Handbook of Creative Writing*. Edinburgh University Press, 2007.

Erstad, Ola, and Kenneth Silseth. "Agency in Digital Storytelling: Challenging the Educational Context." *Digital Storytelling, Mediatized Stories: Self-representations in New Media*, edited by Knut Lundby, Peter Lang, 2009, pp. 213–232.

Fimrite, Peter. "Dana Winslow Atchley." *SFGATE*, 26 Dec. 2000. https://www.sfgate.com/news/article/Dana-Winslow-Atchley-2689271.php. Accessed 4 July 2017.

Fisanick, Christina, and Robert O. Stakeley. *Digital Storytelling as Public History: A Guidebook for Educators*. Routledge, 2021.

Fletcher, Christopher, and Carolina Cambre. "Digital Storytelling and Implicated Scholarship in the Classroom." *Journal of Canadian Studies*, vol. 43, no. 1, 2009, pp. 109–130.

Freidus, Natasha. "Our Stories, Their Decisions Voter Education Project." *Telling Stories to Change the World: Global Voices on the Power of Narrative to Build Community and Make Social Justice Claims*, edited by Rickie Solinger, Madeline Fox, and Kayhan Irani, Routledge, 2008, pp. 119–126.

González-Tennant, Edward. "Digital Storytelling in the Classroom: New Media Techniques for an Engaged Anthropological Pedagogy." *Deep Stories, Practicing, Teaching, and Learning Anthropology with Digital Storytelling*, edited by Mariela Nuñez-Janes, Aaron Thornburg, and Angela Booke, De Gruyter, 2017, pp. 162–179.

Gubrium, Aline. "Digital Storytelling as a Method for Engaged Scholarship in Anthropology." *Practicing Anthropology*, vol. 31, no. 4, 2009, pp. 5–9.

Gubrium, Aline. "Digital Storytelling: An Emergent Method for Health Promotion Research and Practice." *Health Promotion Practice*, vol. 10, no. 2, 2009, pp. 186–191.

Gubrium, Aline, Amy L. Hill, and Sarah Flicker. "A Situated Practice of Ethics for Participatory Visual and Digital Methods in Public Health Research and Practice: A Focus on Digital Storytelling." *American Journal of Public Health*, vol. 104, no. 9, 2014, pp. 1606–1614.

Harden, Fred. "A Story about Dana Atchley." *While I Remember It*. https://www.whileiremember.it/a-story-about-dana-atchley-2/. Accessed 4 July 2017.

Hardy, Pip, and Tony Sumner, editors. *Cultivating Compassion: How Digital Storytelling is Transforming Healthcare*. Palgrave Macmillan, 2018.

Hartley, John. "Problems of Expertise and Scalability in Self Made Media." *Digital Storytelling, Mediatized Stories: Self-Representations in New Media*, edited by Knut Lundby, Peter Lang, 2009, pp. 197–212.

Hartley, John, and Kelly McWilliam, editors. *Story Circle: Digital Storytelling around the World*. Wiley-Blackwell, 2009.

Helff, Sissy, and Julie Woletz. "Narrating Euro-African Life in Digital Space." *Story Circle: Digital Storytelling around the World*, edited by John Hartley, and Kelly McWilliam, Wiley-Blackwell, 2009, pp. 131–43.

Herman, David. "Multimodal Storytelling and Identity Construction in Graphic Narratives." *Telling Stories: Language, Narrative, and Social Life*, edited by Deborah Schiffrin, Anna de Fina, and Anastasia Nylund, Georgetown University Press, 2010, pp. 195–208.

Hertzberg Kaare, Bridgit, and Knut Lundby. "Autobiography and Assumed Authenticity in Digital Storytelling." *Digital Storytelling, Mediatized Stories: Self-representation in New Media*, edited by Knut Lundby, Peter Lang, 2008, pp. 105–222.

Hull, Glynda A. "At Last: Youth Culture and Digital Media: New Literacies for New Times." *Research in the Teaching of English*, vol. 38, no.2, 2003, pp. 229–33.

Hull, Glynda A., and Mark Evan Nelson. "Locating the Semiotic Power of Multimodality." *Written Communication*, vol. 22, 2005, pp. 1–38.

Hull, Glynda A., and Mira–Lisa Katz. "Crafting an Agentive Self: Case Studies of Digital Storytelling." *Research in the Teaching of English*, vol. 41, no. 1, 2006, pp. 43–81.

Iseke, Judy, and Sylvia Moore. "Community-Based Indigenous Digital Storytelling with Elders and Youth," *American Indian Culture and Research Journal*, vol. 35, no.4, 2011, pp. 19–38.

Jamissen, Grete, et al., editors. *Digital Storytelling in Higher Education: International Perspectives*. Springer, 2017.

Kannengießer, Sigrid. "Digital Storytelling to Empower Sex Workers: Warning, Relieving and Liberating." *Feminist Media: Participatory Spaces, Networks, and Cultural Citizenship*, edited by Elke Zobl, and Ricarda Drüke, Transcript, 2012, pp. 238–49.

Klaebe, Helen. "The Problems and Possibilities of using Digital Storytelling in Public History Projects." XIIII International Oral History Conference - Dancing with Memory, Sydney, 2006.

Klaebe, Helen, Marcus Foth, Jean Burgess, and Mark Bilandzic. "Digital Storytelling and History Lines: Community Engagement in a Master-Planned Development." 13th International Conference on Virtual Systems and Multimedia (VSMM'07), Brisbane, Springer, 2007.

KPIX. "Travelling with Ace Space." *YouTube*, uploaded by Bart Friedman, 06 Mar. 2017, https://www.youtube.com/watch?v=ZDvVMyf8r7w. Accessed 4 July 2017.

Lambert, Joe. "The Memory Box: The Role Of A Community Arts Aesthetic In The Information Technology Revolution." Center for Digital Storytelling, https://www.storycenter.org/memoryboxnew.html. Accessed 1 May 2008.

Lambert, Joe. Personal Interview. 27 March 2022.
Lambert, Joe. "Where It All Started." *Story Circle: Digital Storytelling around the World*, edited by John Hartley, and Kelly McWilliam, Wiley-Blackwell, 2009, pp. 79–90.
Lambert, Joe. Zoom Interview. 19 July 2022.
Lambert, Joe, and H. Brooke Hessler. *Digital Storytelling: Digital Storytelling: Capturing Lives, Creating Community*. 5th ed., Routledge, 2018.
Lambert, Joe, and H. Brooke Hessler. *Digital Storytelling: Story Work for Urgent Times*. Digital Diner Press, 2020.
Lenette, Caroline, et al. "Digital Storytelling as a Social Work Tool: Learning from Ethnographic Research with Women from Refugee Backgrounds." *British Journal of Social Work*, vol. 45, 2015, pp. 988–1005.
Li, Ying. *Digital Storytelling as Participatory Media Practice for Empowerment: The Case of the Chinese Immigrants in the San Gabriel Valley*. 2007. University of Southern California, PhD Dissertation.
Lundby, Knut, editor. *Digital Storytelling, Mediatized Stories: Self-Representations in New Media*. Peter Lang, 2009.
Manuelita, Brenda. *Creating Space for an Indigenous Approach to Digital Storytelling: "Living Breath" of Survivance within an Anishinaabe Community in Northern Michigan*. 2015. Antioch University, PhD Dissertation.
Max, Ulrike. "Digital Storytelling." *Emotional Branding: Playing with the Senses: A Conceptual Approach, Diplomarbeit*, Diplomarbeiten Agentur diplom.de, 2002, pp. 30–32.
Meadows, Daniel. "Digital Storytelling: Research–Based Practice in New Media." *Visual Communication*, vol. 2, no. 2, 2003, pp.189–93.
Nelson, Mark Evan, and Hull, Glynda. "Challenges of Multimedia Self-Presentation: Taking, and Mistaking, the Show on the Road." *Written Communication*, vol. 25, no. 4, 2008, pp. 415–440.
Nuñez-Janes, Mariela, et al., editors. *Deep Stories: Practicing, Teaching, and Learning Anthropology with Digital Storytelling*. De Gruyter, 2017.
Ong, Walter J. *Orality and Literacy*. 1982. Routledge, 2002.
Pink, Daniel. "What's Your Story?" *Fast Company*, 31 December 1998, www.fastcompany.com/36331/whats-your-story. Accessed 4 July 2017.
Poitras Pratt, Yvonne. *Digital Storytelling in Indigenous Education: A Decolonizing Journey for a Métis Community*. Routledge, 2020.
Reed, Amber, and Amy L. Hill. ""Don't Keep It to Yourself!": Digital Storytelling with South African Youth." *Seminar.net: International Journal of Media, Technology, and Lifelong Learning*, vol. 6, no. 2, 2010, pp. 268–279.
Rice, Carla, and Ingrid Mündel. "Multimedia Storytelling Methodology: Notes on Access and Inclusion in Neoliberal Times," *Canadian Journal of Disability Studies*, vol. 8, no. 1, 2019, pp. 118–148.
Rosenberg, Scott. "Lest We Forget." *Wordyard*, n.d., www.wordyard.com/dsf/97fest1.html. Accessed 4 July 2017.
Saper, Craig J. *Networked Art*. University of Minnesota Press, 2001.
Silberman, Steve. "Digital Storyfest Finds Heart among Bits: Narrative and the Web will be the Focus of this Fall's Digital Storytelling Festival." *WIRED*, 23 May, 1997. https://www.wired.com/1997/05/digital-storyfest-finds-heart-among-bits/. Accessed 4 July, 2017.

Şimşek, Burcu. *Using Digital Storytelling as a Change Agent for Women's Participation in the Turkish Public Sphere*. 2012. Queensland University of Technology, PhD Dissertation.

Spurgeon, Christina. "The Art of Co-creative Media: An Australian Survey." *Journal of Cultural Science*, vol. 6, no. 1, 2013, pp. 4–21.

Spurgeon, Christina "The Ethics, Aesthetics and Practical Politic of Ownership in Co-Creative Media." *Digital Storytelling: Form and Content*, edited by Mark Dunford, and Tricia Jenkins, Palgrave Macmillan, 2017, pp. 119–135.

Spurgeon, Christina, et al. "Co-creative Media: Theorising Digital Storytelling as a platform for researching and developing participatory culture." ANZCA09 Communication, Creativity and Global Citizenship. Brisbane, July 2009.

Tacchi, Jo. "Finding a Voice: Participatory Development in Southeast Asia." *Story Circle: Digital Storytelling around the World*, edited by John Hartley, and Kelly McWilliam, Wiley–Blackwell, 2009, pp. 167–75.

Tufte, Edward. *Envisioning Information*. Graphics Press, 1990.

Vandendorpe, Christian. *From Papyrus to Hypertext: Toward the Universal Digital Library*. University of Illinois Press, 2011.

White, Hayden. "The Value of Narrativity in the Representation of Reality." *Critical Inquiry*, vol. 7, no. 1, 1980, pp. 5–27.

Woo, Elaine. "Dana Winslow Atchley III; Pioneered Digital Storytelling." *LA Times*, 30 Dec. 2000. https://www.latimes.com/archives/la-xpm-2000-dec-30-me-6346-story.html. Accessed 4 July 2017.

Wu, Qiongli. "Digital Storytelling in China." *Story Circle: Digital Storytelling around the World*, edited by John Hartley, and Kelly McWilliam, Wiley-Blackwell, 2009, pp. 230–244.

3 The Politics of Storytelling
Stakeholders in Collaborative Media Creation

Situating the Author in Autobiographical Storytelling

Personal narratives are formed by outside forces before their authors even consider putting them into words for an autobiography. The narratives we tell about our lives, and in fact, the narratives that others have told us about our lives, influence how we comprehend our autobiographies. These narratives are shaped and molded throughout the years, changing with new perspectives and narratives that come into our lives. Additionally, we learn how to formulate and organize stories into recognizable structures and genres.

Digital storytelling concentrates on stories that are self-revelatory, personal, experiential, make use of photos (more so than video), and underscoring. They are created minimally (in terms of time and effects), and prioritize process over product (Lambert and Hessler 37). Developing a story based on a moment or moments speaks to the experiential nature of digital stories, one of the seven defining characteristics of the genre (Lambert and Hessler 37). The memories of the moment(s) become the building blocks for the autobiographical story:

> The memories associated with our most important life lessons are inevitably those with strong emotional encoding at the moment, as in traumas or events involving those close to us. When we describe these events, and their meaning to our lives, we inevitably drop out of argumentation and into story. Story in this sense works biologically to ensure the total recall of those events we have ingrained as being of greatest emotional importance to us.
>
> (Lambert and Hessler 7)

Compounding the impact of moments with the genre's highlighting of the self-revelatory invites moments that become transformative for the storyteller. For literary theorist Jerome Bruner, narratives that showcase the author's personal growth and the ways in which these moments have changed their outlook and future decision making is a key feature of autobiography, which he describes in the following manner:

DOI: 10.4324/9781003200826-3

> A narrator, in the here and now, takes upon himself or herself the task of describing the progress of a protagonist in the there and then, one who happens to share his name. He must by convention bring that protagonist from the past into the present in such a way that the protagonist and the narrator eventually fuse and become one person with a shared consciousness. Now, in order to bring a protagonist from the there and then to the point where the original protagonist becomes the present narrator, one needs a theory of growth or at least of transformation. You need a prescription that will allow the callow pear-stealing boy to turn into the thoughtful St. Augustine now caught in a struggle between faith and reason. The boy, of course, becomes an instrument in the telling. His life becomes dedicated to the theory or story into which his destiny is fitted.
>
> (27–28)

Bruner acknowledges that the specific act of "marking turning points," that is, the self-revelatory transformation of key moments in life heavily influences Western autobiography (31). For digital storytelling, self-revelations show that "the author is aware of a new insight that is being shared in the story, giving the story a sense of immediacy and discovery" (Lambert and Hessler 37).

The concept of focusing on moments of change and growth, on Bruner's "turning points," is one that I have long followed as a digital storytelling facilitator and one that I still use to this day. In my Introduction to Oral Communication courses, my students create a digital story focusing on "A Defining Moment." While in line with the general theme of digital storytelling as autobiographical writing, the theme was also influenced by a university campaign of the same name that began around the time I started working at St. Mary's University. My student's work showcases moments that they feel defined their lives in some way. For some, that was the moment they chose their college, the moments loved ones got sick or died, or the moments where parents introduced them to video games or books. The diversity of stories reflects the diversity of students and is a similar project to the *I am UCF* digital storytelling campaign I helped bring to life while at the University of Central Florida (Underberg-Goode, et al.; Hill, et al.; Hill). The project's goal is to "celebrate personal identity, diversity, and community on campus through its collection of personal digital stories" (97). The project, *A Defining Moment*, has a similar goal at St. Mary's University. With both of these projects, I worked with predominantly college-age students to engage them in a narrative writing process that grows out of a Western autobiographical style. While this may not be surprising, considering that both universities are in the United States, it is important to understand that this stylistic framework is just a binding. As I facilitated the creation of the stories in each program, I worked with the storytellers to craft their stories around the perspective of turning points and those moments that define how we see ourselves in the world. This guideline generally goes unchallenged as it is a key component of autobiographical writing and one that students are generally familiar with through their everyday media intake.

Autobiographical narratives are built from retellings and reframings of these moments that occur first within the minds of these storytellers and in their retellings to others over the years. The reactions of these others greatly influence subsequent retellings of the stories. In our telling and subsequent retellings of life stories, we continually edit with regard to what went well in previous tellings and what didn't. Such changes can come from both the audience response and also the constraints of the medium through which the story was told. Even if the story took place in a three-minute conversation, storytellers will discover which pieces of the narrative really moved the audience (based on their verbal responses and nonverbal reactions) and which parts of the story felt off-track, irrelevant, or time-consuming (story structure). Moreover, the storyteller will learn whether the story is worth telling again or not, or how tellable a story is. Thus, our life stories are both ours and not ours – private and public. They are ours in that we fashion them after our own memories, each author deciding for themselves what is "true," and not ours in that to gain a bigger understanding of "what is true," we should seek the help of others.

But, of course, the creation of autobiography is itself a fictionalization, forged within the prevalent narrative tradition. As Jonathan Gotschall explains:

> Our life stories are who we are. They are our identity. A life story is not, however, an objective account. A life story is a carefully shaped narrative that is replete with strategic forgetting and skillfully spun meanings.
>
> (161)

We sift through the past, selecting which moments to include, and refine over time based on the audiences' reactions, even those that come in daily interactions. When creating a narrative, this process is formalized as writers will consider which parts of a narrative will be included or excluded from their finalized tale. This act of editing works to shape a more effective story within narrative norms of their society and culture. Authors will try to shape their narratives into ideal story shapes, or patterns with which their audience will be familiar (consider how many Western narratives that follow traditional story structures such as those found in Freytag's pyramid, Vonnegut's G-I/B-E graph, or Campbell's Hero's Journey). Additionally, the writer, often unconsciously, hones their narrative to match the cultural folk psychology of morality, history, and expectation. Both of these edits are further impacted by the traces left by those involved in the digital storytelling process.

The "Why Tell" Function

Understanding the tellability of a story influences whether people continue to tell a story and how they adapt their narratives for future tellings. Digital storytelling, like all storytelling, also strives to find those stories worth telling and this impacts the kinds of narratives that are shared. Bruner identifies this principle through what he calls the "why tell" function of narratives (29). Bruner writes,

> Not everything that happened is worth telling about, and it is not always clear why what one tells merits telling. We are bored and offended by such accounts as 'I got up in the morning, got out of bed, dressed and tied my shoes, shaved, had breakfast, went off to the office and saw a graduate student who had an idea for a thesis.'
>
> (29)

This kind of narrative is too ordinary, too banal. Bruner goes on to explain,

> The 'why tell' function imposes something of great (and hidden) significance on narrative. Not only must a narrative be about a sequence of events over time, structured comprehensibly in terms of cultural canonicality, it must also contain something that endows it with exceptionality.
>
> (29)

Digital storytelling works to find those stories worth telling with ordinary people, it is important to consider how the "why tell" function impacts the kinds of narratives that are shared. Considering Bruner's "why tell" function in combination with the vernacular creativity (Burgess) of digital storytelling, we begin to see that asking someone to tell the story of a specific moment also asks them to consider the story's tellability in relation to this trope of turning points. Because the concept of turning points is so embedded in our cultural understanding of telling personal stories, storytellers naturally want to find moments of their lives that imbue a sense of change or growth, as this is what influences tellability. Telling a story about the moment I put on my shoes today seems banal unless that was the exact moment I learned about the death of someone I love, in which case the unfinished tying of the shoe might represent something greater than the mere act itself.

Understanding the tellability of a narrative depends on understanding the audience for whom the story is being told. As Marie-Laure Ryan addresses,

> We may for instance produce narratives as a response to questions from a doctor, a prosecutor, a teacher, or a parent who wants explanations for our behavior, and these stories can satisfy the questioner without fulfilling the felicity conditions that pertain to what Mary Louise Pratt

calls 'narrative display texts,' such as conversational storytelling or the production of literary fiction.

(4)

Ryan argues,

> there is a continuum that runs from strict conditions of narrativity to conditions of tellability, and from tellability to full-fledged aesthetic principles, such as the Aristotelian principles that recommend exposition, conflict, climax, and a resolution brought up by a dramatic turns of events.

(ibid.)

The combination of understanding tellability within narrative display texts and the aesthetic principles of storytelling are key to understanding the writing process that exists within the digital storytelling workshop. Teaching participants to write within this discourse is the primary focus of the digital storytelling facilitator.

Bruner suggests the idea of what makes something worthy of telling is based on what is "culture confirming" (29): "We laugh at what is canonically funny, sorrow for what is canonically sad" (30). These standards in culture guide our narrative-making processes, and because these norms are guided not by one person, but by a collective culture, it is impossible to understand any narratives as individually created. Bruner argues, "If it is all 'givens', then there is no individuality, no modern Self" (30). We are, in a sense, defining and shaping ourselves through repeated interactions with others. The self is co-created and politically and socially constructed. This understanding of the external forces shaping personal narratives is contrary to the ethos and ideals embedded in the genre of digital storytelling, which so highly prides itself on the agency of writers as autonomous individuals. But most of today's digital storytellers are already engrossed in learning these norms through their everyday media experience and narrative intake. Further, digital storytelling facilitators generally have training in crafting narratives that are guided by Western "culture conforming" norms, and thus these considerations are reinforced to the storytellers. This raises questions about the true agency afforded to digital storytelling writers. What does agency look like when we consider that there is "no modern Self"? What aspects of the writing process afford agency? Is there a lasting sense of agency for participants?

I, too, am aware that I help craft such narratives with writers in my digital storytelling workshops. What, if any, role am I playing in infringing on the rights and agency of storytellers? Is it better to assist writers in learning the cultural norms of effective storytelling or to let them write based on what they've already consumed? Is this, in fact, even cause for concern, as they have already experienced so many "culture conforming" narratives?

What could a digital storytelling workshop look like that didn't conform to these standards? In what ways do I reinforce power structures inherent in these political schemas and in what ways do I work to dismantle them?

These are questions I examine with each storytelling project. Examining the role of the facilitator in digital storytelling writing workshops is essential to considering how outside influence impacts narrative creation. It is this impact that drives conversations about digital storytelling as being co-creative or co-productive. If there is "no modern Self" and all stories are written (consciously or unconsciously) to meet a set of culturally-defined narrative standards, then all storytelling is automatically collaborative between author and culture. The facilitator and other storytellers in the workshop (as well as others who may have heard the author share this story at previous points) act as an intermediary between the two, helping the author discover how such narrative standards can shape their writing to make it more effective in reaching their audiences. Thus, the creation process of narratives exists within the framework of co-creative media including digital stories.

Digital Storytelling as Co-creative Media

Viewing personal narrative creation as a co-productive practice calls into question the authenticity of personal narratives like digital stories, which previous scholarship claims are based on the reliance of digital storytelling on the author's own words, voice, personal archives, and personal experiences (Wu; Thumim; Hertzberg Kaare and Lundby; Helff and Woletz). Yet public influence affects the way in which storytellers compose, produce, and share personal narratives. Thus, there is no such thing as an "individual" story; instead, personal narratives are constantly compounded by the agendas, experiences, and expectations of others. Digital storytelling, too, is co-creative media that is compounded by the agendas, goals, and ideas of both inside and outside forces.

The collaborative creative production process that digital storytelling workshops employ is not simply because of the role of technology in its creation and consumption (Sprugeon et al.). Instead, as narrative theorist Christina Spurgeon et al. argue, "participatory media are facilitated by people and organizations, not just technology" (274). In short, participatory media is a public, social production. Moreover, while they acknowledge that participatory media is predicated on the relationships between stakeholders and the agents involved in the creation process, the rhetorical and dialogic practices among these constituents reinforces the social and political processes through which stories are produced. Digital storytelling works to equalize power dynamics by positioning the participants as experts alongside the facilitators, thereby putting them in cooperation with one another. This often results in giving or failing to give participants more agency in the telling of their personal narratives. This is what is commonly referred to in digital storytelling scholarship as "giving voice," a term I contest for its

Figure 3.1 Chart depicting the immediate influences on the storyteller in a Digital Storytelling workshop.

reliance on the assumption that voice can be given by an outsider. Rather, facilitators should focus on the way in which we can remind participants of the power they hold in the creation space; power that is not *given*, but rather amplified.

Yet unearthing the ways in which diverse individuals hold power in a room will not eliminate the political and social aspects of co-produced narratives. As digital storytelling scholars William Hartley and Kelly McWilliam write, "digital storytelling is a good way to explore how individuals can help each other to navigate complex social networks and organizational systems, which themselves rely on the active agency of everyone in the system to contribute to the growth of knowledge" (15). For the storyteller, the most direct influences in the room are the facilitator, the other storytellers, and the potential audience (Figure 3.1).

These are just the influences the storyteller is likely to meet in the creation room. It does not consider, for example, the outside influence of family and friends as separate from potential audience members the storyteller may not know. However, these influences also equally impress on the storyteller's creation process and therefore exemplify the co-creative media processes of digital storytelling. Ideally, then, the co-productive process of digital storytelling works to disrupt the traditional producer/consumer relationship of mass media, by putting the creative power into the hands of the storytellers.

Storytelling Is Political

Philosopher Hannah Arendt suggests that telling a story can never be a completely personal or individual experience. Rather, she argues that storytelling is a part of the subjective-in-between where private and public interests constantly struggle with one another. Arendt argues "the greatest forces of intimate life ... lead an uncertain, shadowy kind of existence unless and until they are transformed, deprivatized and deindividualized, as it were, into a shape to fit them for public appearance." She considers storytelling a form of transformation that reframes and reworks the private in the context of a public (50). Using Arendt as a guide, anthropologist Michael Jackson emphasizes,

> When one tells stories, therefore, one is never simply giving voice to what is on one's own mind or in one's own interests; one is realizing, or objectifying, one's own experience in ways that others can relate to through experiences of their own.
>
> (15)

In considering the words of Arendt and Jackson, we begin to see that stories are continually narrated in relation to an audience who may or may not be aware of their role in the co-created stories. Implied in this is the idea that stories can never be created solely by or for a single person. Arendt's "greatest forces" need a shape, created for and informed by a public audience. Stories are one of the most influential and understandable ways to synthesize and organize knowledge and from which to create meaning (Erstad and Wertsch). Creating meaning from stories occurs in the relational space between the teller and the listener, or potentially the teller and the presumed listener. Because of this, storytellers narrate tales to meet the needs of others in addition to serving to meet their personal needs and agendas. Even if these considerations are not consciously evaluated, narratives cannot remain private in thought or when spoken. They always enter into larger contexts that grapple with socio-cultural constructions and perceptions seeking to unearth how and why storytellers thought about, felt, and narrated their personal stories.

Personal narratives thus become cultural artifacts where private meets public and wherein storytellers make meaning out of their social experiences in inherently collaborative spaces created both socially and by the methodology of co-creative storymaking processes. Composing personal narratives brings storytellers' experiences, beliefs, and emotions, all formed in social contexts, to their narratives, which frames the way in which they tell and share their digital stories. In other words, their stories are subjective, rather than objective, and express narratives of unique perspectives established by and situated in the tellers' cultural, historic, geographic, and social positions. Personal narratives, then, balance between the public and the private in the liminal space of Arendt's subjective-in-between. In this understanding personal narratives are both unique – an individual's representation of these events or experiences, their personal mindset, emotions, and understandings of which are unique unto them – and publicly and socially framed. It is this social framing that makes them political.

This understanding of the political nature of personal narratives informed one of its more famous variations, the second wave feminist slogan: "The Personal Is Political." The use of the phrase dates back to Carol Hanisch's influential 1971 article of the same name. Hanisch, in speaking of women's therapy sessions she attended, noted the primary discovery of the group sessions was that the individual problems of the women were communal problems, political problems (76). In sharing their experiences in group story-sharing practices, Hanisch found the women could identify common oppressive patterns stemming from the kinds of interpersonal relationships significant to the women in the group. From these private, personal stories, she recognized larger public, political constructs. She suggested the individual feelings and experiences of these women offered a way to think about the role of women on a macro scale and to develop a deeper understanding of women's struggles and determine effective solutions (77). She suggests that in listening to stories of the everyday experiences of various people, we can achieve connection between diverse individuals and perspectives. Sharing private stories from everyday citizens thus creates a broader range through which to understand our public culture. While this may sound a little romantic, it is important to remember Hanisch wrote her seminal essay at the height of the second wave of feminism. Still, scholars such as Arendt make similar arguments about sharing personal experiences.

Arendt recognized the importance of everyday storytelling practices such as those found in Hanisch's therapy sessions: "Each time we talk about things that can be experienced only in privacy or intimacy, we bring them out into a sphere where they will assume a kind of reality which, their intensity notwithstanding, they never could have had before" (50). This focus on the everyday, ordinary transaction of storytelling is mirrored later in digital storytelling scholarship by Jean Burgess and her theory of vernacular creativity, which "describe[s] and illuminate[s] creative practices that emerge from highly particular and non-elite social contexts and communicative conventions" (205). For Burgess, digital storytelling "[amplifies] the ordinary voice" as it aims to "legitimate it as a relatively autonomous and worthwhile contribution to public culture" (207). Still, even the idea that these stories will reach public culture might be an optimistic one, as "reach" implies a two-way communication pattern: Sending and receiving. Jackson suggests that following Arendt's theory, the subjective-in-between, implies and leaves room for political power structures of oppression: "For every story that sees the light of day, untold others remain in the shadows, censored, or suppressed" (31). Those that do see the light of day are often the dominant narratives of the culture and can be either substantiated or countered by personal narratives.

The unique perspective of each storyteller will account for the ways in which their personal stories mirror or contrast the dominant cultural narratives communicated through historical narratives and mass media. Thus, personal narratives are a reaction, whether in favor or against, to dominant cultural narratives, another instance of the subjective-in-between, or a meeting of the private and public. Dominant narratives tend to be taken as the presiding narrative of an event or experience by the majority of people within a community, but counter-narratives help fill the gaps left by dominant personal narratives.[1]

According to political scientist Iris Marion Young, dominant narratives are part of the process of cultural imperialism, wherein a dominant group of people determines and shapes the interpretation of the history and culture of a society. Young writes, "as a consequence, the dominant cultural products of the society, that is, those most widely disseminated, express the experience, values, goals, and achievements of these groups" (59). This invites gaps and stereotypes underrepresented storytellers can help close and change, as Young argues:

> Assumptions of the universality of the perspective and experience of the privileged are dislodged when the oppressed themselves expose those assumptions by expressing the positive difference of their experience. By creating their own cultural images they shake up received stereotypes about them.
>
> (155)

Yet counter stories can also be seen as threats to the status quo, or to cultural imperialism. Further, sharing these experiences can, in some situations, jeopardize the safety of the storyteller. In his fieldwork in New Zealand researching narratives of Iraqi and Somali refugees, Michael Jackson found:

> one often finds that the truth will get you nowhere or get you into trouble. One has to learn to carefully select, censor, and misrepresent one's reality in order to get one's way—to escape from terror, to cross a border, to be selected for emigration, to avoid racist insults and condescending expectations in the country of asylum; and persuade state officials to look kindly on one's petition for family reunions. Stories are often cover stories, defenses against danger and hurt. They downplay any disparity between the truth of one's own experience and the truths enshrined in the dominant narratives of the state, which expects gratitude from refugees, not grievances, conformity not criticism.
>
> (14)

Thus, counter stories can be seen as threats to the status quo, or threats to cultural imperialism, "mark[ing] and stereotyp[ing] some groups at the same time that it silences their self-expression" (Young 24). Young reminds us that "Victims of cultural imperialism cannot forget their group identity because the behavior and reactions of others call them back to it" (123). Such group identity is collected in public narratives created by those outside of the group for group members, thereby eliminating the impact or value of distinct voices or narratives in larger cultural contexts.

Storytelling or story-like practices dominate many, if not all, cultures as a practice that helps to share and collect memories; preserve and create culture; understand community, events, and identity; and problem-solve personal, community, and global issues. As a method of communication, it can be didactic and entertaining and can serve to instill cultural mores and values:

> Stories are one of the most powerful and personal ways that we learn about the world, passed down from generation to generation through the family and cultural groups to which we belong. As human beings we are primed to engage each other and the world through language, and stories can be deeply evocative sources of knowledge and awareness.
>
> (Bell 16)

It is easy to see, then, that storytelling is a cultural practice. Bettina Stumm faces a similar challenge in her process of co-writing biographies. She writes, "Collaborators create spaces for subjects to speak and to assert their marginalized voices, voices that are affirmed in the collaborators' responses. Truth telling, listening, and engaging empathetically with vulnerable subjects become significant political activities in the process," (764). Inviting the influence of complex relationships between the storyteller and workshop participants, participants engage in an (often) unconscious act of molding identity. In turn this phenomenon extends to power structures of cultural citizenship that can affect the overall message and context participants may want to share. Aiwah Ong, in her examination of cultural citizenship, identifies this as a "dual process of self-making and being-made within webs of power linked to the nation-state and civil society" (qtd. in Klaus and Lünenborg 202).

Co-creation is especially interesting when considering authors who discuss their individual identity within a community whose other members are part of the same digital storytelling workshop. Effectively, the persistent presence of a community identity in the writing environment might exert pressure over the individual storyteller to share a story that positions her as a member of the community. It follows that digital storytelling can also be seen as an instance where cultural citizenship can be formed. Most notably the "self-making and being-made" can be seen in the story circles as participants share the stories they want to make and seek advice and critique. These moments of the process usually happen under the guidance of the facilitator, which invokes questionable and flexible power structures within the workshop. Story circles place a single member of the group in a vulnerable place in relation to all the other workshop participants as both a collective and as individuals. Although a microcosm (and typically a positive experience) of what a person might face in sharing her story in broader cultural settings, digital storytelling remains a site where people can attempt to "self-make," but instead define themselves in relational contexts to others. This also helps shape the final message and context, inviting a process of "being-made" into the creation of self. Thus, while digital storytelling spaces work to unveil storied moments of authentic identity, they often gloss over the complex web of relationships that influence identity and storymaking processes, failing to recognize the problems inherent in the idealization of an "authentic identity."

The Role of the Institution

As collaborators, institutions leave traces on participants' digital stories. Hence, it is important to question "[w]hat and whose interests shape our programs and practices" (Taub-Pervizpour 246) as a whole and how

> we navigate between multiple agendas which may be at odds with each other and which almost inevitably at moments collide: the agendas of the institutions that support and fund our work, the agendas of community partners, [participants], not to mention our own agendas.
> (246–247)

John Hartley writes that personal narratives are at best "coloured" by and at worst "determined by" facilitating institutions (Smiling 207). For Hartley, this is not so much a criticism as an expectation. It is simply not possible to remove the story from the organization that produced it. Personal narratives are not created in a vacuum. Rather, digital storytelling is "an *embedded* practice, one that happens within institutions and is mediated by institutional values and discourses" (Dush 627–628). The amount to which an organization influences participants' digital stories further has to do with the ways in which the organization engages with the participants. Where some institutions may truly want only to amplify participants' stories, others may wish to garner stories that specifically meet their needs, beliefs, and perspectives as a method to reinforce their institution. Some institutions will even retain the rights to the created works, enabling an unethical ownership and power over the storyteller and their story (Dush).

There are often conscious and unconscious institutional rules enforced by the facilitating institutions that affect the narratives participants tell. For instance, projects conducted in classrooms, face the "constraints of course objectives, assessment regimes, timetables and large classes," among others (Gachago and Sykes 91). Additionally, institutions often hold values that drive their programs in greater ways than structural and organizational limitations. In an analysis of a digital storytelling workshop held for youth members of a faith-based congregation, Brigit Hertzberg Kaare and Knut Lundby identify a reciprocity of identity formation, explaining that the participants negotiate their individual identity based on the collective, and the collective is in turn shaped by the individuals, since the "young narrators are connected to the collective identity of the congregation" (117). In their analysis of the project *Faith Stories*, Hertzberg Kaare and Lundby write,

> The Digital Faith Stories are supposed to have a positive message, and the supervisors use their influence to discuss with the youths how they

might interpret their narratives in a positive way (DFS 14), thus putting their impress on both the content and structure of the narratives.

(113)

In this example, we again see how the institutional organization plays a role in the message and narratives of the stories created, complicating the authenticity and perspective of "personal" stories in favor of a more "public" and institutionalized, co-created "self."

Jerry Watkins and Angelina Russo point out that presumed interference from the BBC can be seen in the digital stories distributed in the *Capture Wales* archive, a digital storytelling project that ran from 2001–2008 produced in a partnership between BBC Wales and Cardiff University's Cardiff School of Journalism, Media and Cultural Studies: "There is little to no profanity, nudity, violence; these stories have been made within creative restrictions and preset themes, with varying degrees of input from workshop" (271). Similarly, the digital storytelling program *I Am UCF*, which I helped facilitate from 2016 to 2018, made political decisions about whether or not to include videos made by undergraduate students that mentioned or made ties to alcohol in the online database collection. In one story deemed suitable for inclusion in the online database, a student uses a video of him dancing saved from the social media app Snapchat. A filter placed on the video serves as an advertisement for Heineken beer. At no point in the digital story is the student seen drinking, nor could audiences infer him to be drinking. He additionally adds the following caveats in his credits in response to the Snapchat filter: "This video is not affiliated or sponsored by Heineken®/ Don't drink and drive" (*Libra Garage*). Another video involving alcohol was not accepted for display in the online collection, even though the student consented to making it public. Like the previous student, he made use of Snapchat videos in his digital story. However, these videos showed, or implied, that the student was drinking alcohol with friends. It was unclear whether all the parties involved had consented to being on display in this way, and it was further unclear as to whether or not all these students were of legal drinking age. Concerned about a potential lack of consent on the part of the other people filmed in the video and further concerned about the depiction of potential illegal activities like underage drinking, the project team did not include the video in the online database as they felt it may reflect poorly on the project and university.

Students in the *I Am UCF* project were given creative freedom in their storytelling, and rules about what could or could not be publicly displayed went unspoken during the creation phase of the *I Am UCF* project. Whether or not these rules were clearly stated by institution officials and/or digital storytelling facilitators remains unclear in the case of *Capture Wales*. Yet some programs make their approval procedures very clear. Amy Hill notes that some of her programs with foster youth require that agency staff members "sign off" on youths' scripts: "staff may ask participants to delete or revise over critical language, factual inaccuracies, material that may incite legal action or details that risk alienating viewers" (27). The youth she works with are aware of this policy before beginning to write their scripts, but some youth retain concerns that "their words were stifled, their stories silenced" (ibid.). Hill writes that the goal of this policy "is not censorship but openness, in terms of a desire that the stories will welcome social worker viewers into a dialogue rather than immediately putting them on the defense" (ibid.). In this example, the institution is working to have the students create stories to reach a specific audience and thus ask that students edit their stories accordingly. Because the facilitators were employed by the organization, there is an added framework of expectations and obligations to ensure that the workshop and produced digital stories meet the desired outcomes. Dush points out that this perceived expectation may additionally push employees, and perhaps workshop participants, if asked, to speak about the hosting or funding organization and/or the workshop itself: "[Participants] may feel that they owe an organization their participation. Similarly, in workplace-based digital storytelling initiatives, employees may feel obliged to both participate and to speak in ways that shine a favorable light on their employer" (634). To varying extents, these institutional expectations on facilitators and story content place constraints on storytellers. These constraints could interfere with the storytellers' ability to tell their stories in truthful ways that meet their own needs as opposed to the needs and expectations of facilitating institutions, especially as they influence the story's ability to be shared publicly and with specific audiences. Further, while not directly implied in any of the above examples, institutions may be concerned with satisfying the needs of their funding institutions and stakeholders, which could further complicate the constraints institutionally placed on storytellers.

Understanding the facilitating institution is important to comprehending fully the produced stories as they can point to organizational intentions. These intentions may have missionary or testifying roots, as in the "positive" faith narratives produced in *Digital Faith Stories*, or they might have corporate roots, such as the case with projects receiving funding from agencies with an outspoken agenda. Projects whose institutional support prioritizes their agenda over the whole range of potential stories to be told may retain more veto power over the types of stories that are created and disseminated. Many times, these personal stories serve as what John Hartley calls "smiling" stories, or stories that reflect the personal aspect, and are "appropriated to signal non-threatening communicative intentions, which would likely be rejected if the tale were understood to be on behalf of industry or government" (Hartley "Smiling" 207). The audience's assumption that digital stories privilege authentic personal, private stories thus advantage the institution through which they are developed, for the precise reason that they seem to be removed from the institution. This can create an intuited trust and acceptance of the story. Everyday consumers may never give a thoughtful consideration of the facilitating institution, leaving consumers to view these stories as solely their own. A digital story might represent the storyteller as its sole creator in the credits or by-line, but any analysis that excluded the local context of the workshop space and its participants would be false. Indeed, many workshops acknowledge the local context within the credits or the text and/or the metadata embedded with the video online. StoryCenter acknowledges its participation in the creation of digital stories by adding an animated logo to the end of all their participants' creations. This addition serves as branding to entice viewers to learn more about StoryCenter and marks the company as co-constructors of the digital narrative.

Digital storytelling thus exists within a capital paradigm, even as it operates as a tactical media. It is supported through institutions that make money off the products created by storymaking participants, whether or not the funding is directly linked to the completed digital stories. Grants and subsequent funding, based in part or wholly on previously conducted digital storytelling workshops, create a sort of monetary exchange for institutions, but not for the participants. In some cases, such as many of StoryCenter's residencies, participants pay to learn how to design and produce digital stories. StoryCenter can then use, should the participant grant permission, the created story not only to further the exchange of ideas, but also as a means of advertising for future participants and as a product that exemplifies their growth and practice, which could be used to establish further institutional funding. The cultural project created more often serves the institution than the individual, especially as academics, myself included, are more likely to focus on digital storytelling programs or institutions than on individual stories. While some stories may be highlighted, rarely will it be in numbers that rival the institutional or programmatic consideration. Because institutional support is developed in a system that continuously seeks recognition – be it prestige, known-ness, funding – there is necessarily pressure to deliver products that will continue to bring such recognition.

Because institutions aim to continue receiving recognition for their works, there are times when they take active measures to ensure what they might call quality control. We saw this in the examples above, where institutions veto story types for production and dissemination. However, the types of stories storytellers are able to tell with institutional support are only one way in which institutions push their agendas in the digital storytelling workshop. Before they can concern themselves with the types of stories participants are telling, they should first gather participants. Some digital storytelling projects may have restrictions on who can participate or cap the number of participants. While some of these restrictions are logistical, they can serve to place limitations on the number and diversity of stories shared within digital storytelling platforms.

In her analysis of the *Queering the Museum* digital storytelling project to develop LGBTQ+ narratives for a museum exhibit, Nicole Robert explains how the Community Advisory Committee (CAC), a group consisting of representatives from local LGBTQ+ institutions, needed to approve "all major decisions" (18). She writes, "This meant that the CAC supervised development of the application to participate, helped recruit applicants, and selected participants based on those applications" (ibid.). This process greatly benefited the needs of the facilitating institution, as the participants ultimately created products that aligned with the desires of the institution. The CAC members marketed the digital storytelling project to their social networks, potentially limiting the applications to people known to one or more CAC committee members. Additionally, CAC members selected applicants for the *Queering the Museum* digital storytelling project based in part on the knowledge that some or all of the produced videos would be exhibited in the museum and thereby determining which stories would be best for dissemination and public consumption.

The suitability of the story as well as the capability of the applicant to tell a story, how widely representative stories were, and story accuracy guided the CAC's selection process: "[the] process was absolutely shaped by its affiliation with the museum exhibit, and the perceived or desired requirements that each CAC member imagined for that Exhibit" (149). In short, the CAC selected participants subjectively, based on the stories they were prepared to tell. Robert writes,

> Part of this selection process for the DSW and for the general content of the exhibit was based in each individual's ideas of what constituted an accurate queer history of the Seattle area .... Accurate representation brings a pressure to conform to pre-existing notions of chronology, identity and even narrative organization. This pressure influences selection, even collaborative selection, to uphold, rather than contest, existing ideologies of identity.
>
> (149)

The CAC placed themselves in a position to determine authentic truth, a problematic turn when considering how memories and subjective truth play into the telling of personal stories, as these stories will necessarily be performed with a specific purpose and audience in mind, as discussed above. Furthermore, the project focused on a vulnerable population. In order for people to participate in the project, they needed to be ready to share their personal histories. It is possible that the most vulnerable among the targeted group continue to remain silent for fear of retribution. It would follow, then, that there are still underrepresented stories unavailable to the committee members.

In addition to the subjectivity of the CAC's selection process, potential storytellers faced a series of limitations before they could participate in the *Queering the Museum* digital storytelling project. First, participants needed to complete an application form, thereby eliminating the stories of those who could not read or write the language of the application form. These applications reached the CAC anonymously, and the members then ranked the applications on a scale of one to five, with five being the top choice. The individual scores were combined into a list of ten finalists, only eight of whom were able to attend the four-day workshop. Robert points to "the ability to have two weekends free," "access to the online application, availability to attend the workshop, [and] transportation" as further barriers to participation (148). The project required an intensive four-day commitment over the period of two weeks, and Robert notes that while this might have made the project more accessible to some storytellers, some selected applicants had work, health, and transportation challenges and could not ultimately participate (90).

All of this is not to call out Robert's digital storytelling project. Indeed, there are challenges and reasonable constraints to participation in every digital storytelling project. These challenges and constraints will differ for each project based on the unique circumstances and needs of that project. As such, I recognize that I am not capable of seeing every angle of a project by looking in from the outside. My assessment here makes use of Robert's detailed account of a specific selection process to show how logistical constraints and institutional agendas account for the continued silencing of select stories in order to consider the implications for responsible facilitation. The application and selection process utilized by the *Queering the Museum* project greatly speaks to the ways in which institutions and stakeholders maintain control over the stories produced in, and subsequently shared by, digital storytelling projects, ultimately raising questions about how future projects can appropriate and learn from the techniques utilized by previous projects to create equitable and ethical participation and storytelling standards.

The relationships a storyteller encounters within a co-productive storytelling environment are complex and even when unconscious, inform the creation of a digital story. In order to comprehend how the public shapes the personal, it is important to look at the influences enacted on an individual storyteller. No story is completely personal. They are all created in social networks. A personal narrative is constantly in struggle with the agendas, experiences, and expectations of others. The responsible digital storytelling facilitator will effectively manage these networks in ways that minimize outside interference, to allow storytellers to take more ownership over the production and dissemination of their narratives.

Note

1 See: Goodall; Yosso; Knight et al.; Bamberg and Andrews; and Delgado for more on counter-narratives; and the value and validity of counter-narratives has been asserted in feminist (McKenzie-Mohr and Lafrance; Godrej; Ross), queer (Vaccaro), critical race theory (Solórzano and Yosso), Black (Sawyer and

Palmer), Latino/a (Castro-Salazar and Bagley), Indigenous (Bishop), and education studies (Muñoz and Maldonado; Roy and Roxas; García).

References

Arendt, Hannah. *The Human Condition*. 2nd ed., University of Chicago Press, 1998.

Bamberg, Michael, and Molly Andrews. *Considering Counter-Narratives: Narrating, Resisting, Making Sense*. John Benjamins Publishing Company, 2004.

Bell, Lee Anne. *Storytelling for Social Justice*. Routledge, 2010.

Bishop, Russell. "Freeing Ourselves: An Indigenous Response to Neo-Colonial Dominance in Research, Classrooms, Schools, and Education Systems." *Qualitative Inquiry Outside the Academy*, edited by Norman K. Denzin, and Michael D. Giardina, Routledge, 2014, 146–163.

Burgess, Jean. "Hearing Ordinary Voices: Cultural Studies, Vernacular Creativity and Digital Storytelling." *Continuum: Journal of Media & Cultural Studies*, vol. 20, no. 2, 2006, pp. 201–14.

Bruner, Jerome. "Self-Making and World-Making." In *Narrative and Identity*, edited by Jens Brockmeier, and Donal Carbaugh, Philadelphia: John Benjamins Publishing Company, 2001, pp. 25–38.

Castro-Salazar, Ricardo, and Carl Bagley. "'Ni de Aquí ni from There': Navigating between Contexts: Counter-Narratives of Undocumented Mexican Students in the United States." *Race Ethnicity and Education*, vol. 13, no. 1, 2010, pp. 23–40.

Delgado, Richard. "Storytelling for Oppositionists and Others: A Plea for Narrative." *Michigan Law Review*, vol. 87, no. 8, 1989, pp. 2411–2441.

Dush, Lisa. "The Ethical Complexities of Sponsored Digital Storytelling." *International Journal of Cultural Studies*, vol. 16, no. 6, 2012, pp. 627–640.

Erstad, Ola, and James V. Wertsch. "Tales of Mediations: Narrative and Digital Media as Cultural Tools." *Digital Storytelling, Mediatized Stories*, edited by Knut Lundby, Peter Lang, 2008, 1–17.

Gachago, Daniela, and Pam Sykes. "Navigating Ethical Boundaries When Adopting Digital Storytelling in Higher Education." *Digital Storytelling in Higher Education: International Perspectives*, edited by Grete Jamissen, Pip Hardy, Yngve Nordkvelle, and Heather Pleasants, Palgrave Macmillan, 2017, 91–105.

García, Alyssa. "Counter Stories of Race and Gender: Situating Experiences of Latinas in the Academy." *Latino Studies*, vol. 3, no. 2, 2005, pp. 261–273.

Godrej, Farah. "Spaces for Counter-Narratives: The Phenomenology of Reclamation." *Frontiers: A Journal of Women Studies*, vol. 32, no. 3, 2011, pp. 111–133.

Goodall, H. Lloyd. *Counter-Narrative: How Progressive Academics Can Challenge Extremists and Promote Social Justice*. Routledge, 2016.

Hanisch, Carol. "'The Personal is Political.' Women's Liberation Notes from the Second Year: Major Writings of the Radical Feminists, edited by Shulamith Firestone, and Anne Koedt, New York Radical Women, 1970, 76–78.

Hartley, John. "Smiling or Smiting?–Selves, States and Stories in the Constitution of Polities." *Digital Storytelling: Form and Content*, edited by Mark Dunford, and Tricia Jenkins, Palgrave Macmillan, 2017, pp. 203–227.

Hartley, John, and Kelly McWilliam, editors. *Story Circle: Digital Storytelling around the World*. Wiley-Blackwell, 2009.

Helff, Sissy, and Julie Woletz. "Narrating Euro-African Life in Digital Space." *Story Circle: Digital Storytelling around the World*, edited by John Hartley, and Kelly McWilliam, Wiley-Blackwell, 2009, 131–43.

Hertzberg Kaare, Bridgit, and Knut Lundby. "Autobiography and Assumed Authenticity in Digital Storytelling." *Digital Storytelling, Mediatized Stories: Self-representation in New Media*, edited by Knut Lundby, Peter Lang, 2008, 105–222.

Hill, Amanda. *Power to the People: Responsible Facilitation in Collaborative Storytelling Practices*. 2018, University of Central Florida, PhD Dissertation.

Hill, Amanda, et al. "I am UCF Digital Storytelling Database," *HASTAC*, 3 Nov. 2017, University of Central Florida, Orlando, FL. Conference Presentation.

Hill, Amy. "Digital Storytelling and the Politics of Doing Good: Exploring the Ethics of Bringing Personal Narratives into Public Spheres." *Community-Based Multiliteracies and Digital Media Projects: Questioning Assumptions and Exploring Realities*, edited by Heather M. Pleasants, and Dana E. Salter, Peter Lang, 2014, pp. 21–43.

Jackson, Michael. *The Politics of Storytelling: Variations on a Theme by Hannah Arendt*. 2nd ed., Museum Tusculanum Press, 2013

Klaus, Elisabeth, and Margreth Lünenborg. "Cultural Citizenship. Participation by and through Media." *Feminist Media: Participatory Spaces, Networks and Cultural Citizenship*, edited by Elke Zobl, and Ricarda Drüeke, Transcript, 2012, 197–212.

Knight, Michelle G., Nadjwa E. L. Norton, Courtney C. Bentley, and Iris R. Dixon. "The Power of Black and Latina/o Counterstories: Urban Families and College-Going Processes." *Anthropology & Education*, vol. 35, no. 1, 2004, pp. 99–120.

"Libra Garage." *YouTube*, uploaded by I Am UCF, 27 April 2017, www.youtube.com/watch?v=Uvuk4x_OeMs.

McKenzie-Mohr, Suzanne, and Michelle N. Lafrance, editors. *Women Voicing Resistance: Discursive and Narrative Explorations*. Routledge, 2014.

Muñoz, Susana María, and Marta María Maldonado. "Counterstories of College Persistence by Undocumented Mexicana Students: Navigating Race, Class, Gender, and Legal Status." *International Journal of Qualitative Studies in Education*, vol. 25, no. 3, 2011, pp. 293–315.

Robert, Nicole. *Queering U.S. History Museums: Heteronormative Histories, Digital Disruptions*. Dissertation, University of Washington, 2016.

Ross, Loretta. "Storytelling in SisterSong and the Voices of Feminism Project." *Telling Stories to Change the World: Global Voices on the Power of Narrative to Build Community and Make Social Justice Claims*, edited by Rickie Solinger, Madeline Fox, and Kayhan Irani, Routledge, 2008, 65–74.

Roy, Laura, and Kevin Roxas. "Whose Deficit Is This Anyhow? Exploring Counter-Stories of Somali Bantu Refugees' Experiences in 'Doing School.'" *Harvard Educational Review*, vol. 81, no. 3, 2011, pp. 521–542.

Ryan, Marie-Laure. "Defining Media from the Perspective of Narratology." n.d. 1–14. http://pure.au.dk/portal/files/7562/M-L_Ryans_paper.pdf. Unpublished manuscript.

Sawyer III, Don C., and Robert T. Palmer. "A Different Kind of Black, but the Same Issues: Black Males and Counterstories at a predominantly White Institution." *Journal of Progressive Policy & Practice*, vol. 2, no. 3, 2014, pp. 255–272.

Solórzano, Daniel G., and Tara J. Yosso. "Critical Race Methodology: Counter-Storytelling as an Analytical Framework for Educational Research." *Qualitative Inquiry*, vol. 8, no. 1, 2002, pp. 23–44.

Spurgeon, Christina. "The Art of Co-creative Media: An Australian Survey." *Journal of Cultural Science*, vol. 6, no. 1, 2013, pp. 4–21.

Spurgeon, Christina, Jean Burgess, Helen Klaebe, Kelly McWilliam, Jo Tacchi, and Mimi Tsai. "Co-creative Media: Theorising Digital Storytelling as a Platform for Researching and Developing Participatory Culture." *ANZCA09 Communication, Creativity and Global Citizenship*, Brisbane, July 2009.

Stumm, Bettina. "Witnessing Others in Narrative Collaboration: Ethical Responsibility beyond Recognition." *Biography*, vol. 37, no. 3, 2014, pp. 762–783.

Taub-Pervizpour, Lora, and Erin Drisbrow. "Digital Storytelling with Youth: Whose Agenda Is It?" *Story Circle: Digital Storytelling around the World*, edited by John Hartley, and Kelly McWilliam, Wiley–Blackwell, 2009, 245–51.

Thumim, Nancy. *Self-representation and Digital Culture*. Palgrave Macmillan, 2012.

Underberg-Goode, Natalie, et al. "I am UCF: Diverse Digital Narrative." *Media Education Research Journal*, vol. 9, no. 1, 2019, pp. 96–110.

Vaccaro, Annemarie. "Toward Inclusivity in Family Narratives: Counter-Stories from Queer Multi-Parent Families." *Journal of GLBT Family Studies*, vol. 6, no. 4, 2010, pp. 425–446.

Watkins, Jerry, and Angelina Russo. "Beyond Individual Expression: Working with Cultural Institutions." *Story Circle: Digital Storytelling around the World*, edited by John Hartley, and Kelly McWilliam, Wiley–Blackwell, 2009, 269–78.

Wu, Qiongli. "Digital Storytelling in China." *Story Circle: Digital Storytelling around the World*, edited by John Hartley, and Kelly McWilliam, Wiley-Blackwell, 2009, 230–244.

Yosso, Tara Joy. *Critical Race Counterstories along the Chicana/Chicano Educational Pipeline*. Routledge, 2006.

Young, Iris Marion. *Justice and the Politics of Difference*. Princeton University Press, 1990.

4 Navigating Authenticity
Challenges and Considerations in Writing Personal Narratives

Authenticity Is Co-created

Personal narratives and the identity created therein are shaped in part by an audience's experience of an individual's performance of self. The presence of other "voices," so to speak, within the creation of personal narratives, challenges our concept of what it means to produce and view "authentic" personal narratives. Digital storytelling facilitators and participants in the workshop space enter into a dialogue with storytellers as they develop their narrative work within this dialectical relationship to establish a line of communication to yet another outside party, the viewing audience. Ethically, facilitators should contend with the impacts of this dialogue within the creation of digital stories, as it can alter the story's narrative and even the performance of identity. The way in which the audience responds to a story, or how the facilitator and other storytellers respond to a storyteller in a digital storytelling workspace changes the situational context of the social interaction.

As feminist theorist Liesbet van Zoonen suggests: "Authenticity is in the eye of the beholder and, as the discussions among reality TV audiences testify, it is part of a negotiation and not an easily and objectively observable 'fact'" (46). This is an important concept for ethical storymaking, because it gives the viewing audience the ability to define the authenticity of the work. As such, the understanding of the storymaker's work as authentic comes from a quasi-dialogic practice, a negotiation to use van Zoonen's term, between digital storytelling viewers and the identification put forward by the collective work of the storyteller, facilitator, and others in the workshop space. Herein lies the case for ethical questioning. If one can never be sure how an audience will respond to a digital story nor what they will ultimately take away from it, then what are the concerns and considerations for a facilitator who wants to assist storytellers in their own authentic representation?

If we understand that identity is not a fixed trait, that it evolves over time and changes depending on the contextual situation, then we call into question the very notion of authenticity as a concept that "points to a wider popular desire to identify 'real selves' that are true, single and consistent" (van Zoonen 46). Therefore, we need to reconsider our understanding of authenticity as co-created, and consider that the works of digital storytelling are co-created first by the storyteller within society, then with the facilitator and other participants within the workshop, and later by the audience. For the sake of responsible facilitation, we thus have to understand how we, as facilitators, are embodied subjects and consider our everyday life so we can properly acknowledge how it plays into our role as a facilitator and our interactions with the storytellers.

On the Creation of Authentic Identity Narratives

As philosopher Charles Taylor writes, "the importance of recognition has been modified and intensified by the understanding of identity emerging with the ideal of authenticity" (47). We can begin to see, then, how the authenticity of these stories is complicated when they are created by or with someone else. Thus, we should ask: How is authenticity conveyed when traces of others' ideas are readily apparent in another's story? This is key to understanding digital storytelling, where viewers not only want, but expect, authenticity since the genre is based in part, on the fact that the narratives are personal reflections. van Zoonen notes that authenticity is "a key asset and value in contemporary western society," and that "it is an ascribed rather than an innate or essential quality" (46). She means here that "authenticity is a part of a negotiation and not an easily and objectively observable 'fact'" (ibid.).

Key to understanding the role of authenticity is what van Zoonen suggests is that "the importance of the concept of authenticity points to a wider popular desire to identify 'real selves' that are true, single and consistent" (ibid.), that is, that authenticity points keenly to identity. An individual's performance of self alters based on the context of the situation one encounters. As van Zoonen sumarizes,

> Cultural and social theories of identity have in common that they assume both individual and collective identities to be multiple rather than single, to be dynamic rather than static and to be volatile rather than consistent. In addition, they propose that identity is something that we do, rather than something that we are.
>
> (44)

Our awareness of being present with others and of their presence influences our actions with those same individuals. This is a defining principle of what identity theorist Erving Goffman calls co-presence: "persons must sense that they are close enough to be perceived in whatever they are doing, including their experiencing of others, and close enough to be perceived in this sensing of being perceived" (17). Story sharing is conducted through a collaborative process, which leads us to consider the importance of ethics in the co-creation of identity within performances of life stories, like those of digital storytelling.

Yet to understand how performance contends with authenticity, we should consider how those viewing the performance, that is, how the audience, approaches and contextualizes authenticity. Thus, performances of identity are indelibly tied to how the audience identifies the subject of the digital story; often this identification happens in the same way a person identifies themselves, seeking out similarities and differences between oneself and those around them, or in front of them as is the case of watching someone on screen. As scholar David Buckingham suggests, people have a predilection toward identifying themselves in terms of how similar and dissimilar they are to those around them: "The fundamental paradox of identity is inherent in the term itself. From the Latin root idem, meaning 'the same,' the term nevertheless implies both similarity and difference" (1). Buckingham sees the potential to form identity on both social and individual levels:

> individuals may make claims about their identity (for example, by asserting affiliation with other members of a group), but those claims need to be recognized by others. In seeking to define their identity, people attempt to assert their individuality, but also to join with others, and they work to sustain their sense of status or self-esteem in doing so.
> (6)

These two levels are important for understanding the creation of identity of the storytellers. First, they make claims about their identity, for which they seek recognition from the facilitator and other storytellers. At the same time, they are seeking to identify themselves within an assortment of communities, for example, as residents of a specific place and as members of specific affiliations or communities. The audience then reads this performance and decides with which components they want to identify, or which speak the most directly to their own self-identification. This is further complicated by the fact that in spaces of distribution and dissemination, facilitators, institutions, and other stakeholders may contextualize the identity of the storytellers without input from the storytellers themselves. As such, we should always consider how an audience contends with authentic identity creation in order to understand how it affects the storymaking process and the choices storytellers make during that process.

Contextualizing Challenges to Authenticity

Questions of authenticity in personal narratives are not new to digital and social media: oral storytellers and audiences also confront these questions, especially with cases of hoaxes, rumors, or gossip. Yet while these were certainly concerns of oral storytelling practices, the abundance of new digital works, the increasing ability for people to create digital narratives, the ability to manipulate the aural and visual components of a story, and the distance between the audience and the author in digital worlds all increase the potential for authors to pass false narratives off as truth. In *Stories and Social Media: Identities and Interaction*, Ruth Page revisits the story of YouTube user Lonelygirl15, who posted a series of fictitious video blogs presumably about her experience as a homeschooled teenager being raised by extremely religious parents. Her episodic posts attracted thousands of viewers and followers, who interpreted her video stories as truthful depictions of her daily life. A few months after her first post, however, sources revealed Lonelygirl15 was really a 19-year-old actress from New Zealand. Furthermore, sources showed that her fictitious video posts were the work of two additional aspiring filmmakers (170). Page asserts that some of Lonelygirl15's followers and viewers saw this revelation as a "betrayal of the countercultural, grassroots, participatory ethos of YouTube" (171). While Page argues that Lonelygirl15

> does not make the claim she is real (in ontological terms), the audience associated the narration of her life experiences on YouTube as implicitly associated with first-person narration, assuming she was genuine, existed in the real world, and was an eyewitness to the reported events (ibid.).

Authenticity is a "social virtue," as Hertzberg Kaare and Lundby suggest, that can be taken to mean "a relation between the individual and society" (110). Perhaps it becomes clear why some audience members viewed Lonelygirl15's posts as deceptive after her outing. Although Lonelygirl15 made no direct claims of authenticity, the stylistic and formulaic components of her narratives made it difficult for audiences to separate the "real" story from the digital performance. This separation removes the digital performance from historicity, and the consensus of the viewers was that the videos implied historicity in the real world. Cases of deception like that of Lonelygirl15 complicate traditional storytelling practices, by making it harder to differentiate fictional performance from truthful narratives, and beg the questions: "Is it important to know before beginning a story if it is authentic?" and "Does fictional art need to identify itself as such for ethical purposes?"

These questions point to another problem of authenticity – that of performance. The authenticity of personal storytelling rests on the assumption and the trust that a storyteller's personal narrative isn't modified, performed, or fictionalized, but is in fact the storyteller's reflection of a real, lived event. Yet performance is a necessary part of any storytelling experience. Further, devices of storytelling can influence and manipulate the way the audience perceives a story. "Jim Lawson's Hoss Trade" was a fictitious radio production recorded in 1903 by performer Cal Stewart. In his analysis of the radio program, Richard Bauman identifies lexical and grammatical aspects of word choice and sentence structure and aural tonalities of the vocal performance in the character of Uncle Josh Weatherby that audiences would recognize as "a general 'country' accent" (26). Although from Virginia, Stewart, who voiced Uncle Josh, used "informal, vernacular, marked by stereotypical 'rural' dialect forms" to position Uncle Josh as a denizen of rural New England (ibid.). Bauman notes that Stewart's vernacular choices were often not isolated to the New England area and in some cases were not current syntactic structures. Bauman seems to claim that with applied listening, Stewart's word choice and accent can complicate an audience's understanding of the Uncle Josh character, who was supposed to serve as a reimagining of the day's common stock character of "the comic rustic Yankee" (ibid. 24). Stewart's performance in this case should negotiate between the iconic sound of his heritage and the accent skills of a good performer, hopefully leading to consensus. In the case of Cal Stewart, the authenticity of the character relies on the abilities of the performer to portray a sense of truth believable enough to audiences to allow them to suspend their disbelief and imagine Stewart as Uncle Josh.

In a different fashion, storytellers may lessen or soften their accents and cultural colloquialisms as a means of telling a story with the potential to reach a larger audience who may not be familiar and/or accepting of these characteristic markers. It is worth considering what sense of authentic performance and/or narrative might be lost when this happens as well. Does changing or omitting language and aural markers that link a speaker to a specific region or background result in a loss or partial loss of the storyteller's authentic identity? How can a storyteller maintain her cultural authenticity while still reaching broad audiences? While consideration of acceptance and voicedness certainly plagued oral storytellers as well, the ability for storytellers using digital technologies to reach larger audiences, tell a greater number and variety of stories, and modify physical and aural body characteristics exponentially increases the challenges for authenticity.

Because of these ontological concerns about the accuracy with which an author can tell a story, the inherent nature of authenticity can be problematic, especially when one considers the ways by which an individual arrives at her perspective of the story. If we consider that identity is learned through political and social processes, then the performance of that identity is also learned and constructed. Storywork focusing on personal narratives is part of such performance. We represent ourselves through stories that have been shaped and molded in social contexts, given over from a private self to a public, and introducing the possibility for the Brazilian pedagogue and philosopher Freire's concept of "prescription," or "the imposition of one individual's choice upon another" (29). At worst, storytellers will learn to embody such prescription, imparting the choices of others in place of their own. Yet, if personal narratives are developed from performed identities within social contexts, then the shaping of narratives to fit the desires of others, should limit the creation of such narratives. Digital storytelling scholars Bridgit Hertzberg Kaare and Knut Lundby juxtapose the idea that personal narratives and assets necessarily constitute authenticity. They conclude that it is impossible to make "too definite" an argument regarding the authenticity found in digital stories (119) since self-representational narratives "[illuminate] culture as an experienced reality, seen from the point of view and personal position of the individual in society" (109). In these concerns about the ability to determine authenticity, we are reminded once again of the position of the storyteller within Arendt's subjective-in-between, and are able to see how digital stories are important subjects within which to consider the challenges of authenticity.

The Challenges of Implied Authenticity in Digital Storytelling

Because digital storytelling focuses on the telling of personal life experience, it has become known as a genre of self-representational narratives. Compounded with the use of personal assets, these stories often naturally invoke a sense of presumed authenticity from the viewing audience. Yet, understanding *personal* narratives as *collaboratively* created through political and social processes, calls into question the very notion that personal narratives like digital stories can be seen as authentic. This is the case even when these stories rely on the authors' own words, voice, archives, and personal narrative. Thus, storytelling "is not something 'invented' by the individual, but renegotiated in a cultural process in which we all participate" (Erstad and Wertsch 26). In digital storytelling this idea is most clearly witnessed in the workshop story circles. Story circles refer to those times in which the workshop participants and facilitators gather in a circle to share story ideas. They are designed to assist the authors as they draft their stories. In the 3rd edition of *Digital Storytelling: Capturing Lives, Creating Community*, Lambert explains,

> we want to help each storyteller not only find and clarify the story being told, but also check in with them about how they feel about it, identify the moment of change in their story, then use that to help them think through how the audience will see and hear their story in the form of a digital story.
>
> (29–30)

With Lambert's mention of how the audience will perceive the message and context of the work, we see how the narrative of each individual's digital story is socially driven and created.

In order to reach a place where critical exchanges between participants take place, workshop facilitators use story circles to create community among the workshop participants. Hartley and McWilliam, who titled their edited collection of digital storytelling after story circles, suggest that story circles are not just communal drafting periods, but "expressive 'limbering-up' exercises, designed to loosen up everyone's storytelling capabilities;" they explain that story circles "may include verbal games, making lists (loves and hates), and writing make-believe scenarios, as well as scripting what will become each person's own story" (3). In addition to sharing drafts of the final product, the pre-writing work and playful activities Hartley and McWilliam mention here are important parts of the story circle process because they allow a sense of community to form among the participants as they exchange ideas and express personal values. Additionally, story circles become a place where storytellers share personal experiences that help establish how each participant relates to the communities of which they are a part and the specific community formed by the digital storytelling workshop. Story circles are never an individual activity; even though Lambert and Hessler hope they "help to focus and inspire each individual," which they may indeed do (70). They are as much about the community as they are about the individual participant, as story circles join the individual to the workshop community and undoubtedly affect the way community identity forms, which in turn may affect the ways in which participants choose to shape and publish their identities within that community in their digital stories.

It is easy to see, then, during such communal drafting processes, how the authenticity of an individual's story might be called into question when it is positioned in relation to larger community identities, especially the one created in the digital storytelling workshop environment. The process of conversation involves probing storytellers with further questions and providing feedback to other storytellers. This is a necessary and important part of story circles, which help to foster the production of "good" stories and a sense of community among participants. Story circles become a place where participants share private, personal experiences that in reality help establish how each participant's social position relates to their community. Other workshop participants act as test audiences for the storytellers and give feedback the storyteller can employ in her continued work. Individuals might be encouraged to change details of their message, context, or narrative structure based on questions and feedback received from other participants. These exchanges serve the basis behind the phrase "listen deeply" in StoryCenter's motto:

> When we speak of 'deep listening,' we are speaking about the interplay of someone working out an idea before an audience, and how that audience demonstrably holds that idea, works through it, and provides insightful commentary and reflection on the idea.
> (Hessler and Lambert 30)

Listening, then, is an exchange; not merely a passive listening, but something active that is intrinsically tied to thinking and response.

While listening and responding fosters dialogue and opens points of discussion among participants, it can also be viewed as a way in which Freire's concept of "prescription" occurs within the digital storytelling workshop. By taking part in the story circle process individual participants are connected to the workshop group's collective identity, and a co-creation of both the individual (private) identity and the group (public) identity occurs. Thus, while identity is fashioned over time through social exchanges within communities and institutional structures before participants come to the digital storytelling workshop, in playing with narrative they are more consciously and knowingly forming the outward appearance and organization of their identity, meaning the process of identity formation extends into the digital storytelling workshop and interactions among participants therein. By understanding personal narratives as co-constructed, such as they are in story circles, it becomes easy to see that participants are offering what can only be an incomplete version of themselves to other workshop participants for review and critique as they continue to shape their representation of identity within the stories they share. The other people present in this co-creative media practice can greatly impact on the way personal narratives unfold over the course of the storymaking process.

The Challenge of Guided Authenticity in Digital Storytelling

Often when facilitators gather community members together to conduct a digital storytelling workshop, that facilitator, and perhaps even the others in the community, may have only a limited notion of the other storytellers in the room. Given that many digital storytelling facilitators are hired by institutions to develop and implement workshops in various communities, time and resource constraints may mean facilitators move in and out of storytellers' lives without forming lasting relationships.

To understand the relationship between the facilitator and a storyteller is to understand that identity is not created in a vacuum. Rather it is created in an ongoing dialogical process. The dialogue that takes place between the facilitator and a storyteller, as well as those that take place among storytellers within the workshop space, is both overt and internalized. This is not to say that the facilitator is always actively and overtly influencing the story. It is also not, however, to say that this is never the case. Often the facilitator and other storytellers can influence the storytellers in subtle ways, for instance by the questions they ask or the tangential branches of the personal narrative that they choose to follow up on. These lines of inquiry from the facilitator and other storytellers should be considered a part of the narrative process in and of themselves.

In this way, the stories developed in the digital storytelling workshop are similar to the narratives that arise in interviews. Linguist Elinor Ochs suggests that interviews are often "dominated by a primary teller, who recounts events with a relatively passive co-teller" (282). The interviewee is the primary teller and the others in the workshop space, in our case, are the passive co-tellers, who shape the narrative process through their passive responses of interest or disinterests, verbal and nonverbal responses, and lines of questioning. Catherine Kohler Riessman suggests that one way to view autobiographical storytelling, then, is to always see it as co-constructed: "the act of storytelling in dialogue *constitutes* the autobiographical self, that is, how the speaker wants to be known in the interaction" (29). Riessman exemplifies the ways interviewers impact the construction of subjects' interviews by relaying an experience she had in which she was acutely aware of her role in the process of narrative creation. In reflection of a particular interview, she posits that if the interviewee, an Indian woman, had been "talking with friends around a dinner table, or with an Indian interviewer, she would have assumed some knowledge was shared, and developed the account (and the 'self' constructed in it) differently" (32). The woman instead shared her narrative using terms to which she thought Riessman might more easily relate as a listener. What's more, Riessman asked specific questions to gain context of the situation and culture, which an Indian interviewer, being familiar with the socio-cultural context, might not have needed. Riessman argues, "Through [the interviewer's] presence, and by listening and questioning in particular ways, we critically shape the stories participants choose to tell" (50). A sense of self is created during the process of an interview as the interviewee actively remembers and relates narratives. This self has a base in prior experiences and the narrative might change in relation to the current cultural context and relationship of the interviewee to the interviewer, reminding us that, "to play with narrative is to play with identity," as Lundby writes (5). In the interview setting, the personal narrative then is dictated by the interviewee, who choose what to share.

Considering the Creation of Personal Narratives in Digital-Storytelling-Based Co-creative Practices

The digital storytelling method developed at the Center for Digital Storytelling is highly formulaic storytelling method, but it is easily modified to meet the needs of community members and stakeholders. For example, due to constraints, some editing processes are not always performed with the original storyteller leading the process. In a project in which she was working with a group of scientists, Ragnhild Larson augmented the process because her participants had limited time to complete their project. She interviewed the researchers, recorded and transcribed them, and finally developed a short script based on the interview. In her process, Larson removed thousands of words and changed word choice in some instances "to make the script readable and understandable" and "to make the story powerful" (171). None of the participants "made any significant changes to the scripts" she wrote (179). While as a facilitator I personally work to avoid having such a heavy-hand as a facilitator, there are often reasons to change the methodology to meet the needs of the community. For instance, in working on a project with high school students, I edited the stories because the students did not have access to the technology required to edit digital stories on their own. In order to help their narratives be heard, Larson took on the editing work. Additionally, she employed a professional photographer to create visual assets to minimize the time requirements on the storytellers and while the storytellers record their own voice-overs from Larson's scripts, she sometimes omitted or edited the voice-overs for inclusion in the digital story (179).

By removing the participants from the editing process, in majority or in total, a new relationship between the facilitator and the storyteller emerges, and a new sort of dialogue begins between them. In some ways, the facilitator is now engaging with the participant of the past (albeit possibly the recent past), since the interview of the storyteller now exists in the hands of the digital storytelling facilitator, revoking the rights of the storyteller to change their narrative, or at the very least limiting their ease of access to do so. Further, after the recording is complete, the storytellers lose the ability to change their interview. Thus, the facilitator and/or editor become responsible for the impression the storyteller makes on the viewing audience. While this is unlikely to happen within ethical digital storytelling practices, the facilitator could, if they wanted, make the interviewee utter entirely new words and still maintain the same pitch, tone, and timber of the interviewee's voice with the use of audio processing tools. Certain software also works to manipulate video as well as audio (Maras and Alexandrou; Siekierski). This sort of digital manipulation, known as deepfake, while possible, remains highly unethical. Although this is an extreme end to what could happen in letting others edit personal narratives, the storyteller should put into the facilitator a certain level of trust and the hope that the facilitator will adhere to the vision the storyteller sees for and of themselves.

At different points in the process, Larson provided the storytellers with drafts of their scripts to ensure that the narrative was heading in the direction the storyteller wanted. Depending on who composed the script the story would likely be told differently, in part due to the fact that this person retains control over what is included or excluded in the narrative. After completing the digital stories, Larson asked her participants to consider whether or not their personal narrative presented in the digital stories she collaborated on felt like the storytellers' stories. She found that

> all the researchers interviewed said they felt the story was their own and that they had got their most important message across, although they said they would not have used exactly the same words or highlighted the same parts of the story.
>
> (179)

Such feedback is important to understanding the authenticity of personal narratives and the collaborative approach of digital storytelling as a method. While Larson doesn't follow the strict protocol of a StoryCenter digital storytelling approach, which allows for storytellers to edit their own stories, digital storytelling in this way broadens the potential storytellers one can partner with, specifically those who might not have access to editing technologies or those who might not be capable of using them for one reason or another. Laron approached tensions over who is telling the story with an intention to ensure that the participants felt the stories were their own. If she wasn't interested in this aspect, she would not have confirmed the narrative being created during the storymaking process, nor would she have followed-up with participants after the digital stories were created. In fact, Larson found that people were grateful for her skills as a story teller (179) and that the researchers felt like they were in control of the storymaking experience without having to put as much of their time into the process (180).

Case Study: "Getting a Job at Nikki's Place"

In my own work I have faced similar challenges when I stepped in as the editor for digital storytelling projects when access to the technology was otherwise unavailable (Hill "Crafting Memory"; Hill "Power to the People"). In the creation of my digital story for the augmented reality (AR) game, "Getting a Job at Nikki's Place" (Argo et al.), I developed the script from an oral history that told the story of Nick Aiken, a restaurant owner in the Parramore neighborhood of Orlando, Florida. The AR game play was designed so that elementary school children could understand some of the complex histories of the swiftly changing neighborhood through the eyes of one the neighborhood's residents. The game play asked students to tour the neighborhood gathering objects needed to create a meal at the restaurant Aiken worked at as a young boy. The game play ended with a digital story, which I edited, playing as you arrived at Aiken's then-current restaurant, Nikki's Place.

To create the game play and digital story, a group of researchers from the University of Central Florida, myself included, conducted an oral history with Nick Aiken. In his oral history, Aiken spoke about the history of Parramore and the well-developed community in which he was raised and raised his family. He spoke at length about his work and how he came to be a chef. Using information he provided about his career path, the research team created a loco-mobile game that enables players to follow Aiken's path as a young man starting out as a young chef in Roser's Restaurant, the restaurant that eventually became Nikki's Place. As such, the game took players on a geo-based tour of Parramore, which included an augmented reality feature showing the business and community that Aiken grew up with. These augmented reality sections additionally featured snippets of Aiken's oral history and the game ended with an abbreviated version of Aiken's oral history as a voice-over for a video featuring photographs and film of Aiken, his family, and his restaurant.

For the project, "We honed in on the aspects more closely associated with personal, everyday life as a business owner in the neighborhood, as opposed to larger, more socio-political narratives" (Argo et al. 58). As such, we were concerned about how much of what we said and did would affect the telling of another person's story. Although the gamification adds another dimension, oral historians have long negotiated the complexity of narratives told in interviews and transcribed by outsiders. For example, Lynn Abrams discusses the questions and difficulties raised by transcribing oral histories and whether to transcribe narratives verbatim or eliminate some of the hesitations and false starts while maintaining the meaning of the interview. Both texts ultimately argue for balance in this process and for creating an interpretation of the interview that provides a clear meaning to the outside audience. The transcriber here becomes an interpreter. Translating oral histories into narratives for digital stories and game play, as was the case with "Getting a Job at Nikki's Place," extends the interpretation beyond transcription into game creation.

Viewing the game in this way makes it easy to see the collaboration at work behind the presentation of Mr. Aiken's history. First, there is the shared authority present in the interview process. When the oral history leaves the interview room, it becomes the responsibility of the interviewer, or perhaps a research team, who dictate the way in which the story is transcribed and shared. Abrams argues that the interviewer should never dictate the course of an interview, sway it, or edit it to meet commercial, academic, or financial gain and that the interviews should not be forced into fitting in with the interviewer's research. But what happens when an interview team goes into an interview with a set objective in mind, as was the case with this project? We knew were looking to create a game using the material Aiken provided. In an effort to maintain an ethics of responsibility, we shared this information with Aiken who supported the project. Even with Aiken's approval, the research team was still greatly concerned with building a narrative around a community of which we were not a part. As the storytellers/historians, we were careful not to see or present ourselves as a spokesperson for the community and, further, that Aiken's story did not belong to us. Yet we shared a common goal with Aiken: A desire to preserve the cultural memory of Parramore and to teach young people about the town's complex history. With this goal in mind, our research team entered into a deeper level of shared authority with Aiken's story as we utilized his words to create a narrative game and edit a digital video based on his life.

The game was tested by local fourth graders who, as residents, were familiar with the neighborhood in its current status. This connection allowed them to understand the historical narrative and photo archives presented within the game to build a relationship with Parramore's history.

The research team aimed to reach these students by using digital mobile technologies with which they were likely familiar and which they might find highly engaging. Combining the physical landscape with digital spaces gives players the sensation of being capable of navigating beyond their present understanding of place into a (perhaps) unknown past. As Flynn reminds us, "To evoke the presence of the past relies on a different treatment of space that creates cultural and social presence" (364). This sense of presence was one the research team hoped to create for students with "Getting a Job at Nikki's Place." Yet creating this space meant that the research team attempted a second layer of shared authority with Aiken's story in creating the game play and digital story. In both of these stages, the research team engaged in open dialogue with Aiken to assure we were moving forward with his continued approval. By engaging him in this way, we strove to share the authority of the creation process and ensure we were not prioritizing our goals and agendas above his. For the digital video, the research team took photographs and videos of Aiken cooking and daily life at his restaurant. We additionally used photographs from Aikens personal archives. I had the task of editing Aikens complete oral history, nearly two hours of interview, into a digital story lasting less than four minutes. To do this, I focused on the parts of Aiken's history that were specifically about his career path to become a chef. This meant removing parts of his oral history from the digital story and in some cases from the overarching game narrative. Some of it, such as Aiken's memory of Parramore, were embedded into the game play outside of the digital video in the form of augmented reality segments. Players walking along the game path stop at specific locations to watch short videos featuring Aiken's voice depicting what life used to be like in the Parramore neighborhood.

Aiken's oral history, then, was featured in three different ways in the game play. First, it was utilized to create the narrative on which the game play was based. Second, it was used in a closing digital video that connected the player to the character they play. Third, it was used as a site remembrance and history in augmented reality sections showing players what once was. These three narrative functions worked to compile a significant portion of Aiken's entire oral history in a medium that the research team hoped would engage youth to experience their neighborhood in a new way. Yet this method raises questions about the researcher's responsibility to the oral history interviewee. While shortening and re-combining the oral history might allow us to better reach and engage a specific audience, it also allows the research team to have a significant impact on which story components and themes are selected for sharing. As researchers, we continually reached out to Aiken to ensure he was satisfied with the direction and narratives we were creating. In this way, we strove to maintain the integrity and agency of the storyteller and his memory. In every action we took, we aimed to speak with Aiken rather than for him, while acknowledging that this is not neatly, easily, nor perfectly accomplished.

The communication of a story requires that one person speaks and the other receives the narrative, the act of listening, and the subsequent actions that follow make personal storytelling a complex political endeavor. Amy Hill, who works with people all over the world to develop personal digital stories, asks, "what responsibility do I have to talk with workshop participants about the complexities of representation?" (32). This is an important question for responsible facilitators to ask, because as we have seen, stories cannot be created in a vacuum and can involve varying levels of oversight or collaborative storytelling measures. As facilitators, we should help storytellers account for and acknowledge the ways in which their stories take shape in social systems, while remaining aware of the developmental stages of the storyteller. Going too deep into this conversation with storytellers who are unprepared to tackle the full complexity of this conversation will not help the storytellers. Yet, understanding how narratives are passed from one person to the next, often shaped and reformed by the hearer's unique understanding of and perspective on the original narrative can help storytellers shape and tell their stories to reach their desired audience. As we have seen, this can also affect the ways in which storytellers finalize their narratives and leave trace imprints of those involved in the story sharing and story development processes on the finished video narratives. In digital storytelling, it is important that we contend with our responsibility in helping to craft personal and community narratives. Anyone who is in the room or involved with the production of the narrative contributes consciously and/or unconsciously to the way in which that story develops and ultimately how it is produced.

References

Argo, Bartley, et al. "The Way It Used to Be: Exploring Cultural Heritage through the Augmented Reality Story of a Neighborhood Soul Food Restaurant." *Visual Ethnography*, vol. 5, no. 2, 2016, pp. 55–78.

Bauman, Richard. "The Remediation of Storytelling: Narrative Performance on Early Commercial Sound Recordings." *Telling Stories: Language Narrative and Social Life*, edited by Deborah Schiffrin, and Anastasia Nylund, Georgetown University Press, 2010, pp. 22–43.

Buckingham, David, editor. *Youth, Identity, and Digital Media*. The MIT Press, 2008.

Erstad, Ola, and James V. Wertsch. "Tales of Mediations: Narrative and Digital Media as Cultural Tools." *Digital Storytelling, Mediatized Stories: Self-Representations in New Media*, edited by Knut Lundby, Peter Lang, 2008, pp. 1–17.

Flynn, Bernadette. "The Morphology of Space in Virtual Heritage." *Theorizing Digital Cultural Heritage: A Critical Discourse*, edited by Fiona Cameron, and Sarah Kenderdine, Massachusetts Institute of Technology, 2007, pp. 439–368.

Freire, Paulo. *Pedagogy of the Oppressed*. Continuum, 1993.

Goffman, Erving. *Behavior in Public Places: Notes on the Social Organization of Gatherings*. The Free Press, 1963.

Hartley, John, and Kelly McWilliam, editors. *Story Circle: Digital Storytelling around the World*. Wiley-Blackwell, 2009.
Hertzberg Kaare, Bridgit, and Knut Lundby. "Autobiography and Assumed Authenticity in Digital Storytelling." *Digital Storytelling, Mediatized Stories: Self-Representation in New Media*, edited by Knut Lundby, Peter Lang, 2008, pp. 105–222.
Hessler, Brooke, and Joe Lambert. "Threshold Concepts in Digital Storytelling: Naming What We Know about Storywork." *Digital Storytelling in Higher Education: International Perspectives*, edited by Grete Jamissen, Pip Hardy, Yngve Nordkvelle, and Heather Pleasants, Palgrave Macmillan, 2017, pp. 19–36.
Hill, Amanda. "Crafting Memory: Where Oral History Meets Narrative in the Creation of a Mobile Game." International Oral History Association Congress, 19 June 2018, University of Jyväskylä, Jyväskylä, Finland. Conference Presentation.
Hill, Amanda. *Power to the People: Responsible Facilitation in Collaborative Storytelling Practices*. 2018. University of Central Florida, PhD Dissertation.
Hill, Amy. "Digital Storytelling and the Politics of Doing Good: Exploring the Ethics of Bringing Personal Narratives into Public Spheres." *Community-Based Multiliteracies and Digital Media Projects: Questioning Assumptions and Exploring Realities*, edited by Heather M. Pleasants, and Dana E. Salter, Peter Lang, 2014, pp. 21–43.
Lambert, Joe. *Digital Storytelling: Capturing Lives, Creating Community*. 3rd ed., Digital Diner Press, 2009.
Lambert, Joe, and Brooke Hessler. *Digital Storytelling: Capturing Lives, Creating Community*. 5th ed., Routledge, 2018.
Larson, Ragnhild. "My Story or Your Story? Producing Professional Digital Stories on Behalf of Researchers." *Digital Storytelling in Higher Education: International Perspectives*, edited by Grete Jamissen, Pip Hardy, Yngve Nordkvelle, and Heather Pleasants, Palgrave Macmillan, 2017, pp. 167–184.
Lundby, Knut, editor. *Digital Storytelling, Mediatized Stories: Self-Representations in New Media*. Peter Lang, 2009.
Maras, Marie-Helen, and Alex Alexandrou. "Determining Authenticity of Video Evidence in the Age of Artificial Intelligence and in the Wake of Deepfake Videos." *Journal of Evidence and Proof*, vol. 23, no. 3, 2018, pp. 255–262.
Ochs, Elinor. "Narrative Lessons." *A Companion to Linguistic Anthropology*, edited by Alessandro Duranti, John Wiley and Sons, 2004, pp. 269–289.
Page, Ruth E. *Stories and Social Media: Identities and Interaction*. Routledge, 2012.
Riessman, Catherine Kohler. *Narrative Methods for Human Sciences*. Sage, 2008.
Taylor, Charles. *The Ethics of Authenticity*. Harvard University Press, 1992.
van Zoonen, Liesbet. "From Identity to Identification: Fixating the Fragmented Self." *Media, Culture, and Society*, vol. 35, no. 1, pp. 44–51.

5 Who's Listening? The Audience as Stakeholder

Audience Reception of Personal Narratives

The audience's storytellers consider when composing and disseminating their stories are a prominent influence in the co-creative spaces of digital stories. This chapter addresses the ways audience reception and digital dissemination affect the storyteller's agency, particularly for storytellers with a political agenda. Additionally, this chapter looks at how facilitators can inadvertently or purposefully control who joins the workshop and thereby the narratives and voices that are shared and heard in the workshop and beyond. As StoryCenter's Joe Lambert writes,

> we want to help each storyteller not only find and clarify the story being told, but also check in with them about how they feel about it, identify the moment of change in their story, then use that *to help them think through how the audience will see and hear their story in the form of a digital story.*
>
> (29–30) (emphasis mine)

Lambert here identifies the push to think about audience at every stage of the development process, because audiences serve as a creative force that influences the storytellers' composition practices while existing outside of the active storymaking space.

Reciprocity is inherent and essential in sharing stories. This narrative communication necessitates audience attention to complete a cycle of exchange. In order to understand the full complexity of the digital storytelling methodology as a co-creative media practice, we should acknowledge the relationship between listeners and speakers and consider the ways digital storytelling, as a methodology, is used to engage the audience's attention.

One way to captivate an audience's attention is to create a story structure that looks like narratives with which the audience is already familiar as this offers a known way for audiences to make meaning from the narrative. Familiar narrative structures "give us a structured way of accessing knowledge in a culture and a way of expressing intentions and how we relate to others" (Erstad and Wertsch 28). When sharing personal experiences, this "structured way of accessing knowledge" often takes the form of a narrative. Mimicking common story structures, often based on mass media narratives, gives audiences a means of understanding the story. However, thinking about narrative in this way can also be prescriptive and can determine the ways storymakers shape their stories both consciously and unconsciously. Digital storytelling participants might find their storytelling abilities limited by the institutions facilitating the digital storytelling workshops. These institutions are embedded in systems of power, which shape the projects in which they engage. Further, in some cases, professionals conducting digital storytelling projects request that their participants "must fit their story into a shape that has ultimately been decided by the professionals" (Thumim 88), as we saw in the case study of Digital Faith Stories, where the authors alluded to the importance of narrating positive messages (Hertzberg Kaare and Lundby 113).

The ways in which people aim to write "good" stories may ultimately lead storytellers to alter their narratives for the sake of their audience. For digital storytelling, this takes on a very specific framework, one that Anna Poletti argues can be problematic for storytellers. Poletti considers how digital storytelling workshops work with storytellers to develop life narratives "through which a range of institutions participate in the construction of an intimate public" (74). In so doing, the life stories developed in digital storytelling workshops can be "coaxed or coerced" (76), and that this can inform the ways in which the narratives take shape. She argues,

> the specific narrative strategies of the digital storytelling form present significant barriers against digital storytelling being used as a means of redefining or challenging existing meanings attached to life experience, given its emphasis on narrative accessibility (Burgess 2006, 207), closure (Lambert 2006, 57), and coherence of theme (Neilsen 2005, 5).
> (Poletti 75)

The narrative production for which digital storytelling as a genre and methodology is known is, thus, highly systematic. In digital storytelling, the author scripts the story, develops the story's structure, and decides the mediation of the story with the audience in mind. This could be potentially at odds with the story the author truly wants to tell, should their ideas not fit into such prescribed narrative structure or theme of what they think an audience expects. Joe Lambert suggests people should learn this "narrative" voice in order to tell "good" stories. He writes that creating narrative voice is a developmental process in which you learn to write by merging "the analytical and the emotive" parts of the brain. He further argues that this is a specific voice used for the purposes of telling stories and should be developed against the "official" voice used for professional and academic writing. As Lambert suggests "We have been taught that this [official] voice carries a dispassionate authority, useful perhaps in avoiding misunderstandings, but absolutely deadly as a story" (22). Thus, in using narrative voice, storytellers utilize a set of codes and signifiers learned through media to shape "good" stories, that is, those stories that follow conventional narrative tropes so pervasive in Western media, in a familiar fashion for the audience.

Personal storytelling traditions, in Western culture, tend to advantage those stories that have a single author with an unwavering moral stance, a high level of tellability – the measurement of a story's value to be told, a linear narrative, and those that can be detached from their original context, are the most privileged (Ochs and Capps). This narrative privilege translates into the ways in which personal stories are passed from one person to the next through oral and mediated means. Digital stories also privilege such narratives. The narratives shared in this space are told by an individual, deemed important and highly tellable by their author, are easily de-contextualized from their author's original context, typically depict an author's unwavering moral stance, and have linear structures. The art of telling stories, learned through everyday experiences of both telling and reading stories, is coded by cultural markers for what makes a "good" story. Digital stories are lauded for their concise approach to narratives that focus on a single moment in the storyteller's life and last only two to three minutes. Further, many facilitators encourage the storyteller to write narratives that are temporally ordered and organized. In the first two editions of *Digital Storytelling: Capturing Lives, Creating Community*, Joe Lambert sets forth seven elements of digital storytelling: (1) point of view; (2) a dramatic question; (3) emotional content; (4) the gift of your voice; (5) the power of the soundtrack; (6) economy; and (7) pacing (qtd. in Poletti 77). In subsequent editions of the book, these were revised as the seven steps: (1) owning your insights; (2) owning your emotions; (3) finding the moment; (4) seeing your story; (5) hearing your story; (6) assembling your story; and (7) sharing your story (Lambert and Hessler). This change was a result of the evolution of the thought process behind teaching the digital storytelling method (Lambert and Hessler 53). However, the original steps remained impactful for the type of narrative work created in Center for Digital Storytelling-style workshops. Poletti argues that this creates a limited and confining storywork structure for the participants. She writes,

> The impact of the seven elements is that, as a site of autobiographical narrative, digital storytelling coaxes life stories in response to very specific expectations about what constitutes a 'good' story (closed structure, dramatic question, economy and first-person perspective) and how that story can be made intelligible to its intended audience (emphasizing affect, reverie, identification and the use of universal themes).
>
> (78–79)

This structure emerges from a Western narrative tradition and, as Cunsolo Willox et al. suggest, it "does not necessarily resonate with non-Western storytelling forms or traditions, which celebrate stories-in-process and do not require stories to conclude succinctly and fully by the end" (141). Digital storytelling that utilizes other narrative forms (perhaps episodically and thematically ordered) are rarer. Yet, they still exist in digital storytelling practices. For example, in a project with youth at the Orlando Union Rescue Mission, participants created digital stories in the form of recipes of self, leading to highly poetic and experimental narratives (Hill, Amanda). Still, many storytellers structure their digital storytelling narratives with a beginning, middle, and end and reflect "collective dimensions of storytelling, learning, and meaning making" (Erstad and Wertsch 23) obtained as a result of constant interaction with stories told in mass media.

Yet increased media literacy might in fact diminish the individual's approach to storytelling structure. As mass media expectations become increasingly pervasive, "stories do not solely reflect authors' backgrounds, their ethnic and cultural experiences and upbringings, but are increasingly formed by story elements that can be neither located in a specific narrative tradition nor in a singular national context" (Helff and Woletz 132). These practices instead develop from our everyday interactions with other media that may make use of blended storytelling and cinematic techniques as well as the communication and performance practices we learn in personal interfaces. If we consider there are a few typically dominant narrative trends in mass media – for instance, linearity and stories following structural patterns featuring a beginning, middle, and end – then we can assume that in the process of composing their own digital stories, authors may be more inclined to gravitate toward a familiar or "standard" style of storytelling they have learned from the media. Learning to author stories that mirror this structure and that are told in multiple and multi-media formats requires access and resources not always available to all storytellers. However, with the continued advancement of technology, these resources are becoming increasingly accessible. Hartley further argues that because "consumers are increasingly also producers, a level of reflexivity about the 'self' and skepticism about *personae ficta* is built into" our performance of self, ("Smiling" 208) and this performance is directed toward an outside audience.

The performance of self is deeply embedded in the composition of a digital story. The way authors structure, construct, mediatize and disseminate their narratives all play a role in how an audience member relates to and values the authors and their stories. This in turn relates to the level of expertise perceived by the viewers of the digital stories, as today's audiences are increasingly more literate in mass media narrative styles. For example, based on the grammar structures an author employs in writing the story the audience might assume the level of education the author has completed or judge the intelligence of the author. These perceptions can affect whether an audience member finds the author credible as a narrator. Additionally, the audience may assume an author has a certain level of proficiency in digital literacy skills based on the way in which the author puts her narrative together, regardless of the medium used. For example, in digital storytelling, some of these skills may be linked to visual composition such as the way an author photographs a subject or the way in which transitions and movement are employed in the digital video. The institutions through which an author disseminates her narrative can also influence the audience's reception of the individual. In the audience member's mind, an institution's wealth, celebrity, or standing, for example, may imbue the author with certain traits. These factors contribute to an assumed audience perception of the storymaker, which storymakers are likely to consider while composing their digital stories. Of course, these factors can also be manipulated purposefully by the storyteller to intentionally give such impressions, as was the case of Lonleygirl15 described in the previous chapter. When Lonleygirl15's true identity was revealed, her audience felt betrayed by the manipulation.

While interpretations and critiques from other workshop participants and the facilitator during the storymaking process serve as a sort of test to consider outside audience interpretations, they by no means indicate that an outside audience will receive and interpret the work's message and context in the way intended by the storyteller. Sharing digital stories in any circumstance opens room for interpretation, as Iris Marion Young reminds us: "the other person may understand my words differently from the way I meant them, or carry my actions to consequences I do not intend" (231). In order to minimize the misinterpretation of the digital stories it becomes important to think about how these narratives will be connected and framed in the process of distribution. Providing context for a collection of digital stories could be useful when framing these narratives together, especially when it comes to framing narratives of social change. When working with stories of social change, the framing of the narratives within a collection can also be a space where more strategic calls to action or source material for further education are placed alongside digital stories to enhance contextualization and clarify intent.

In order to maintain the most democratic effect in this instance, participants should be part of the contextualization process rather than allowing the facilitating and/or hosting institution to contextualize the works on their own. The contextualization process should be a collaborative effort between these institutions and the participants that continues the process of digital literacy education begun in the workshop space. Although contextualization will help, it will likely not erase all erroneous or unintended interpretations by viewers, because the audience is an important part of cultural meaning production. Facilitators cannot control the responses and actions of an audience, but Amy Hill suggests that "adopting a disclaimer to share with viewers, reminding them to respect the dignity of storytellers, who are much more than what their digital stories may reveal" might influence an audience's response to the storytellers and their works (27). These disclaimers can be used to remind audiences that these personal narratives reflect the views of the author as informed by the particular moment or moments in time around which they revolve. They can further ask audiences to remain open to new perspectives or perspectives that might be difficult to hear because they differ from their own.

Storytelling as Resource

Narratives are always positioned in relationships between teller and listener, or in the case of co-creative storymaking, multiple listeners. Klaus and Lünenborg argue the process of cultural production and those involved, their products, and their audiences "fundamentally remain dependent on each other" (204) and this dependency can be seen in the co-creative practices that dominate digital dissemination spaces. Klaus and Lünenborg have devised a model to examine the processes of cultural production embedded in cultural citizenship, a term that "entails all those cultural practices that allow competent participation in society and includes the rights to be represented and to speak actively" (ibid.). The model considers cultural citizenship as a circuit that factors in production, media text, and reception as influences that enable meaning-making. The model supports that production leads solely to media text, but that reception responds to and is responded to by both media text and production, indicating that the reception of a text or work in progress can be influenced by the audience's process of meaning-making. Their model is particularly relevant to digital storytelling as it perfectly identifies not only the process of sharing the digital story with an outside audience, but also the co-creative story-making processes such as the story circle. Reception cycles into future production and continues the co-creative schema for storytellers.

The audience reception of personal narratives, and the ways in which storytellers comprehend the audience in the storymaking process, create a cycle of co-creative cultural citizenship, and this citizenship is predicated on the potential for democratic participation and voice, which has profound implications for whether stories are heard, listened to, and valued.

Narratives thus act as a way to frame democratic participation. Indeed, where subjects are removed from telling their own narratives, we see an important loss of voice. Linda Tuhiwai Smith argues that narratives form the basis of etic research practices by creating curiosity about people encountered on exploratory expeditions. In *Decolonizing Methodologies: Research and Indigenous Peoples*, she argues that stories helped shape the idea of the "other" in European research circles. She suggests original interest in indigenous populations stemmed from untrained "travellers' tales and adventurers' adventures ... which became fixed in the milieu of cultural ideas" (41). These storytellers provided an outside, typically white, perspective on these diverse peoples built on Eurocentric contextual understandings of social norms, perspectives that "became fixed" as these stories were told and retold. The power of narrative created, shared, and used in this way shaped generations of research and cultural assumptions about Indigenous peoples. Narratives told from outside storytellers about others effectively silenced the perspectives and voice of the peoples in question. In silencing these voices, the travelers, and ultimately researchers, created a divide wherein the peoples whose voices were silenced could no longer effectively participate in their own societies. By creating a schema where the voices of outside travelers became the go-to perspectives of different peoples, the voices of the Indigenous peoples were rendered not valuable, and therefore not invited to participate in the cultural storytelling processes that most affected their lives.

Digital technologies have the capacity to expand the voices that participate in storytelling in contemporary culture. Using a combination of narrative and digital technologies, as digital storytelling does, we can see the rise of new voices that enable a broader awareness and perspective of the diverse individuals that make up the greater collective. Further, as media scholar Nick Couldry shows, voice is intrinsically linked to critical discourse of participation and democracy. To understand voice in this way is to understand it as a deeply political function that enables civic engagement. Couldry recounts Barak Obama's victory speech on the night of the 2008 election where Obama alluded to the story of a black woman who had voted for the first time that day at 106-years-old. This, to Couldry, pinpoints the effect of narrative in political arenas and argues that in "choosing to focus the election's significance for a national global media audience through its impact on the narrative of a single life" Obama "faced down the neoliberal insistence that nothing matters more than markets, and declared that at least one thing mattered more: a vision of democracy as acting together through voice" (ibid.). Connecting voice to narrative then becomes a way to view narratives as a resource.

Yet, the creation and dissemination of the narrative is not enough for political efficacy. According to Couldry, spaces need to be "created that enable the exchange between narratives normally regarded as irrelevant to each other; that means challenging the blocks that prevent certain types of narrative being heard" (146–147). He argues that this will ultimately take a "rethinking [of] the space of politics," to encourage society to shift its value perception about diverse narratives to a position of credibility (150).

Rethinking narrative communication practices and digital infrastructures to allow for more attention is critical in achieving this:

> Acts of writing, the social networks and cultural contexts in which they occur, and the technological networks in which they take place and are disseminated still involve systems of power, still reflect relationships between individuals and groups within those systems, and still entail questions of what it means to be and how we come to see, hear, sense, and know the world with all of those technologies, power relations, social networks, and cultural contexts.
>
> (Banks 154–155)

This holds true in the digital storytelling space as well. Facilitators need to engage the storytellers in the dissemination practices of their digital stories in strategic ways in order to responsibly facilitate workshops. While facilitators cannot guarantee the attention of an audience, they can help storytellers build networks and understand avenues for dissemination.

While the co-creative practice does engage in tactical media creation, whereby ordinary folk create artistic personal narratives, the broader structuring of the digital storytelling methodology invites the oversight and strategy of those in higher positions of power. If we align this understanding with Couldry's understanding of the potential to expand voice to include participation, we can easily see how the combination of strategy and tactics creates new voices, awareness of voices, new methods and perspectives of political organizing, and how it possesses the ability to generate "new intensities for listening." By strategically structuring the workshop around the goal of expanding participation, the narratives produced in the workshop can be resources for their storytellers to captivate audiences' attention. If we understand a resource as something that produces a benefit, digital storytelling has the capacity to teach storytellers how to tell and use their stories to reach wider audiences. Julian Rappaport also argues for a framework wherein narratives are considered resources. He writes,

> If narratives are understood as resources, we are able to see that who controls that resource, that is who give stories social value, is at the heart of a tension between freedom and social control, oppression and liberation, and empowerment versus disenfranchisement. If we view the power to create, select, and tell stories (that are positively valued) about one's self and one's community as a resource, we quickly see that like most resources it is distributed unevenly, in about the same proportion as other resources, such as money and social prestige. Those most in need are least likely to have control over the valued resources.
>
> (805)

Narratives can operate as a beneficial resource for the storytellers, and for some populations, the ability to tell their own story, to have narratives act as resources, is a critical power. Especially in Western narrative history, a colonization endemic, this power omitted "silenced" storytellers, especially those who have been historically marginalized and who have not typically been afforded the chance to tell their own stories. Storytelling facilitator Yvonna Lincoln argues that "in becoming producers, analysts, and presenters of their own narratives, storytellers cease to be the objects of their histories and knowledge. They are enabled instead to become the agents and instruments of their own change processes" (43). The empowerment that comes from the process of production and presentation can be amplified through "using the language of the dominant" as scholar Ananda Mitra suggests, which allows for the potential that the storyteller "may be able to co-opt the authoritative discourse to produce a new voice which can demand to be heard and acknowledged by others" (32), disrupting the traditional pattern of whose voices are heard and listened to. The benefit a storyteller receives from being able to author her own story is intrinsically connected to another resource: Audience attention. In fact, I would argue that the ability to reach the audiences is often a primary benefit for storytellers.

Imparting social value on a narrative necessarily involves reaching an audience. While Rappaport suggests that "the power to create, select, and tell stories" is a resource unto itself, it should necessarily be accompanied by an audience's attention, which can be understood as another resource. Narrative as resource is a useful framework by which to help storytellers understand the power of story; however, understood by itself, the framework assumes that narratives will all be heard and regarded equally, an assumption that dismisses the audience's attention as an additional resource. The mere creation and telling of narratives is not enough; it is also important that narratives are heard and valued by listening audiences. This understanding is missing from Rappaport's assessment. Instead, he suggests that the resource of telling stories is "distributed unevenly." However, everyone has the power to "create, select, and tell stories," and they do so constantly in their everyday lives through traditional oral storytelling, conversations, social media, and the like. This indicates that the framework of narrative as resource should be compounded by the resource of audience attention or visibility and spaces "that enable the exchange between narratives" (Couldry 146).

In effect, it is not enough to say that all stories are resources for their tellers, because this assumes equal opportunities for stories to reach an audience and a unilateral sense of value placed on every story. It is not enough to simply have a narrative; it is equally important to have a space to tell the narrative, a way to share it with an audience, and an audience to engage with the narrative. Often, to obtain these three needs, it is important to have technical and theoretical understanding of narrative creation in a chosen medium, the ability to communicate your narrative clearly and effectively, and a communications network to reach an audience. The Internet, social media, and other digital tools have made it more accessible for consumers/users to produce stories, but the imbalanced power structures between strategic and tactical operators in society are mirrored still in the digital spaces. Biases against marginalized and vulnerable peoples result in a lack of attention and listening in online spaces as they do in physical ones. Community literacy initiatives and citizen's media practices, like digital storytelling, work to dismantle these structures. In digital storytelling workshops, the facilitator can help participants build and shape the skills needed to tell efficient narratives for the purposes of gaining greater attention and visibility. Additionally, the institutional support from hosting and facilitating organizations and those involved with these organizations can provide the space, medium for sharing, and audience via the Internet.

Teaching these skills allows participants to become resources in and of themselves, and this strategic turn is needed for responsible co-creative media practices. As Ananda Mitra suggests, the Internet becomes a place where it is possible to have a voice, produce alliances, and "renegotiate identities" (30) and "[elicit] a response" (32). In working with facilitators, participants in co-creative media spaces like digital storytelling workshops gain a greater "access" to an audience by sharing their stories on the Internet, which can often be expanded through institutionally-supported means, but the Internet does not provide equal broadcast capabilities to each story nor does it mandate responses of the kind for which Mitra calls. Rappaport acknowledges, "Stories are not a scarce resource, but often the stories of people who are 'outsiders' are an ignored or devalued resource" (805). Ignoring and devaluing select stories potentially silences the voice of the storyteller and limits the chance for storytellers to gain attention.

Audience Attention and Listening

The amalgamation of inexpensive and user-friendly digital media platforms now available has broadened opportunities for content development and dissemination for many everyday storytellers, which provides the ability for more "information" and "stuff" to make their way onto a platform where they have the potential to be seen and heard. Yet, what has been discovered is an inequality in attention to digital items created by marginalized peoples. Scholar Richard Lanham suggests there is a key difference between "information" and "stuff" and that this difference is important to the new understanding of what he calls "the economics of attention." He understands economics as the "study of how human beings allocate scarce resources to produce various commodities, and how those commodities are distributed for consumption among the people in society" (6). For Lanham, the current scarcity in economics is attention, specifically "the human attention needed to make sense of information" (7). "Stuff" is no longer the driving economic factor in a digital world; instead, our top commodity is what we think about "stuff." Lanham argues that information is more valuable because it is active and connected to emotion, and for this reason, people collect it, and it stays with those who have collected it: "Information, unlike stuff, can be both kept and given away at the same time" (Lanham 259). The more attention a specific object or topic procures, the more "stuff" it will produce and thus the more attention it will have. For this reason, attention becomes capital in the new economy and focuses and organizes the economy of information.

Still, digital creations placed on the Internet do not guarantee an audience. They are primarily relegated to the classification of "stuff." Without attention from an outside audience to produce information about or around this new content, there is little political efficacy available to the content creators. Couldry writes, "A system that provides formal voice for its citizens but fails so markedly to listen exhibits a crisis of political voice" (101). Couldry here points to a limited response-ability that ultimately reflects

Lanham's consideration of "stuff" versus "information" and key civic considerations of the Internet era. Digital platforms certainly open new arenas through and with which citizens can engage, but without sufficient attention paid by an outside audience, they do not guarantee that these engagements are not equivalent to muting their voices.

Far too often in digital storytelling, the focus is on amplifying the voice, but rarely on the listening or reception of that voice. If audiences do not pay attention to vulnerable voices in the digital world, then the response-ability of voice – the ability to respond to others and be responded to by others (Oliver) – becomes nullified because no one is listening, or giving attention, to their creations. Much of the focus, even within media and cultural studies relating to inequality, is on the expression of voice. However, as media scholars Penny O'Connell, Justine Lloyd, and Tanja Dreher argue, mediated communication practices are relational and the response of an audience affects the ability for the author's voice to reach people. Tanja Dreher argues that digital storytelling as a methodology isn't doing enough to encourage this sort of critical reception. Perhaps these concerns stem from what Pamela Hendry considers Western culture's privileging of speaking over listening (494), a concern we can see in the scholars and facilitators' case studies that focus on giving or amplifying voice, but rarely on the listening or reception of that voice. In light of Dreher and Hendry's concerns, it is important to identify ways in which digital storytelling could promote better opportunities for "receptivity, recognition and response" (Dreher, "A Partial Promise" 159) in an age when we are oversaturated with "stuff." The plethora of digital stories available, especially those made publicly available digitally, marks a vast departure in media studies scholarship of the early 2000s, which assumed the Internet and digital infrastructures built greater spaces for underrepresented voices. While this has certainly proved true in many ways, the abundance of narratives mean we should contend with even more substantial questions: Whose stories are audiences hearing? And, what does this mean for digital storytelling storytellers? In order to begin to answer these questions, we need to understand the spaces in which outside audiences are likely to encounter digital stories to examine these areas as potential sites of response and attention.

Spaces of Audience Encounters

John Hartley breaks down the genealogies of digital storytelling into two distinct groups, divided by their distribution method: The "*artist + festival*" model of California's StoryCenter and the "broadcasting" model developed by Daniel Meadows with BBC Wales (who acknowledges he learned the genre methodology from the late Dana Atchley of the Center for Digital Storytelling). These genealogies primarily differ in their dissemination practices. The "*artist + festival*" model gears itself toward live screening events and the "broadcasting" model makes use of digital dissemination, although as digital storytelling practices have developed, we have come to see a combination of the two models ("Problems of Expertise").

Perhaps we can find that at the core of Hartley's distinction between live and digital dissemination practices is the value these facilitating institutions place on different audiences. Broadcasting projects, such as the BBC-produced digital storytelling project *Capture Wales*, aims to reach local and global audiences through digital archives and televised viewings. In contrast, the "*artist + festival*" method of StoryCenter appears to focus on reaching a more local audience. The stories are created during local group workshops and shared in community spaces when finished as if they were gallery exhibits. The span of the reach is more immediate and perhaps limits the future reach of the texts. Audience members are unable to revisit the digital stories at a later time if they are not provided with external access to digital copies. This approach privileges engagement within communities and sharing digital stories with those connected geographically. While the potential reach of projects distributed via broadcast might be considered greater, the festival element is essential to creating community dialogue. These two audiences look and act very differently and likely influence storytellers' creative practices in different ways. Still, both types of audience are valuable to dissemination practices and should be made available to all storytellers if they desire them.

Live Screenings

I am particularly interested in the ways live screenings can operate to open dialogues that act as a means of resistance. Digital storytelling participants engage with audience members in ways that cross presumed lines of hierarchy and ask both sides to reconsider power and identity. For digital storytelling scholar Megan Alrutz, these interactive frameworks provide audiences the opportunity to engage in a similar disruptive and reflective process that the participants have undergone during story creation. The end-of-workshop screenings that occur for many digital storytelling programs act as a moment of "disturbance." These presentations are given to honor the storytellers and their hard work, voice, and perspective, and in some cases to advocate for a particular social change action. Moreover, the storytellers, workshop facilitators, and people with relationships to the storytellers or the facilitating and/or hosting institutions also attend these presentations. Occasionally, these presentations also attract the interest of local community members; however, it is rare to see a broader audience than this because they are typically specifically aimed at engaging the local community. The gathering of these people to watch the digital videos expands the audience and creates opportunities for direct engagement, disrupting the normal reception of these narratives. It allows for critical thinking by providing the necessary situation to send new "signs, messages, and narratives," (6) as tactical media scholar Rita Raley writes, into the community, which often results in a shared critical discussion between digital storytelling workshop participants and the audience.

For digital storytelling and co-creative media practices it is important to consider how the audience present for a final screening is perhaps privileged over those watching the narratives later from home. Media scholar Chris Atton suggests a connection occurs within the physical space that gathers diverse community members in dialogue and reflection and has large implications for social change. While this sort of dialogue may occur with those watching digitally at a later time, a live presentation creates the opportunity for the audience to discuss the stories directly with the creators and those who helped support the digital stories' creation and places those storytellers as experts in that space. In their digital storytelling project with school-age youth, Lora Taub-Pervizpour and Erin Disbrow saw the same hierarchical disruption. Screenings of the youth-created documentaries, "opened up vital avenues for dialogue in which youth who are regularly silenced by community institutions are positioned – position themselves – and recognized by adults as part of the solution, rather than the problem" (106). These screenings created space for the storytellers to become cultural meaning-makers not only in the process of creating their digital story, but also in the act of sharing it. In so doing, these storytellers occupied positions of power that changed how the audiences perceived these youth.

For digital storytelling processes, the performance and "consensus zones" created in final screenings exists only temporarily in lived space and the works produced often take up residence on the Internet. While they are still ephemeral in this space, the Internet provides a second life for the works and perhaps a chance to create a new "consensus zone" for critical thought. Digital storytelling in this way becomes a critical link between tactical and digital media. As Raley argues, tactical media is viewed as a "performance rather than as static art object emphasizes viewer experience and engagement" (12). In moving from a live performance space to the digital network, digital storytelling may seem to lose this key connection to performance and audience. Unlike in the face-to-face screening, however, the audience for these digital interactions do not always get to build a relationship with the storytellers unless certain digital infrastructures such as a comments section or contact form are included in the digital space. More often audiences are left to interact only with the contextualization the hosting and/or facilitating institutions have put in place as well as the messages and contexts of the digital stories. Thus, digital storytelling spaces should work to maintain and consider the importance of audience in the knowledge-making process.

In these live spaces, digital storytelling authors should continually renegotiate their relationship with members of the audience. Their narratives have been solidified in their final digital stories presented to the audience. Yet storytellers may feel an additional need to perform identity and defend their stories to live audiences in a more immediate way than might happen in digital dissemination spaces. Additionally, these performances and justifications will likely change depending on the person to whom the storyteller is speaking, just as we saw in the story circles or interviews of Catherine Kohler Riessman, since the diversity of people in the audience might be more readily apparent to the storyteller. Tanja Dreher writes that her digital storytelling projects facilitated by Information Cultural Exchange (ICE) in Sydney, Australia, typically attract political figures at their events, which seemingly engages the authors in the political realm. Yet, Dreher cautions that a simple presence in the room does not guarantee efficacy:

> It is not uncommon for a local mayor or dignitary to attend a launch event but then provide no indication of engagement with the stories being told. Rushing off to another engagement, a disappearing dignitary can function as a promise of listening that is not fulfilled.
> ("A Partial Promise" 164)

We are forced to contend with the fact that even in these spaces, the impact of the shared narratives may remain low. Determining in what ways live community digital storytelling events impact diverse audience members and the tactics and strategies we might employ to enhance audience engagement is a topic of study that needs further research, as most scholarship on dissemination considers the broadcast or digital dissemination practices, uses, and benefits.

Digital Dissemination

Access is one of the most notable ways in which digital technologies are expanding everyday conversational storytelling traditions, making it possible for more people to author texts that can be heard by larger audiences than ever before and helping to erase the gap in production between professional media composition and citizen composition. With more access to digital communication technologies in daily life allowing nonprofessionals and professionals alike to author stories and ideas (think Facebook, email, and blogs), we are seeing a rise in storytelling production in a variety of formats. If we understand the communicative and storytelling practices utilized in these new spaces with digital and distributive technologies, we begin to see a larger understanding of the ways stories authored by non-professionals can reach greater audiences and act as critical cultural resources for storytellers. In *Spreadable Media*, Henry Jenkins, Sam Ford, and Joshua Green argue digital audiences are as, and possibly more, important to the circulation of media than their commercial counterparts, because "spreadability is determined by processes of social appraisal rather than technical or creative wizardry and on the active participation of engaged audiences" (192). They call for a strategic approach to ensure successful spreadability of media in which "creators understand the strategic and technical aspects they need to master in order to create content more likely to spread, and they think about what motivates participants to share information and to build relationships with the communities shaping its circulation" (196). In the context of digital storytelling, this implies that in order to achieve the most reach, those in charge of distribution, usually the hosting organization and/or the facilitating institution, should think strategically about the dissemination of digital stories, especially if they are to be used for the purposes of social justice. The authors put forward five key principles to employ in order to maximize the potential for spreadability of content: 1) it is "available when and where audiences want it;" 2) it is "portable;" 3) it is "easily reusable in a variety of ways;" 4) it is "relevant to multiple audiences;" and 5) it is "part of a steady stream of material" (197–198). Effective digital storytelling projects that aim to reach a larger audience with social justice narratives should make use of these principles. In so doing, digital stories created with the aim of social change "[act] as fodder for conversations that audiences are already having" (199), thereby adding a more effective way for the digital storytelling authors and institutions to connect to outside audiences. Effectively, this practice serves as a way to entice digital "consensus zones" to become consensus networks.

While the majority of digital storytelling practices operate through private facilitating institutions, there are notable exceptions of projects facilitated by public service broadcasters. The most renowned of these exceptions is *Capture Wales*, one the most commonly analyzed early digital storytelling project with a myriad of authors using it as a case study,[1] because of the power of institutional support from the BBC. The project ran from 2001 to 2008 and was produced in a partnership between BBC Wales and Cardiff University's Cardiff School of Journalism, Media and Cultural Studies. *Capture Wales* is a key case study in addressing the relationship between audience and everyday storymakers because it highlights the gap between the means of everyday people to tell and share their own stories and the means of a large broadcast corporation. Because of this, the project speaks to a larger, corporate, mass media process of how digital storytelling can reach broad, diverse, and international audiences. The project began as a way for the BBC to create and sustain better relationships with their communities, to teach "the latest media technologies," and "to boost the Welsh creative economy – which is a crucial aspect of the development of the so-called 'new economy' in Wales" (Meadows 192–193). The project's website states:

> Everyone has a story to tell. All over Wales, people are making Digital Stories about real-life experiences and each story is as individual as the person who made it. Each Digital Story is made by the storyteller themself, using his or her own photos, words and voice.

The project archives all of their stories online[2] and additionally "experimented with various ways of incorporating the stories into TV and radio schedules" (Hartley, "Problems of Expertise" 201). The implications for the reach of these endeavors are large. Not only could *Capture Wales* reach local and regional audiences through television and radio, they additionally reach a potential global audience through their archive. Additionally, they make accessible every story created during the project's tenure. These endeavors exemplify Hartley's broadcast method.

Daniel Meadows, who served as creative director for the project from 2001–2006, began his media career as a photographer and quickly expanded into the field of digital storytelling after an introductory workshop with what was then the Center for Digital Storytelling (Meadows 189–191). He views digital storytelling with the ardor of a fervent optimist and describes it as "not just a tool," but also a "revolution" (192). Meadows speaks passionately about the ability of digital storytelling to enable democratic participation among citizens, but it is important to recognize his perspective stems from a well-funded, well-received project with significant strategic, institutional support.

Welsh citizens served as the participant group for the project, enabling a means of democratic participation in partnership between citizens, the university, and a major media and news network. Yet, where these three entities might appear to exist in different levels of power, Meadows wanted to be certain each entity, and especially the citizen participants, held equitable levels of respect and power. In his analysis of *Capture Wales*, Meadows says he was interested in sharing stories from Welsh citizens from all walks of life. For Meadows, even the terminology used in *Capture Wales* needed to recognize the power of the individual authors. He disapproved of the term "ordinary people," because he felt it implied that "individuals' stories [were] not each extraordinary" and because it raised questions about hierarchical power between the storytellers and their professional partners (Thumim 87). Indeed, Meadows saw *Capture Wales* as "explicitly political" (Thumim 91) and "argued that enabling self-representation within the BBC, and in broadcasting more generally, constituted a significant contribution to the health of the democracy" (ibid. 96).

Regardless of whether or not a facilitating institution is private or public, the second life of digitally disseminated stories is a key factor to thinking through the audience of a digital story. Notably, workshop participants may retain little control over the distribution of their digital stories once they are publicly shared. Although it is customary for workshop participants to have consent over whether or not their videos are shared digitally or publicly, and participants typically reserve the right to request their digital stories be removed at a later time, these procedures do not ensure their stories will not have an unintended second life if a viewer replicates their videos. Once the narrative moves beyond the walls, so to speak, of the digital distribution site, the distributing institution no longer has ultimate control over that content. Although this could prove problematic for some participants, Atton argues having the hosting and/or facilitating institution in charge of the dissemination process also could be valuable to the spreadability of the content, as often one of the biggest assets to the institutional facilitator is their ability to reach a larger audience. As Atton explains, "An élite of experts and pundits tends to have easier and more substantial access to a platform for their ideas than do dissidents, protesters, minority groups and even 'ordinary people'" (11). Still, while an alliance between participants and experts is useful for spreading the participants' ideas and narratives, it cannot come at the price of privileging this elite form of dissemination. Access to spaces of, and avenues for, dissemination and the techniques used therein should be made accessible and employable by the everyday citizen as well if we are to facilitate co-collaborative storymaking spaces responsibly. This is particularly important when considering that many dissemination practices are led by project facilitators rather than participants, affecting decisions as to whose stories are shared with audiences.

Facilitator Influence on Dissemination

Determining which stories are shared, where they are shared, how they are shared, and for how long they are shared often falls to the facilitator and facilitating institution, which invites room for bias and censorship. For instance, StoryCenter shares some of the stories created by participants in their workshops online, as do other facilitating organizations, but they do not archive a complete collection of all the stories created through their outreach, raising the question: What determines how stories are selected for dissemination? While storytellers may release their narratives for public distribution on their own, facilitators might retain the right to ultimately decide which narratives to disseminate. As we saw, this selective dissemination occurred in the projects *I Am UCF* and *Queering the Museum*. That some films in each project were selected while others were not, indicates bias and privilege within dissemination practices can potentially dismiss certain voices and narratives from being included in public and digital showcases. This encourages a consideration of those storytellers who are excluded from digital storytelling spaces.

Stakeholders in the storytelling process other than the storytellers (i.e., the facilitator, the hosting institution, the organization running the gallery and/or the workshop, etc.), hold control over whose narratives are showcased in public places. Additionally, the inclusion of videos in screenings may be selected by outside institutions who did not participate in the storymaking process, as was the case in the *Revealing Queer* exhibit and the film festivals in which select videos were showcased. In this case, digital stories were selected for inclusion based on content (Robert 149). Vetoing the video from *I Am UCF* was done to protect some college students present in the digital story who did not give written consent to have the content publicly shared. Amy Hill discusses a similar case where her concern for the wellbeing of her storytellers informed her decision on whether or not to disseminate certain digital stories. She conducted a project in which storytellers told narratives of abuse that implicated the people to whom they were married. Hill encouraged sensitivity in disclosing certain information, especially in cases where she felt that it jeopardized the safety of the storytellers, but she did not ultimately insist they tell alternative narratives. The women did not change their narratives and agreed to share their stories publicly, but as Hill explains,

> I didn't ultimately include their work as part of a compilation DVD that, according to a contractual agreement with the project funder, was to be widely duplicated and distributed (and I didn't ask the funder for permission to exclude these stories, which reveals an imbalance between that contract and my allegiance to community members, to whom I feel I must ultimately be accountable).
>
> (35)

Hill's decision silenced certain narratives from being disseminated but it also speaks to a consideration of a facilitator's responsibility. Her role as facilitator gave her the power to promote what she perceived to be the wellbeing of the participants over the goals of the project and project stakeholders. Hill ultimately argues that "...the line between an ethic of 'do no harm' and a decision that some might see as patronizing or tinged with censorship was difficult to pinpoint" in this specific case (35), and it could be argued that her actions dismissed a challenging problem too easily. This is a line that responsible facilitators should continually walk as they negotiate not only the dissemination process, but the storymaking process as well.

The dissemination of narratives on the behalf of others becomes a question of representation, as Cunsolo Willox et al. show in their case study of the *Changing Climate, Changing Health, Changing Stories* project:

> Once the stories were created, and our team and the story creators were discussing when, how, and where to make the digital stories public, we were confronted with the 'burden of representation' (Fine et al., 2003: 169). Indeed, our team became acutely aware of the responsibility held by the community, the facilitators, and ourselves over story dissemination, as issues and questions around participant privacy and the potential for the perpetuation of stereotypes were foremost in our minds.
>
> (140)

In their consideration of dissemination practices, the authors address the ways that the dissemination of narratives not only affects the wellbeing of the individual storyteller, but how such narratives will ultimately affect and influence socio-cultural representation. Representation, then, has, (at least) two important concerns: How people are represented and how people are served by such representations.

Responsible facilitators should include storymakers in their discussion of where, when, and how to disseminate their digital stories, thereby including them in conversations about representation. Helping storytellers understand the potential impact of their digital stories is important and can help storytellers make better informed decisions for the dissemination of the stories created during workshop as well as stories they may author later. Storytellers should consider how these influences will affect their own story creation process. The ability to author narratives should be seen as a resource for the storytellers. I believe this resource should be extended to include the methods of a story's distribution. Acknowledging the relationship between listeners and speakers is essential to understanding the full complexity of digital storytelling as a co-creative media practice. It is equally essential to discuss the importance of these relationships with storytellers.

Notes

1 See: Burgess; Klaebe and Burgess; Hartley and McWilliam; Meadows; Meadows and Kidd; Thumim; Lewis and Matthews.
2 At the time of this writing, this archive could be accessed at www.bbc.co.uk/wales/audiovideo/sites/galleries/pages/capturewales.shtml.

References

Alrutz, Megan. *Digital Storytelling, Applied Theatre, & Youth: Performing Possibility*. Routledge, 2014.

Atton, Chris. *Alternative Media*. Sage, 2002.

Banks, Adam. *Digital Griot: African American Rhetoric in a Multimedia Age*. Southern Illinois University Press, 2011.

Burgess, Jean. "Hearing Ordinary Voices: Cultural Studies, Vernacular Creativity and Digital Storytelling." *Continuum: Journal of Media & Cultural Studies*, vol. 20, no. 2, 2006, pp. 201–214.

Couldry, Nick. *Why Voice Matters: Culture and Politics after Neoliberalism*. Sage, 2010.

Cunsolo Willox, Ashley, et al. "Storytelling in a Digital Age: Digital Storytelling as an Emerging Narrative Method for Preserving and Promoting Indigenous Oral Wisdom." *Qualitative Research*, vol. 13, no. 2, 2012, pp. 127–147.

Dreher, Tanja. "A Partial Promise of Voice: Digital Storytelling and the Limits of Listening." *Media International Australia*, vol. 142, no. 1, pp. 157–166.

Erstad, Ola, and James V. Wertsch. "Tales of Mediations: Narrative and Digital Media as Cultural Tools." *Digital Storytelling, Mediatized Stories: Self-representations in New Media*, edited by Knut Lundby, Peter Lang, 2008, pp. 1–17.

Hartley, John. "Problems of Expertise and Scalability in Self Made Media." *Digital Storytelling, Mediatized Stories: Self-Representations in New Media*, edited by Knut Lundby, Peter Lang, 2009, pp. 197–212.

Hartley, John. "Smiling or Smiting?–Selves, States and Stories in the Constitution of Polities." *Digital Storytelling: Form and Content*, edited by Mark Dunford, and Tricia Jenkins, Palgrave Macmillan, 2017, pp. 203–227.

Hartley, John, and Kelly McWilliam, editors. *Story Circle: Digital Storytelling around the World*. Wiley-Blackwell, 2009.

Helff, Sissy, and Julie Woletz. "Narrating Euro-African Life in Digital Space." *Story Circle: Digital Storytelling around the World*, edited by John Hartley, and Kelly McWilliam, Wiley-Blackwell, 2009, pp. 131–143.

Hendry, Pamela. "The Future of Narrative." *Qualitative Inquiry*, vol. 13, no. 4, 2007, pp. 497–498.

Hertzberg Kaare, Bridgit, and Knut Lundby. "Autobiography and Assumed Authenticity in Digital Storytelling." *Digital Storytelling, Mediatized Stories: Self-representation in New Media*, edited by Knut Lundby, Peter Lang, 2008, pp. 105–222.

Hill, Amanda. "Food for Thought: Constructing Multimodal Identities through Recipe-Creation with Homeless Youth." *Community Literacy Journal*, 2020, pp. 162–170.

Hill, Amy. "Digital Storytelling and the Politics of Doing Good: Exploring the Ethics of Bringing Personal Narratives into Public Spheres." *Community-Based Multiliteracies and Digital Media Projects: Questioning Assumptions and Exploring Realities*, edited by Heather M. Pleasants, and Dana E. Salter, Peter Lang, 2014, pp. 21–43.

Jenkins, Henry, et al. *Spreadable Media: Creating Value and Meaning in a Networked Culture*. New York University Press, 2013.

Klaebe, Helen G., and Burgess, Jean E. *State Library of Queensland Oral History and Digital Storytelling Review*. Queensland University of Technology, 2008.

Klaus, Elisabeth, and Margreth Lünenborg. "Cultural Citizenship. Participation by and through Media." *Feminist Media: Participatory Spaces, Networks and Cultural Citizenship*, edited by Elke Zobl, and Ricarda Drüeke, Transcript, 2012, pp. 197–212.

Lambert, Joe. *Digital Storytelling: Capturing Lives, Creating Community*. 3rd ed., Digital Diner Press, 2009.

Lambert, Joe, and H. Brooke Hessler. *Digital Storytelling: Digital Storytelling: Capturing Lives, Creating Community*. 5th ed., Routledge, 2018.

Lanham, Richard. *The Economics of Attention: Style and Substance in the Age of Information*. University of Chicago Press, 2006.

Lewis, Karen, and Nicole Matthews. "The Afterlife of Capture Wales: Digital Stories and Their Listening Publics." *Digital Storytelling: Form and Content*, edited by Mark Dunford, and Tricia Jenkins, Palgrave Macmillan, 2017, pp. 103–118.

Lincoln, Yovanna S. "I and Thou: Method, Voice, and Roles in Research with the Silenced." *Naming Silenced Lives: Personal Narratives and Processes of Educational Change*, edited by Daniel McLaughlin, and William G. Tierney, Routledge, 1993, 29–47.

Meadows, Daniel. "Digital Storytelling: Research–Based Practice in New Media." *Visual Communication*, vol. 2, no. 2, 2003, pp.189–193.

Meadows, Daniel, and Jenny Kidd. "Capture Wales." *Story Circle: Digital Storytelling around the World*, edited by John Hartley, and Kelly McWilliam, Wiley–Blackwell, 2009, pp. 91–117.

Mitra, Ananda. "Marginal Voices in Cyberspace." *New Media & Society*, vol. 3, no. 1, 2001, pp. 29–48.

Ochs, Elinor, and Lisa Capps. *Living Narrative: Creating Lives in Everyday Storytelling*. Harvard University Press, 2002.

Poletti, Anna. "Coaxing an Intimate Public: Life Narrative in Digital Storytelling." *Continuum: Journal of Media & Cultural Studies*, vol. 25, no. 1, 2011, 73–83.

Raley, Rita. *Tactical Media*. University of Minnesota Press, 2009.

Rappaport, Julian. "Empowerment Meets Narrative: Listening to Stories and Creating Settings." *American Journal of Community Psychology*, vol. 23, no. 5, 1995, pp. 795–807.

Riessman, Catherine Kohler. *Narrative Methods for Human Sciences*. Sage, 2008.

Robert, Nicole. *Queering U.S. History Museums: Heteronormative Histories, Digital Disruptions*. 2016. University of Washington, PhD Dissertation.

Taub-Pervizpour, Lora, and Erin Drisbrow. "Digital Storytelling with Youth: Whose Agenda Is It?" *Story Circle: Digital Storytelling around the World*, edited by John Hartley, and Kelly McWilliam, Wiley–Blackwell, 2009, pp. 245–251.

Thumim, Nancy. *Self-Representation and Digital Culture*. Palgrave Macmillan, 2012.

Tuhiwai Smith, Linda. *Decolonizing Methodologies: Research and Indigenous Peoples*. 12th ed. Zed Books, Ltd., 2008.

Young, Iris Marion. *Justice and the Politics of Difference*. Princeton University Press, 1990.

6 Ethical Collaboration
The Responsible Facilitator in Theory

The Elephant in the Room

In creating responsible digital storytelling practices, facilitators should assess and understand the roles and power structures within the relationships among the people in the room and with those beyond the creative space such as institutions and audience. To begin this conversation, it is also important to look at the benefits a facilitator brings to the digital storytelling environment. Expertise grows out of embodied action. It is formed through lived experience and makes use of "domain-specific knowledge" (Charness and Krampe 245) and is often rooted in education, "one of the central socializing agencies in society," which "provides the individual with the cultural means to participate in society" (Klaus and Lünenborg 199). Digital storytelling workshops can provide educational instruction in storytelling and digital literacy skills so participants can practice such storymaking skills in an effort to increase their expertise in these fields. This could perhaps be their most benign role within the creation experience, although it is still possible for facilitators to dictate the ways in which participants produce stories using that software, which in and of itself could be seen as restrictive and oppressive. Additionally, many digital storytelling facilitators work with participants to shape their narratives, which in turn often adhere to dominant Western narrative structures. At the same time, the shaping of narratives could be seen as a benefit for participants who desire to tell stories like those they see in mainstream media, as most facilitators are also well versed in the story structure and components of those genres.

In his discussion of zines, alternative media theorist Chris Atton points out that "what in mass media enterprises are discrete roles, in zine culture become collapsed into one: an editor is often the sole writer, designer, paste-up artist, finisher, and distributor," thereby giving a single person creative control over the knowledge making process (5). With the rise of digital media, these roles are even more easily combined and navigated. Digital storytelling certainly makes use of intuitive and accessible digital technologies to merge these positions, but as a movement it struggles to hand over unconditional power to the storytellers in the workshop. Zines, on the other

DOI: 10.4324/9781003200826-6

hand, often empower their authors with unsupervised control. The creators of the US-based zine project *Grrrl Zines A-Go-Go* advocate for works like zines to be completely uncensored, able to be single-handedly produced, and created "without the need for experts" (qtd. in Zobl 267). For this collective, the ability for people to say what they desire in the way they desire encourages "active participation in the creation of one's own culture and independence from mainstream media" (ibid.).

On the other hand, the zines of the 1990s were created using cut and paste techniques that were then photocopied, combined, and distributed physically. Digital storytelling in theory makes use of these same techniques, but does so within a digital infrastructure. For those unfamiliar with digital tools and technologies the learning curve might be considerably higher than it is with zines. Unlike those working on zines, Atton maintains that following in theorist Michael Traber's notion of grassroots alternative media, where media "are produced by the same people whose concerns they represent," expert involvement need not be totally dismissed. He writes, rather, that "they will be firmly in the role of advisers, their presence intended to enable 'ordinary people' to produce their own work, independent of professional journalists and editors" (16). It is from Traber's position that we begin to shape the role of the responsible digital storytelling facilitator. Understanding the facilitator as filling the role of advisor renegotiates the expert paradigm common in educator/student and researcher/participant dichotomies, accomplishing the aims of many digital storytelling projects. Because of this, we should assess the ways in which the facilitator as advisor is responsible for engaging with the storytellers as subjects.

An Ethics of Responsibility

The key to being an ethically responsible facilitator is listening. The work of Kelly Oliver explores this by considering how what we listen for in a narrative impacts its reception. Using the story of a screening of an eyewitness testimony from a survivor of the Auschwitz uprising collected by Dori Laub, Oliver argues that the logic of fact and recognition cannot account for the entirety of the testimony. The witness "reported four chimneys going up in flames and exploding, but historians insisted that since there was only one chimney blown up, her testimony was incorrect and should be discredited in its entirety because she proved herself an unreliable witness" (Oliver 1). Because of what might be considered a faulty memory, historians chose to discredit her testimony as inaccurate. Meanwhile, psychoanalysts who heard the account argued that the survivor "was not testifying to the number of chimneys blown up but to something more 'radical' and more 'crucial' – namely, the seemingly unimaginable occurrence of Jewish resistance at Auschwitz, that is to say, the *historical truth* of Jewish resistance at Auschwitz" (ibid.). Oliver writes that unlike the historians who were listening solely for confirmation, the psychoanalysts were listening for what was new. In testimonies such as this, the narrator is not merely seeking recognition, but also "retribution and compassion," what Oliver would call the ability to respond (8). The historians who discredit this testimony take away the address-ability and the response-ability of the narrator, and in so doing, other her, placing her in the position of object rather than as a knowledgeable subject with a valuable story perspective.

Oliver argues that intersubjective dialogue enables moments of address and response, and calls this "the ethical obligation at the heart of subjectivity" (15). This dialogue "implies that subjectivity is constituted *across* subject positions, as both an 'I' who can address oneself to others and a 'me' who can respond and be responsible for others," (Stumm 777). She argues that "our conceptions of *ourselves* determine our conceptions of others and our conceptions of our relationships with others" (3) (emphasis mine), inviting subjectivity that is created dialogically between subjects. Therefore, if we treat the other person as a subject, we facilitate their existence as a subject. Subjectivity in this sense cannot exist without others. It is created relationally, enabled by and arising from interactions with others. I need to be able to respond to you in a way that enables you to respond to me and to others. Key to this concept of subjectivity as dialogically created is Oliver's insistence that each subject has the ability to address and respond. To make this happen, each subject needs to serve as a witness in relationship to the other. Oliver writes, witnessing "both reconstructs damaged subjectivity and constitutes the heart of all subjectivity" (8).

Construing subjectivity in relation to witnessing enables the other's ability to respond or response-ability:

> Subjectivity requires the possibility of a witness, and the witnessing at the heart of subjectivity brings with it responsibility, response-ability and ethical responsibility. Subjectivity as the ability to respond is linked in its conception to ethical responsibility. Subjectivity is responsibility: it is the ability to respond and be responded to. Responsibility, then, has the double sense of opening up the ability to respond, response-ability and ethically obligating subjects to respond by virtue of their very subjectivity itself.
>
> (91)

Subjectivity in this sense becomes a form of ethical responsibility and response-ability. Oliver positions witnessing as a process of "address and response" (2) and makes use of the double-meaning of the term to speak to both the process of "seeing with one's own eyes" and bearing witness, or testifying, that moves beyond understandings of recognition to "that which cannot be seen" (16). Perhaps then, facilitators need to approach storytellers with what Pamela Hendry calls "faith," which calls for listeners to cast storytellers in a relationship of trust: "Trusting in the stories and the storyteller" (494). This faith serves in resistance to approaching storytellers with what we might regard as suspicion as the historians do to the Holocaust survivor in Oliver's account. Hendry writes,

> Listening to stories we are often engaged in a dual conversation. One conversation with the interviewed and one in our own head where we are constantly engaging in a meta-analysis of the story. What is really going on here? What is the meaning? How might I get more? What am I missing? We are in a state of doubt in relation to our interviewee. Our stance is one of distrust. So busy capturing 'experience' that we can't listen. We have so many strategies for 'getting it right' that the real experience is obscured.
>
> (ibid.)

Hendry argues that we should trust storytellers to tell us stories that do not require the listener to interpret or analyze the teller's meaning. When co-productive dialogue translates into the analytical process, there is a danger of creating even further distance between the listener and the storyteller, and at times "interpretation becomes an act of colonization" (ibid.). Colonization of this nature applies to all marginalized communities who, too often, have had their stories told *for* them by an outsider. Digital storytelling practitioner Loretta Ross has first-hand experience in feeling as though her story were being told for her. From her perspective as a woman of color, she often feels as though "others often tell our stories *for us* in a colonizing way, denying us the right not only to tell our own stories but to decide what the stories mean. Anthropologists study us, economists objectify us, historians dismiss us" (67). She argues that owning and defining her story is not solely about authoring it, but also about producing and distributing it, as I took up in earlier chapters.

While using different terms, I believe both Oliver and Hendry are defining a key component to rendering storytellers as subjects. Hendry's concept of faith allows listeners to position storytellers so they are able to be addressed and to respond: "Faith in the story is a political act in which we acknowledge our participants, not as incomplete, but as meaning makers and central to our own meaning making" (494). Like witnessing, faith is political and reciprocal. Hendry suggests that when we listen for factual evidence to support our bias and enable confirmation and recognition, "our questions operate as interrogation" (495). To respond to people with faith, on the other hand, is to "'[plug] into' the experience of listening" (ibid.). Hendry quotes Gadamer who argues that "anyone who listens is fundamentally open. Without this kind of openness to one another there is no genuine human relationship" (ibid.). The importance of listening as the basis, arguably, of both witnessing and faith becomes the key to the ethical responsibility of the facilitator in co-creative relational storymaking spaces like digital storytelling, because it has the capacity to invigorate the storyteller's voice.

Bettina Stumm writes, "Collaborators create spaces for subjects to speak and to assert their marginalized voices, voices that are affirmed in the collaborators' responses. Truth telling, listening, and engaging empathetically with vulnerable subjects become significant political activities in the process" (764). The facilitator is one such collaborator and thus a key practice in their work is political listening (Bickford). The impact of voice is dependent on listening. As digital storytelling scholar Darcy Alexandra writes, "the 'promise' of digital storytelling has primarily focused not on listening, or even visibility per se, but on the power and possibility of 'voice.' But what impact does 'voice' have if no one is listening?" (43). There are two connotations of listening inherent in listening. The large-scale socio-political framework of audience listening discussed in the previous chapter and the small-scale one-on-one social listening that takes place between two entities. How can the facilitator engender this second connotation within the workshop? That is, how can facilitators' listening create response-ability for all workshop participants? Susan Bickford writes, "To highlight the role of listening is to confront the intersubjective character of politics" (4). It is precisely in this intersubjective character that the facilitator takes part. For Bickford, political listening does not necessarily invite the presence of care or good-naturedness. In fact, she argues that political listening is needed as conflict and difference occur (2). Here then, we might suggest that political listening may involve the ability to listen even when the dialogue or ideas become difficult to hear. Bickford suggests that such

> communicative interaction – speaking and listening together – does not necessarily resolve or do away with the conflicts that arise from uncertainty, inequality, and identity. Rather, it enables political actors to decide democratically how to act in the face of conflict, and to clarify the nature of the conflict at hand. Deciding democratically means deciding, under conditions in which all voices are heard, what course of action makes sense.
>
> (2)

Yet while Bickford contends that political listening may not always be based in an understanding of care, she does account for listening as an empathetic and active process. She writes, "Listening means 'I will put myself in his place, I will try to understand, I will strain to hear what makes us alike, I will listen for a common rhetoric evocative of a common purpose or a common good'" (13).

In digital storytelling, listening should take place throughout the process of production and through the process of distribution (Alexandra 41). This ongoing approach enables response-ability as the facilitator is listening for what is being said and from where the sentiment originates. This will, in turn, enable the facilitator to be critically reflexive about their own practices so they can respond to workshop participants as needed to open spaces of address and response. Facilitators should be instrumental in ensuring political listening happens within the workshop. Story-sharing spaces such as the story circle are critical for engaging in response-able political listening. This is important for effectively navigating the dialogue among participants, and allowing space for participants to share the stories they are interested in sharing. It is additionally important to remember that participants will communicate in many ways through both verbal and non-verbal actions. Facilitators should not only listen to the participants' words, but also note their body language when communicating with others. Listening to the whole person can help clarify the meaning of what is being communicated and can help guide the trajectory of the workshop's facilitation.

Responsibility and Voice

Facilitating the ability for these actions to occur is no small task, and facilitators should contend with ethical considerations including responsibility and voice. Biographer Bettina Stumm suggests that "navigat[ing] relational space in order to bear witness to another person's suffering and story is ... a question of ethical responsibility ... that shapes how we receive, respond to, and recount the narrative of others" (763). Stumm makes the same case for biography that I make here for digital co-creative practices: "What is called for, then, is the responsibility to recognize and restore the marginalized identities of vulnerable subjects through their narrative voices without usurping those voices in a new power hierarchy" (764). This is the challenge of the facilitator. Facilitators should assess their presence in the room within every facet of co-creative media practice. In so doing, they practice an important ethical responsibility. Our responsibility to the storytellers in the room, then, is to move away from the seemingly hierarchical notion of the expert, from whom storytellers are expected to seek adjudication and recognition. As Stumm writes, "If agency hangs solely on another's recognition, then the recognizer is put in a position of power and the sufferer's dependent position is reinforced" (765). Recognition in and of itself does not imply a balanced relationship between two people. In fact, in simply recognizing another person, one runs the risk of silencing the person who seeks recognition, because it stops the line of reciprocal dialogue. Stumm further explains, "In [recognition's] very acts of 'giving voice' and 'taking responsibility' for the other's marginalized identity and empowerment, the respondent can create relational imbalance, a one-sided dialogue, and in collaborative writing, an alternate form of narrative control" (777). Likewise, assuming the digital realm eliminates hierarchical barriers and provides a means of "giving voice" to participants, works against the idea of responsibly-facilitated digital storytelling.

The phrase "giving voice" implies underlying power structures whereby the facilitator, as the expert, has the right and the resources to *give* another person their "voice" through recognition. It is then simultaneously about others "taking responsibility," as Stumm indicates, for the identities of the participants. In essence, the act ensures that we first "take" something away in order to "give" something back. "Giving voice" implies that the "voice" of these participants is missing prior to their coming into the digital storytelling workshop and that facilitators are responsible for and have the authority to give it back to them. People are not "voiceless" in the sense that they are missing their "voices" or that they have been lost. Rather, voices can be silenced and repressed in structures of oppression and discrimination. This perspective insinuates that the voice and the person are constantly unified, even if that person feels as though they cannot use or express their voice. The understanding of voice suggested by the phrase "giving voice" assumes that the gift of voice will then be recognized by the facilitator and outside audience. Voice, understood in this way, cannot be obtained alone, it should be given by someone in a greater position of power.

Perhaps most troubling is the common perception that "giving voice" is a form of generosity, a kindness we can bestow on others. In that fraught notion of "giving voice," facilitators revoke the response-ability of the storytellers since voice becomes something *given by* the hands of others and not formed through the storyteller's own volition. This causes storytellers to relinquish the ability to take responsibility for their lives and experiences. Still, digital storytelling promotes itself as a platform that allows everyday storytellers to take ownership of their experiences and perspectives, in essence, as a platform that promotes authentic voice. StoryCenter founder Joe Lambert suggests digital storytelling practices are a way "to develop our own sense of voice and story" (1). Lambert's remark is subtle, but notably different as "develop" suggests each storyteller is the architect of their own story.

Despite the fraught nature of the term, many scholars still make use of it. In her scholarship on digital storytelling, Jo Tacchi broadly defines "voice" when she explains it "references inclusion and participation in social, political, and economic processes, meaning making, autonomy, and expression" (169). Tacchi claims that to give voice is to give "access to modes of expression and more generally to freedom of expression" and "can be about opportunity and agency to promote self-expression and advocacy, about access and the skills to use technologies and platforms for the distribution of a range of different voices" (169). She additionally points to the use of voice in development communication and wellbeing studies and explains the traction it is receiving from larger organizations such as World Bank for its focus on inclusivity in determining whose voice counts (170). Voice, then, in Tacchi's analysis, becomes a democratic tool of digital storytelling that enables individuals from cultures and communities around the world to author often-untold discourses and histories of their experiences in the hopes of reflecting on, and promoting change in, their communities and cultures.

In her work with women from India, Sri Lanka, Nepal, and Indonesia, Tacchi argues that the power of storytelling enabled the women to define and tell their own stories in ways that allow for wider audiences to access their narratives. In this project, Tacchi claims digital storytelling has the ability "to empower poor people to communicate their 'voices' within and beyond marginalized communities" (169). Too often, "giving voice," the act of bestowing voice, becomes the responsibility of the facilitator and prepares participants to expect recognition from others rather than opening a process of address and response that participants can use once they leave the digital storytelling practice. As Stumm argues, "Agency and responsibility must be held in tandem to assert one's subjectivity and to flourish as a whole person," (777). Holding these in tandem positions them inter-subjectively. As facilitators, we should constantly strive to understand how agency and responsibility grow across subjects as Stumm suggests. This will ensure we facilitate responsibly in co-creative media practices.

I don't write this here to blame Tacchi or any others for any previous use of the term. I recognize it was born from a systemic oppression that views others as less-than and own that I too made use of it in previous publications, as the idea of "giving voice" was prevalent in early digital storytelling scholarship. Upon further reflection, the hierarchical and structural implications of such terminology have caused me to give more consideration to what it is I truly hope to accomplish and how I can continue to work to facilitate more inclusive spaces that enable an ethic of care.

An Ethic of Care

A scholarly understanding of care was first put forward by Carol Gilligan in her 1982 work, *In a Different Voice: Psychological Theory and Women's Development*. Contending with scholars like Freud, Piaget, and Kohlberg who trace justice and moral development primarily among boys (sidelining or eliminating female voices), Gilligan examines how women's care work structures their sense of morality. In response to the previous theories, she writes, "for the very traits that traditionally have defined the 'goodness' of women, their care for and sensitivity to the needs of others, are those that mark them as deficient in moral development" (18). For Gilligan, an ethic of care develops in a relationship, similar to the ways in which subjectivity develops in Oliver's work. Gilligan writes that an ethic of care "reflects a cumulative knowledge of human relationships [and] evolves around a central insight, that self and other are interdependent" (74).

Since Gilligan's book, literature about caring and an ethic of care has flourished in numerous fields. Many differences between subsequent works in various fields exist, but a driving factor to all of them is a recognition "that care so far has taken place under oppressive conditions" (Skærbæk 43). Witnessing, too, takes place in such a division, as it is also concerned with the powerlessness of one and the institutionalized power of another within the relationality of response-ability. Of particular importance to this work is Nel Noddings's 1992 work, *The Challenge to Care in Schools*, which applied Gilligan's ethic of care directly to education. Noddings argues that care should be at the forefront of education and looks closely at the relational aspects of caring, especially between the "cared for" and the "carer." She describes a caring relation as, "a connection or encounter between two human beings" (15). Like Oliver's witnessing, caring is not only relational, but also reciprocal. Without this reciprocity, a caring relationship cannot form. Noddings writes, "A failure on the part of either carer or cared-for blocks completion of caring and, although there may still be a relation ... it is not a *caring* relation" (ibid.). Although Noddings and Oliver use different words, their ideologies are similar. Oliver's witnessing opens up "response-ability," to the ability for individuals to respond to and be responded to by others. Response-ability is inherently relational and reciprocal, as it is based in the processes and ability of each person to address and respond to one another. This attentiveness that Noddings describes is the foundation of the process of caring: "When I care, I really hear, see, or feel what the other tries to convey" (16). Attending to another with this kind of open acceptance opens up the ability to respond in a manner that opens up further response-ability.

Looking at witnessing and caring side-by-side, we can see a need to look at the relationships formed between people as a method for understanding the complexity of subjectivity. Because we are looking at the relationship between people, it feels important to begin with a study of conversation, the ways they share information with each other. A significant portion of relational communication comes from the dialogue people use to converse. In the relationality of caring, Noddings suggests dialogue should necessarily be open-ended and undetermined, if it is to be considered genuine (23). That is, genuine dialogue does not have any predetermined outcomes. All parties involved should be willing to be open to the nature of the conversation, to accept what comes, and to see what arises. Dialogue in this way "is a common search for understanding, empathy, or appreciation" as well as what "connects us to each other and helps us maintain caring relations" (ibid.).

Noddings's use of dialogue as a specific practice of response-ability has practical uses in the digital storytelling workshop. Noddings writes, "We respond most effectively as carers when we understand what the other needs and the history of this need. Dialogue is implied in the criterion of engrossment" (ibid.). The knowledge we gain about each other through dialogue "forms a foundation for response in caring" (ibid). Understanding of this nature allows for Oliver's witnessing, because it allows for the carers to respond to another cared-for. In turn, I believe, this would enable the cared-for to have the ability to respond. Oliver argues that intersubjective dialogue enables moments of address and response, and calls this "the ethical obligation at the heart of subjectivity" (15). This dialogue "implies that subjectivity is constituted across subject positions, as both an 'I' who can address oneself to others and a 'me' who can respond and be responsible for others," (Stumm 777). Dialogue that produces response-ability thus becomes critical to establishing and maintaining subjectivity. Considering how dialogue creates relationality and provides opportunities for response-ability is essential for the digital storytelling facilitator, who actively works with a community to construct narratives collaboratively. Critical, then, to this discussion is the importance of interdependency. The subjectivity afforded through response-able dialogic practices necessarily relies on the interdependence between two subjects. Skærbæk writes, "By taking ontological interdependency as a point of departure the question is no longer whether to interfere or not. Interdependency means that every one of us holds some of the life of the other in our hand" (44). If we consider care and witnessing in the context of interdependency, our ability to enable subjectivity is dependent on the response-ability of another, formed through our own responses to that individual. We are responsible for caring and witnessing in a way that opens up the ability for individuals to respond to and to be responded to by others, to create subjectivity, interdependently, because even if we do nothing, we are still responsible for the effects that has on others: "We are interdependent in the sense that we influence each other with what we do and say and by what we do not say and do; we are each other's authors, to use a metaphor of Max Frisch" (Skærbæk 44).

It is in an understanding of interdependency that Noddings's understanding of care as an ethic of relation is most prominent and frames Oliver's witnessing as an ethic of relation. Oliver's witnessing stems from an interest in the relationality and the subjectivity "of those othered within dominant culture" (6). Her ideology contends that the oppression of the "other" prevents that person from engaging in acts of address and response by taking away their place as subject. Oliver writes that "beginning with the subject position of those othered [we can learn] that the speaking subject is a subject by virtue of address-ability and response-ability" (7). Thus, the two subjects become linked in an interdependent system of address and response that one could argue operates in a similar relational fashion as the ethic of care, concerning itself with the wellbeing of another person with whom one is connected, whether briefly or for tenured durations of time.

In a 1993 letter in response to *In a Different Voice*, Gilligan discusses how at the time of writing, she found that many women were not privileged with such subjectivity. Gilligan writes,

> many women feared that others would condemn or hurt them if they spoke, that others would not listen or understand, that speaking would only lead to further confusion, that it was better to appear 'selfless,' to give up their voices and keep the peace.
>
> (x)

Her research focused on providing space to allow women to speak. Gilligan's work was created to allow for the witnessing of women and the amplification of their voices, concerns, and care work. Understanding Gilligan's approach to considering an ethics of care and care work further requires an acknowledgment of the perspective of care work. Female voice has long been equated with the ethic of care. Gilligan's experience examining the responses from male and female children ultimately led her to view an ethic of care as ingrained in femininity. This understanding of care as singularly feminine has complicated our relationship with the methodology of the ethic. As Lynch et al. write in their article,

> The reluctance to name care as work arises also from the public allegiance to the traditional feminine (as opposed to feminist) ethic of care which defines care as a moral obligation (for women in particular) governed by rules of selflessness and self-sacrifice (Gilligan, 1995). It is defined in this deeply patriarchal code as a 'duty' not a job.
>
> (55)

Such work is ingrained through gender social norms as practiced in socialization. It is thus often viewed in direct opposition to masculine work. As Amanda Kennedy writes, "[Gilligan] situated the feminist ethic of care against the masculine ethic of justice, which celebrates objectivity and reason" (219). Yet Gilligan puts both an ethics of justice and an ethics of care as "the ideals of human relationship" that work together to create "the vision that self and other will be treated as of equal worth, that despite differences in power, things will be fair; the vision that everyone will be responded to and included, that no one will be left alone or hurt" (63). Her work, overarchingly, is about "our perceptions of reality and truth: how we know, how we hear, how we seek, [and] how we speak" (xiii). Each of these concerns is built relationally and are created through a process of inter-subjectivity. For the digital storytelling workshop facilitator, these questions are ones we should ask of ourselves and of our workshop participants in order to ensure we are working within an ethics of care and to enable response-ability within the workshop setting.

While digital storytelling workshops do not always take place inside a classroom, or between teachers and students, the relationship dynamic can be similar to that found between the digital storytelling facilitator and the workshop participant. As such, we can learn much from understanding how education and pedagogy have made progress using theories such as an ethic of care to promote the growth and development of people as a whole and to encourage response-ability within such relationships. Digital storytelling work can also be amplified and grown through the use of critical pedagogy.

In considering an ethic of care as a desired cornerstone in education, Noddings understands that educators are advocates for their students. Care, within this context, is a relational practice that can invite more effective ways of learning into the classroom. This also holds true for digital storytelling workshops, which involve both the exchange of information and giving advice. Noddings writes that educators "should suggest, persuade, inspire, encourage, negotiate compromises, offer concrete help. Above all they should engage students in dialogue so that decisions are well informed" (157). In digital storytelling workshops, helping participants make well-informed choices can sometimes be complicated by the needs and desired outcome of other stakeholders. In this case, the facilitator's job is to still enable care and response-ability within the workshop space. Such navigation can be complicated by organizational stakeholders and the timely completion of desired outcomes.

Case Study: *Healthy Young Peer Education* (HYPE)

While many digital storytelling workshops try to enhance participant engagement by including participant-led techniques within their work, the expert paradigm maintains a privileged status in the digital storytelling genre. Digital storytelling scholar John Hartley argues that digital storytelling practices "[require] a dialogic approach to production, relying on a tactfully handled exploitation of a highly asymmetric relationship: the formal, explicit, professional, expert knowledge of the facilitator and the informal, tacit, 'amateur' or 'common' knowledge of the participant" (*Uses* 126). Co-productive media practices require teaching complex digital literacy skills and some argue tighter supervision is needed in such practices. However, when the hierarchical nature of the roles moves beyond the realm of digital literacy into interference in the story creation, it can compromise and complicate the authenticity of the story's message and context and the value of the participant as author.

In "Detours through Youth-Driven Media: Backseat Drivers Bear Witness to the Ethical Dilemmas of Youth Media," digital storytelling facilitators Lora Taub-Pervizpour and Erin Disbrow discuss the methodology and findings of a youth-created documentary project, *Healthy Young Peer Education* (HYPE), an after-school and summer public advocacy program for Latino and African-American high school students. HYPE serves as a space for creative expression where students can voice their concerns through media such as digital storytelling, performance, and documentary. The authors write, "HYPE students unanimously view the community as unwelcoming to young people in general and adults as distrusting of youth of color in particular" (99). In response to this perceived problem, the documentary centered on a student-led interview with the principal.

In their analysis, Taub-Pervizpour and Disbrow maintain the *zone of proximal development* is a good framework for ensuring the best partnership between the facilitator and the participant. In the best practices, this positions the two in "co-constructing knowledge" within the zone (110), a method which implies a dismantling of the expert paradigm commonly seen in research settings. They provide an example of a participant named Jessie who did not know how to use the digital technologies, but knew artistically what she wanted them to do. The facilitator "created a situation in which Jessie was able to accomplish complex editing tasks that she could not yet complete independently" (110). Jessie eventually took over the role of editor and taught another student what she had learned. While this is a powerful example of the way in which the facilitator can work with the participant to learn digital literacy skills, it only affects one part of the dialogic function of the expert in the room. Participants need to learn the digital literacy skills necessary to produce works in digital media, and facilitators are great resources for helping them achieve this goal. The relationship between facilitator and participant thrives when the facilitator serves as an advisor and educator in the techniques of storytelling and digital tools and assets. However, tension between facilitator and storyteller is most clearly present when the facilitator steps in to guide the direction of a story, as also happened in the HYPE project, when the project coordinator stepped in to sway the editing of the documentary work in the students' depiction of their principal. In so doing, the coordinator shifted the relationship between the institution and the participants toward the authoritarian.

Taub-Pervizpour and Disbrow recognize and address the tensions that arose when the program coordinator stepped in to direct the editing of the story content of the youths' documentary:

> she was alert to the potential backlash the young filmmakers faced if they were perceived to be portraying [the principal] in a bad or unfair light .... [It] also raised the risk of turning the principal against the program, which could potentially undermine wider community support.
> (101)

Primarily, this quote exemplifies the controversy between perspectives on issues. The coordinator challenged the students' agenda and their perspective on their principal and asked them to completely change their representation to depict their principal in a light that was neither "bad" nor "unfair." In this way students' voices were limited by institutional control. From this, we can infer that school and community support are as important as, or of greater importance than, authentic student voice and perspective. This implies the coordinator has an institutional (and perhaps capitalistic) agenda, as evidenced by her fear of the principal and/or community rejecting the program, which disadvantages the students' goals. The students made the requested changes, but in making the adjustments, perhaps lost a potentially powerful space of debate within their school community. If the students had been seen to be portraying the principal in a "bad light," might it have served as a catalyst for reflection and maybe even change within the school community? It seems as though these students hoped to challenge the hierarchies of power within the educational institution and were led away from this at the risk of lost capital and partnership. Additionally, Taub-Pervizpour and Disbrow express concern for the safety of the students. The authors observed the students were anxious and reticent when they approached the principal before the editing began (99); they explain this nervousness as stemming from a fear of being in trouble: "the 'principal's office' is, for inner-city students, almost always marked as a space of conflict, punishment, and – above all else – control" (100). These statements do not indicate a sense of safety for the students to begin with and indicate a need for cultural change, which the students potentially could have impacted if they had been allowed to articulate their perspectives without the prescriptive institutional oversight of the coordinator.

Taub-Pervizpour and Disbrow's case study of their facilitation raises questions about the interactions between institutional facilitators and coordinators and the ability for participants to voice the change they wish to see within the digital storytelling program and the educational institution. Taub-Pervizpour and Disbrow rationalize that the coordinator's "concerns reflect her awareness of [their] responsibility to ask the students critical questions that challenge them to think through the implications of their production choices" (102). In getting them to think about the larger picture of representation they hoped they could "empower youth to make production choices that serve the larger social justice objectives at stake" (102). While it does seem possible to justify the intentions of the facilitators overseeing the process, it also brings into question whose social justice objectives were at stake and whom they most directly impacted. It seems important to challenge whether or not the these larger "social justice objectives" were student-driven, were served, and whether or not the digital storytelling facilitating team steered participants away from creating an actual change within their community when they convinced the participants to re-edit their documentary.

On the other hand, this story might be seen as one in which the facilitation team acted responsibly to protect the students from harmful retaliation. Although their decision silenced certain perspectives from being heard, their concerns speak to a larger ethics of responsibility, in which the facilitators consider the perceived wellbeing of the participants. This case is particularly tricky to decipher because of the interconnectedness of the relationship of the storytellers to their subject, who also happened to be a key stakeholder in the overall project. It proves Amy Hill's point that is "difficult to pinpoint" a balance between censorship and ethical responsibility (35).

Ultimately, it is important to remember that my perceptions of this project are based solely on a single paper authored by two members of the project team. My interpretations of their words cannot account for the complexity of the entire project, and only represent the voices of project team members. Critically missing from Taub-Pervizpour and Disbrow's case study, in addition to a majority of digital storytelling case studies, my own included, is the perspective of the participants, and perhaps research continues to force imbalanced relationships between facilitator and participant. This idea is critical because digital storytelling acts as a research methodology in addition to its co-creative practice of narrative creation. As such, we need to investigate the relationships between facilitator and participants in research paradigms.

Facilitators as Researchers

Especially in fields with intersections in feminist, queer, and Indigenous studies, researchers are considering the ways in which subjects can move into more empowered positions within the research. Digital storytelling, with its emphasis on co-productive media, is often viewed as a research practice capable of disrupting the traditional researcher/subject paradigm. Cunsolo Willox et al. make a case for digital storytelling as a methodology that challenges such traditional views of research. They note "research is a project full of power dynamics, colonization, knowledge appropriation, and the recognition that 'the pursuit of knowledge is deeply embedded in the multiple layers of imperial and colonial practices' (Smith, 1999: 2)" (129). For the *Changing Climate, Changing Health, Changing Stories* project they produced, they believe it was important that participants have control over the story creation process. This was a multiyear research project that examined the impacts of climate change on the cultural wellbeing of Indigenous people in Labrador, Canada. Their project was intentionally community-oriented and participant-led in order to disband the expert/amateur paradigm. The authors chose digital storytelling for the project because they felt it "transforms the research process, and requires that the roles of 'researcher' and 'researched' begin to change. This process requires a level of trust between the research team and the communities—a trust that enhances the partnership and the project" (137).

Uniquely, their project removed the traditional role of facilitator, opting instead for the role of researcher. The researcher in the context of their project "is removed from the storytelling and facilitation process, and instead assumes the role of listener" (142). While the term "researcher" semantically might be seen as being coded already within an expert paradigm, the distinction in the role between researcher and facilitator that Cunsolo Willox et al. make shows there are ways to significantly lessen the influence of a hierarchical expert paradigm within the digital storytelling workshop. However, even as listener it is still possible for the researcher to influence the narrative and construction of the digital story. The way in which that person responds or appears to respond to a participant while listening can cause the participant to take a certain direction within their storytelling. Additionally, a number of factors may inhibit a participant from telling a story she wants to tell or even telling a story in the way she wants to tell it to someone whom she may not know or feel comfortable with. This informed Cunsolo Willox et al.'s call for trust between researchers and participants, inviting broad discussions on what trust means, how you get it, and how you sustain it.

114 *Ethical Collaboration*

Cunsolo Willox et al. argue digital storytelling serves as a modern accompaniment to the Indigenous oral storytelling practices embedded in Canadian culture as "a participant-led and participant-created story-based data-gathering strategy" (130). Their analysis makes use of Indigenous and narrative research methodologies to highlight a community-led digital storytelling project that "reflected, preserved, and promoted the culture, histories, and narratives of the community" (131) and "a way to celebrate the individual and the collective" (132). The authors additionally argue that affording Indigenous populations opportunities to participate in the creation and dissemination of cultural narratives in this way, counteracts the traditional colonized approaches to research (129). However, they caution that if not employed conscientiously, especially when working with vulnerable populations, research "can be used to reify, objectify, essentialize, and/or further marginalize individuals and communities" (129).

While Cunsolo Willox et al. address important concerns for digital storytelling as a research methodology, it is unclear to what extent they incorporated participant voices in their academic analysis of this project. Although they list "'My Word': Storytelling and Digital Media Lab" and the "Rigolet Inuit Community Government" in the by-lines, they do not specify how much was written by these populations, who within those communities participated in the writing process, and what contributions they made. Cunsolo Willox et al. are not alone in this. My own research practices rarely make use of participants in the dissemination of academic scholarship, yet I see this as the next step for creating truly response-able and responsible research practices.

A dialogic approach to research practices and the dissemination of research and narratives where researchers "[speak] with and not for" participants (Fielding 305) would enable more democratic storymaking practices. In his discussion of the place of student voice in research settings, Fielding identifies two ways in which students can participate in research: As co-researchers or as researchers (307). As co-researchers, the students work alongside their teacher, and "the enquiry lies with the teacher and its conduct and completion rely heavily on her his [sic] experience and expertise" (ibid.). He adds this method, "cannot succeed without the engagement of students as researchers, enquirers and makers of meaning" (ibid.). Engaging students as researchers gives them control over the enquiry: "the issues for investigation are identified by students who are trained in the skills and values of research and enquiry and supported in their work by teachers who have also been learners at the training events" (ibid.). Digital storytelling practices can run the spectrum between these two methods and both can produce significant research; an important next step, however, lies in making the *research*, separate from the produced narratives, participant-driven, also.

Most commonly, we see digital storytelling research that is ethnographically-based, where the researcher(s) use their own impressions to write academic scholarship. While this scholarship is not generally a reflection of the facilitator's own practices, the work of Darcy Alexandra stands in stark contrast. Alexandra approaches her research with a self-reflexive look at her presence in the room and how that affects the storymaking experience.

Case Study: Digital Storytelling in Ireland

Digital storytelling facilitator Darcy Alexandra is a former interpreter, human rights investigator, and teacher ("Digital Storytelling as Transformative Practice" 101). Her insightful case studies show a great consideration for the co-productive nature of digital storytelling. Alexandra's work is unique in that she reflexively engages with places where her fingerprints linger. As she writes,

> Instead of conceptualising the role of the educator, media mentor, or "story specialist" as a "hands off" position in which one "leaves no fingerprints," we would benefit from recognising the ways in which we influence, shape, and inform the process as well.
>
> ("Implicating Practice" 350)

It is no longer an option to think about the narratives generated in digital storytelling workshops as solely personal; we should dissect the ways in which they are simultaneously public. Alexandra begins the process of dissection by recognizing the traces facilitation leaves behind. She actively documents her interactions with participants during the story creation process using field notes and approaches such as documentation from the perspective of an ethnographer. Her methods serve as a valuable starting point for larger conversations about the implications of dialogic practices between researcher and participants in digital storytelling settings. Like Alexandra, I believe it is time we delve further into the influential process, questioning the dialogue we use as facilitators as it pertains to the development of others' personal narratives.

Participants navigating the stories they want to tell is essential to ensure minimal prescription. Facilitated writing prompts and conversational starters are useful for generating stories, but can retain the traces of the facilitators' ideas. As we saw with the example of Faith Stories, institutional guidelines often scaffold the project and alter the facilitator's approach to workshops. Because workshops generally pull from a specific population or community, this affects the ways storytellers shape and tell their narratives and what kinds of narratives are told. Alexandra's digital storytelling project specifically selected migrants to Ireland as participants because her research focused on issues of migrant life in the country and was supported institutionally by hosting and funding agencies devoted to working with this specific population. Because of this, participants entered the storymaking space with a preconception of the types of stories Alexandra wanted to hear.

This is certainly a useful practice for researching a specific topic, yet there is power in participant-led research practices that allow the participants to identify the research scope, including, but not limited to, the stories they wish to share.

Perhaps equally useful is the ability for the participants to decide which stories are worth sharing in certain contexts. In her article "Are We Listening Yet," Alexandra narrates interactions that occur between herself as facilitator and participants. She shares an experience in which a participant, Omar, argued for the telling of "positive stories" that affirmed the gratitude of the teller for Ireland rather than sharing any other sort of story. As an immigrant, Omar may have wanted to win favorable relations in his new country, suggesting a consideration for how an audience would respond to his narrative. Alexandra explained all sorts of feelings and ideas were valid and valuable for the purpose of digital storytelling research (46). Later, Alexandra asks, "But what would have happened if I had not contradicted Omar's strategy to focus on the positive? If I had agreed with him that yes, it was indeed best (and perhaps strategically imperative) to focus solely on 'happy' stories" (47)? Alexandra wonders whether handling this interaction differently might have promoted a great viewership, yet justifies her reaction by arguing, it supported "the aim of learning from and through the stories participants created, and affirmed a commitment to participants' rights to tell heterogeneous stories" (ibid.). Alexandra leaves the narrative here without interrogating the implications of this interaction; instead, she focuses on the interactions among participants.

Alexandra's response to Omar is a direct instance of the facilitator shaping and guiding participants' narratives, and Alexandra finds herself questioning the boundaries of direct minimal intervention in her reflection. Yet, had she not responded either by neglecting to respond to Omar at all or by agreeing with him, she would have shaped and guided the creation process in the opposite way. In both cases, her presence in the room, as expert, gave her authority within the workshop setting, with participants looking to her for guidance. What might have happened if she had turned the remark back to the participants, letting them debate the effects of telling only "positive stories?" This chance might have let the participants identify the pros and cons of formulating such a decision. While I, wearing my facilitator hat, would hope that the participants reach the same conclusion Alexandra did, the role reversal might have given more agency to the participants in guiding the creation process. As it is, we could argue that Alexandra's seemingly innocuous response to Omar served as a rhetorical move that kept her in a position of expertise above her participants. The workshop space of digital storytelling practices can and should be sites of political listening. However, as indicated by Alexandra's interaction with Omar, there is still room in even the most considerate of practices for reflecting on our ethical responsibility to ensure and practice response-ability.

References

Alexandra, Darcy. "Are We Listening Yet?" *Participatory Visual and Digital Research in Action*, edited by Aline Gubrium, Krista Harper, and Marty Otañez, Taylor and Francis, 2015, 41–55.

Alexandra, Darcy. "Digital Storytelling as Transformative Practice: Critical Analysis and Creative Expression in the Representation of Migration in Ireland." *Journal of Media Practice*, vol. 9, no. 2, 2008, pp. 101–112.

Alexandra, Darcy. "Implicating Practice: Engaged Scholarship Through Co-creative Media" *Digital Storytelling in Higher Education: International Perspectives*, edited by Grete Jamissen, Pip Hardy, Yngve Nordkvelle, and Heather Pleasants, Palgrave Macmillan, 2017, pp. 335–354.

Atton, Chris. *Alternative Media*. SAGE, 2002.

Bickford, Susan. *The Dissonance of Democracy: Listening, Conflict and Citizenship*. Cornell University Press, 1996.

Charness, Neil, and Ralf T. Krampe. "Expertise and Knowledge." *Handbook of Cognitive Aging: Interdisciplinary Perspectives*, edited by Scott M Hofer, and Duane F. Alwin. Sage Publications, 2008, 244–258.

Cunsolo Willox, Ashley, et al. "Storytelling in a Digital Age: Digital Storytelling as an Emerging Narrative Method for Preserving and Promoting Indigenous Oral Wisdom." *Qualitative Research*, vol. 13, no. 2, 2012, pp. 127–47.

Fielding, Michael. "Transformative Approaches to Student Voice: Theoretical Underpinnings, Recalcitrant Realities." *British Educational Research Journal*, vol. 30, no. 2, 2004, pp. 295–311.

Gilligan, Carol. *In a Different Voice: Psychological Theory and Women's Development*. Harvard University Press, 2003 (1982).

Hartley, John. *//the_uses_of_digital_literacy//*. University of Queensland Press, 2009.

Hendry, Pamela. "The Future of Narrative." *Qualitative Inquiry*, vol. 13, no. 4, 2007, pp. 497–498.

Hill, Amy. "Digital Storytelling and the Politics of Doing Good: Exploring the Ethics of Bringing Personal Narratives into Public Spheres." *Community-Based Multiliteracies and Digital Media Projects: Questioning Assumptions and Exploring Realities*, edited by Heather M. Pleasants, and Dana E. Salter, Peter Lang, 2014, pp. 21–43.

Kennedy, Amanda. "Landscapes of Care: Feminist Approaches in Global Public Relations." *Journal of Media Ethics*, vol. 31, no. 4, 2016, pp. 215–230.

Klaus, Elisabeth, and Margreth Lünenborg. "Cultural Citizenship. Participation by and through Media." *Feminist Media: Participatory Spaces, Networks and Cultural Citizenship*, edited by Elke Zobl, and Ricarda Drüeke, Transcript, 2012, 197–212.

Lambert, Joe. *Digital Storytelling Cookbook: January 2010*. Digital Diner, 2010.

Noddings, Nel. *The Challenge to Care in Schools: An Alternative Approach to Education*. Teachers College Press, 2005.

Oliver, Kelly. *Witnessing: Beyond Recognition*. University of Minnesota Press, 2001.

Ross, Loretta. "Storytelling in SisterSong and the Voices of Feminism Project." *Telling Stories to Change the World: Global Voices on the Power of Narrative to Build Community and Make Social Justice Claims*, edited by Rickie Solinger, Madeline Fox, and Kayhan Irani, Routledge, 2008, 65–74.

Skærbæk, Eva. "Navigating in the Landscape of Care: A Critical Reflection on Theory and Practise of Care and Ethics." *Health Care Analysis*, vol. 19, 2011, pp. 41–50.

Stumm, Bettina. "Witnessing Others in Narrative Collaboration: Ethical Responsibility beyond Recognition." *Biography*, vol. 37, no. 3, 2014, pp. 762–783.

Tacchi, Jo. "Finding a Voice: Participatory Development in Southeast Asia." *Story Circle: Digital Storytelling around the World*, edited by John Hartley, and Kelly McWilliam, Wiley–Blackwell, 2009, 167–75.

Taub-Pervizpour, Lora, and Erin Drisbrow. "Digital Storytelling with Youth: Whose Agenda Is It?" *Story Circle: Digital Storytelling around the World*, edited by John Hartley, and Kelly McWilliam, Wiley–Blackwell, 2009, 245–51.

Zobl, Elke. "From DIY to Collaborative Fields of Experimentation: Feminist Media and Cultural Production towards Social Change: A Visual Contribution." *Feminist Media: Participatory Spaces, Networks and Cultural Citizenship*, edited by Elke Zobl, and Ricarda Drüeke, Transcript, 2012, 265–271.

7 Ethical Collaboration
The Responsible Facilitator in Practice

A Framework of Response-able Facilitation

While we all hope that our digital storytelling workshops will make a difference in the lives of our participants, we have to remember there are factors beyond our control as facilitators that can impact – for better or for worse – the storytellers and their work. While sometimes the things that might cause harm are unforeseeable or out of a facilitator's control, there are things that are possible for facilitators to anticipate and plan for to promote care, witnessing, and response-ability within their digital storytelling workshops, and this can be accomplished by adopting a framework of response-able facilitation.

So, what constitutes responsible facilitation in co-creative environments? Following Oliver and Hendry's work, respectively, the fundamental considerations are response-ability created by active witnessing and faith-based listening. Witnessing and listening become ethical obligations in interacting with other subjects. In the co-creative storymaking space, this is the primary responsibility of the facilitator. Because of this, response-ability and listening provide a critical approach to interpreting the facilitator's interactions within storymaking spaces.

In digital storytelling practices, the facilitator typically serves a professional function that places them in a position of "other" in relation to the storytelling participants. This compounds the fact that the facilitator often has a markedly different historical, institutional, and cultural background than the participants. Yet, in digital storytelling practices, the facilitator is the one who either leads or appears to lead the narrative-producing processes. And, this is not without reason. Facilitators are typically experts in story development and narrative as well as in the tools and digital literacy skills needed to create digital stories. This expertise further others the facilitator from the participants. While facilitators trained in digital storytelling methods can come from inside the community in which they work, they often do not. It is not uncommon for facilitators to travel great lengths to reach specific communities whose stories might be under-represented in

DOI: 10.4324/9781003200826-7

larger cultural spheres. And, it is important to note that in such cases facilitators may not be a part of these communities.

Digital storytelling facilitators are often placed in roles of power that position them as a professional/expert guiding novice or amateur storytellers. Professional expertise is most often associated with technical and scholastic knowledge rather than knowledge about people, cultures, and communities. As such, it lends itself to viewing the person in charge as hierarchically above participants. Digital storytelling facilitators are knowledgeable about the process of digital storytelling and the technical knowledge of the programs and tools they use, making them experts in this sense. As Uma Kothari argues, "'professional', 'expert' and 'expertise' ... are not neutral categories" (427). The very notion of "expert" creates power relations between those in conversation with the "expert." It is important to recognize the hierarchical relationship that can form between the facilitator as expert and the amateur participant and to counter this with an approach that acknowledges and values the expertise both parties can contribute to the project.

Institutions can exacerbate this hierarchy by how they position participants' expertise, which can affect the overall story outcome. In her analysis of the digital storytelling project conducted at the Australian Center for the Moving Image (ACMI) and tallstoreez productionz Pty Ltd, Kelly McWilliam frames how the participants' outlook affected the entire narrative creation process. She writes, "By and large, ACMI constructs its participants as *amateurs*, or as learners that need to 'be taught', whereas tallstoreez productionz constructs its participants as *experts-in-training* or as learners whose active learning is facilitated by tallstoreez productionz" (153). McWilliam argued that differences in the produced digital stories were a direct result of this positioning of participants. She observed that the digital stories created through the ACMI's program were more filmistically simplistic, focusing on scanned images and artifacts, but that those created through the tallstoreez productionz program included more video footage (154). She concludes that, "While digital stories are never 'straightforward examples of the discourses of dominant 'institutions' (Burgess, 2006), they can nevertheless be understood as the product of a discursive engagement with their producing institution." (155–156). In this case, it is not only the facilitator that plays a role in the expert paradigm being refashioned into spaces of digital storytelling; the hosting organizations, too, can actively shape the ways in which participants are invited to inhabit the digital storytelling workshop.

User-generated media, like those utilized in many digital storytelling programs, can challenge this idea of expertise in the storymaking space. Digital storytelling employs user-generated media with the assumption that this could empower the everyday citizen as authors with expertise and thus challenge the consumer and producer relationship. Yet, the expertise of the everyday citizens is called into question by the expert paradigm digital storytelling employs to facilitate digital story creation, which invokes questions of authenticity, accuracy, and reliability. While impressions and constraints imparted on participants' work by facilitators pose a serious threat to their authenticity, scholars like McWilliam suggest the threat is unavoidable in an "expert-led media pedagogy" like digital storytelling (146). While McWilliam acknowledges that although digital storytelling sought to move "away from one-way, top down models of communication ... toward two way, bottom-up models of communication," it ultimately landed in between the two because of the use of a facilitator in the role of the expert (146). Power relations revolving around the expert/facilitator and the participant are important in digital storytelling environments as the practices advocate for the participant to lead the creation process. This insistence on participants guiding the collaborative process acknowledges that they additionally have expertise, especially as it stems from their lived experience and pertains to the telling of their personal stories. Recognizing the expertise of the participant, especially when the facilitator feels there is a better way forward, is one of the biggest concerns for responsible facilitation. Valuing storyteller voice is particularly important in story-sharing and storymaking spaces where participants' expertise is based on their personal histories, identities, and experiences.

Considerations of Preparation

Informed Consent

Before beginning any work with participants, it is important to get their voluntary, informed consent to participate and share work. Ensure that you give participants as much transparency in the program and process as possible. Tell participants the project goals and anticipated outcomes, the program's expectations for them, and what they can expect of you as a facilitator. Ensure they understand who is hosting and funding (these may be different) the project as well as their goals and desired outcomes. Lead participants through the workshop experience and beyond into the sharing and distribution processes that could happen after their digital stories are complete. Let them know that they are free to leave the program or revoke their consent to distribution at any time. While it may be difficult to fully prepare participants for all the intricacies and complexities that are to come, transparency up front and throughout the workshop and dissemination processes will provide participants with more agency over their decision making within the program. Indeed, you may find that as expectations change throughout the process, that you need to re-ask participants for their consent.

Considerations on Building the Appropriate Atmosphere

Space and Place

The importance of having a defined and continuously used space for a workshop is significant to minimize distractions, confusion, and tension (Freeman and Hill; Poitras Pratt 90). Space can refer to the physical space of the establishment that will house any sort of residency or community-engaged work and should be carefully considered especially during the collaborative production stage and the sharing stage. It is additionally important to note that the space may change from week to week or from stage to stage. These changes will impact the relationship participants have with the location as well as with each other and with the facilitator. Space also encompasses the physical setup of the rooms in which the facilitator engages with the participants. The room's setup is important for thinking through how space invites participation and reiterates or decentralizes structures of power among those in the room during a digital storytelling workshop. For example, hosting story circles with participants and facilitators seated in a circle can invite a sense of equality by ensuring everyone can see everyone else and that no person is physically higher, lower, or apart from the others.

Considerations of space should also include considerations of place. That is, both the physical location of a place as well as the abstract identifiers of a place. This includes the history and atmosphere of the physical location and whether or not it is welcoming to all community members. For example, is it compliant with the codes of the Americans with Disabilities Act (ADA)? As facilitators we should recognize the ways in which space works to "[make] estranged bodies better fit normative expectations" through "architectural, aesthetic, and moral spaces of inclusion that, paradoxically, strictly police ways of being different for the bodies they include" (Mitchell et al. 304). On the other hand, it is equally important to recognize that there are no "universal design best practices [for inclusion] because difference cannot be fully anticipated, planned for, known, or mastered" (Rice et al. 523). To better support our storytellers, we can ask participants or potential participants what would they need to participate? What would make the physical space and workshop atmosphere accessible to them?

We should also recognize how the space will be experienced by others because of historical and cultural signifiers. Facilitators should ask: What demographic of people are most likely to come to this location? Whose voices might be left out in choosing this location? What cultural, political, and historical signifiers surround the space metaphorically and/or are present materially that might affect how individuals view, inhabit, and interact with and within the space? Does it sit on a site of atrocity for a certain minority group that might affect the tone of the residency or a participant's engagement? Is the location in an area of town where you are likely to see a diversity of people? Will diverse participants feel comfortable and safe with the location? Will they be able to comfortably and confidently walk down the street or park their vehicles should they have one? Is there public transportation available nearby? Are they likely to see people who look like them as they walk toward the residency? Space and place work together to address levels of inclusiveness and accessibility that could affect the participation of community members. The amount of attention and intentionality paid to the space and place of community work can enhance your response-ability of the collaborative work taking place, especially if one is considering the often "otherness" of the facilitator.

The facilitator thus becomes a person who needs to reflexively approach the space and place of any community-engaged work. Especially as an outsider, the chosen space and place can often leave the facilitator feeling cast out, othered, and foreign. This can make the outsider feel uncertain about the social norms and ethics embedded in diverse locations. It can leave facilitators wondering what the boundaries of any given social setting are, be they physical, dialogic, or otherwise. It is further important to recognize that social norms differ from individual to individual and from community to community. In fact, what might be socially acceptable to one person in your community group, may be wholly unacceptable to another. Facilitators should then grapple with the complex social dynamics that take place between a group of individuals to ensure a respectful and culturally responsible atmosphere for all participants.

In considering the atmosphere surrounding a workshop, we often think about a sense of "safe space" as a way to invite participants to take healthy risks and challenge themselves to grow. That is, we hope to create a safe space for risks and growth, rather than creating a space to keep a participant comfortable and stagnant. We can imagine this as a space where workshop participants feel enabled to have dialogues about issues that might be challenging or uncomfortable or to disclose personal information that will help others understand their perspective and life story. Creating a safe space requires that participants and facilitator enter into the workshop with open minds, maintain a sense of curiosity, and withhold judgment. It asks those in the room to take a step back from their immediate assumptions about what a person shares and to ask clarifying questions to engage the storyteller to share more. Enabling a safe space that affirms each storyteller's right to share and be heard reinforces practices of response-ability.

Group Guidelines

To create an atmosphere where response-ability is at the forefront of the creation space, begin by setting up guidelines with your participants. If time allows, the facilitator can ask participants to brainstorm community guidelines before presenting their own ideas. Building guidelines as a community is useful for ensuring that participants feel comfortable and safe within the workshop space. It helps the participants feel they have power to create and define the workshop space in a way that meets their unique needs. It gives them ownership over the guidelines and the creation of safe space. The following instructions for developing guidelines are based on years of contract building and space creation in youth programming (including in the arts, theatre, digital storytelling after-school and summer programs), as well as technical training in arts education, digital storytelling facilitation, and community building. Additionally, facilitator training from Essential Partners, an organization that works with community-based practitioners to host difficult or nuanced conversations about society and community, guides how I approach community-building work. The components you include in your facilitation process will depend on the amount of time available to conduct this space-creating work. While I understand that limitations on time exist, I would strongly argue for including group guidelines in the setup of your workshop space.

If you have a significant amount of time to conduct this work, begin by first asking participants how they would like to communicate with one another. What would be most effective for how they interact with one another? What do they need to broach difficult conversations or sensitive subjects? What will make them feel comfortable voicing their opinion even if it goes against the majority? As participants brainstorm answers to these questions, write their answers down. In my experience, it is easier for people to remember the guidelines if it is a shorter list that is easily digestible by your participants. I start by asking participants to identify things that would help them feel comfortable sharing and having conversations with one another, especially reminding them that sharing personal work can sometimes make people feel vulnerable. I ask participants what they need to do and what they need from others, including myself as the facilitator, to create respectful participation in group work. I collect a long list from participants before working with them to collate and unify the longer list into a few key ideas. For instance, if two points listed by participants can be compartmentalized under a single phrase, I ask participants to identify the phrase and agree to combine the original two. This way participants will understand that the shortened phrase encompasses both meanings that were originally presented. At each step of the unification, I ensure that all participants agree. I have found that a thumbs up is an easy way to scan a room (physical or virtual) to ensure all participants agree. If someone disagrees, invite dialogue about the disagreement. I suggest keeping the list of phrases short, too; that way, they'll be more readily memorable for participants. In my experience, having approximately three to five guidelines for youth and approximately five to eight guidelines for adults provides the best results. If time does not permit a brainstorming session, the facilitator can introduce a short list of standard guidelines. The facilitator can then invite the participants to review the list and ensure that the participants do not feel anything is missing. Invite additions or revisions if participants want them.

When the guidelines are complete, ensure that all participants agree to them. You can use verbal or nonverbal communication to approve each item on the guidelines as well as the contract as a whole. You can also invite the participants to sign the guidelines as a contract after it is written. During sessions where you know a particularly difficult conversation or a problem

Ethical Collaboration 125

between participants may arise, ensure you revisit the guidelines in a meaningful way that informs the conversation you need to have. You can also think of the guidelines as a living document that can be amended as needed. When there are times of struggle within the workshops, revisit the guidelines and ask participants what needs to be upheld and what if anything needs to be revised. Revision of the guidelines can happen at any time. It is important to include the participants in this revision process as well. If something comes up for them in the middle of the workshop series, invite them to discuss adding, removing, or revising existing guidelines. Again, ensure that all group participants come to an agreement about these revisions.

During my first digital storytelling workshop with StoryCenter, the guidelines were listed as follows:

- Each storyteller gets equal time to process story
- Each storyteller tells story without interruption
- Hold questions. Ask storyteller if she is seeking feedback
- Start with Affirmation
- "If it were my story ..."
- Step back, step up.

(Kershaw, "Story Circles")

These guidelines came with rules to ensure that were meaningful to participants, and they reminded participants of what they needed to do in any given moment. Some key components we see represented in these guidelines are the importance of not interrupting someone while they are speaking, ensuring that people take turns so that everyone has a chance to speak, and using neutral phrasing to engage with storytellers about their work. I was presented with these guidelines again in a StoryCenter workshop training digital storytelling facilitators eight years later. While the language has evolved, the key practices remain the same:

- Wait until the Storyteller is done before asking questions or making comments
- Share an appreciative comment first
- Frame feedback as questions or conditional opinions "If it were my story, I might ..."
- Manage assertiveness – Step Back, Step Up
- Keep discussion on topic of story and storyteller, not issued raised by story, or your version of their story
- Signaling Group Affirmation.

(Kershaw, "The Story Circle")

Respecting storyteller's speaking time, providing affirmations, framing feedback, and managing assertiveness remain present. The training also instructs facilitators to thank each storyteller after they share, pause before each storyteller, ask storyteller's if they are seeking any specific feedback from their audience, and synthesize the feedback for each storyteller (ibid.)

In my practice, participants ask before they give feedback, even if that feedback comes in neutral phrasing. In working with the organization Essential Partners to host difficult dialogues, I have also come to value including guidelines that allow for the ability to pass, to listen even when you don't agree with things (what Essential Partners calls "Listening with resilience"), and to consider how your assumptions affect your perception of and speech about the question at hand (Eckles). For me, this involves looking again at how your assumptions about a topic will affect your output. In spaces where I use these guidelines, I ask participants to comment about things they observed and what they inferred from those observations, rather than focusing on their judgments about a topic.

Essential Partners also puts forth a need to maintain confidentiality both within and beyond the workshop setting (Eckles). This concept is not one that I had seen explicitly stated in prior digital storytelling spaces yet is profoundly important to developing ethical and response-able facilitation practices. Within the workshop space, stories should remain relatively anonymous, an especially important consideration when working in small communities where participants might know those people named in a story. This is not always practical in story work, of course, as some stories rely on character relationships. Yet there is a difference between telling a story that references "my father" or "my oldest friend" and calling those people by their name. As digital storytelling facilitator Amy Hill reminds us, it is almost impossible to produce "complete anonymity when it comes to digital stories – though names can be changed or omitted and images can be blurred, voices are unique and cannot easily be altered without negatively affecting sound quality" (29). Responsible facilitators should address the implications of this with storytellers as in some instances this can affect their wellbeing and safety. Hill asks facilitators to consider the following questions:

> When are deliberations about safety based on the real possibility of retaliation or harm, and who defines what is 'real,' in a context where dreams are taken seriously as harbingers of good or bad fortune? When does discussion about safety inadvertently give rise to self-censorship on the part of participants, who may be basing story content decisions on unfounded fears or rumors they've heard about the consequences of speaking out about their experiences, rather than on real risks?
>
> (31)

Whenever possible, anonymizing stories can be helpful for maintaining the confidentiality of others and keep storytellers safe. Additionally, confidentiality of the stories told within the workshop space and that of the storytellers should be maintained by all participants so that they are not shared outside of the workshop.

Further, as digital storytelling asks us to tell personal narratives, it becomes ethically important that storytellers only share their own story and not another's. This eliminates concerns that a storyteller might share a story on behalf of someone else or on behalf on an entire group.

You may also need to include a statement about technology as it becomes increasingly inculcated into our daily lives. While a digital storytelling workshop will make use of mobile and digital technologies, participants may not always need to have mobile devices accessible and, except in emergencies, audio notifications should be turned off during workshop time. Minimizing distractions will help enable response-ability, witnessing, and listening among participants.

Write out your guidelines and make them visible for all participants at the beginning of each session. If you have a single-use physical space, keep the guidelines hanging on the wall. Ensure that the guidelines are always available for participants to see and remember, and return to them as often as is needed to ensure effective communication and feedback take place within the creation space.

Considerations for Story Composition

In the storymaking phase, as with story-sharing, it is important for the facilitator not to over impose or impress too heavily on participants projects. Facilitators need to interrogate the verbal and nonverbal responses they use to critique and question storytellers' works in the workshop space, as they contribute to the local context, the conditions surrounding the production of the work. I can recall times when one question I asked as the facilitator led to a conversation that completely reshaped the storyteller's product. For instance, I worked with one storyteller in the *I Am UCF* project who shared the story of the first date she had where there was significant circumstantial evidence that her date was going to murder her before the evening ended. I asked her to define the ending tone she wanted the story to have. She stated she wanted to end on a light note and with a sense of hope and moving forward. She also wanted to emphasize the humor in the circumstances of the moment that unfolds in her digital story. I asked her to consider how this perceived near-death experience might not be initially humorous to all her audience members, especially considering that the circumstance she describes comes at the beginning of her story before the audience knows whether or not she suffered any actual physical harm.

Upon reflection, the storyteller added a tonal shift to the middle of her story. She used a light tone and the phrase "As you have probably guessed by now, I was not murdered" to take the mood from potentially scary to a place where the audience realizes the humor in her circumstantial exposition (*My Favorite Murder Date*). Based on our conversation, she rewrote the second half of her story so it transitioned into a period of her reflections on her mental state and ended with a sense of hope. This question obviously had large implications for the overall story, and although the initial question was worded in a way that let the storyteller decide the ending of her story, it remains my "expertise" as a workshop facilitator that dramatically changed the story she was telling. When I revisit this story today, I still see and hear this mark of myself on what was supposed to be *her* story. Because of this experience, I question and reflect on the relationship and communicative dynamic between the facilitator and storytellers, especially considering the implications of co-production on the "personal" narrative.

In "Implicating Practice: Engaged Scholarship through Co-Creative Media," Alexandra talks openly about select communications between herself and research participants in the practice of media production. While she states clearly the conversations that happened, she does little to interrogate how her involvement in the conversation affected the stories' production. One example she gives is a conversation she had with Ahmed, a participant who struggling to discover a topic and felt there was "too much to say" in response to the workshop's writing prompts. Alexandra then asked him how he learned English, which he answered with stories about his ex-girlfriend, his relationship with religion and God, and his current living situation. Alexandra's prompt had major impacts on Ahmed's story in which he spoke about his relationship with his ex-girlfriend, his living situation, and his relationship to English.

This example demonstrates one of the challenges facilitators face when helping people tell their stories. While facilitator-led writing prompts and conversation starters can be effective and useful in helping participants find stories to tell, they also hold the potential to force a direction, which may move a participant away from the story they want to tell. Ahmed appears to have struggled with developing a script, and it is clear that the prompts employed had an effect on the story Ahmed told. The prompt may have pushed him to develop a narrative differently than he would have if his writing process had been self-motivated. He may also have been affected by the digital storytelling workshop timeline, which could have made him feel as though he needed a script to reach a set deadline. Influences such as these from outside forces remind facilitators to consider the co-collaborative nature of digital storytelling.

Collaborative dialogic creation process is part of the process of digital storytelling. Where my experience showed me a need to survey digital storytelling as a methodology in more nuanced ways, I also discovered a need to frame the digital storytelling co-creative space as a reflective site for facilitators. It is through the collaboration between facilitator and participants that digital storytelling practices can affect the greatest change. To affect this change, we, as facilitators, should ensure that the storytellers guide the creative process through their storytelling, composition, and dissemination practices.

In all our activities, we should work to help participants understand the complexities and entanglements of how narratives are created. In some instances, such entanglements are rooted in systems beyond the relationships described in this book. For example, Spurgeon acknowledges that some of the systematic pressures that occur within a digital storytelling workshop are even larger than the immediate surrounding stakeholders. She argues that larger systems (such as legal systems) also affect the outcome of the narrative and how facilitators of digital storytelling workshops work with participants to create the "best" narratives using copyright-free materials. She writes, there is

> a frequently encountered storyteller desire to use copyrighted materials as a deficit that co-creative methods are well suited to address; and/or an assumption that one scheme of knowledge production (for example, a digital story told using assets generated by the storyteller) is superior to another (for example, borrowing assets to re-tell or elaborate on existing narratives) because one is legitimated in the law.
>
> (128)

Facilitators not only work with storytellers to develop their scripted stories, they also work with participants to learn where to gather assets; how to create assets like audio recordings, pictures, and video; how to compose with these assets; and how to use digital technologies to compose. As Darcy Alexandra writes, co-creative media facilitators should also pay "significant attention to media production values, and consistent mentoring in photography and audio-visual editing constituted productive ways of taking storytellers, their stories, and the labor of documentary story production seriously" ("Are We Listening Yet" 48). Often facilitators are teaching participants the digital literacy skills and techniques needed to tell the stories participants ultimately want to tell. Facilitators should teach these tools in ways that do not impress, too heavily, their own personal media look and feel on the participants as well as give enough information that allows facilitators to have options that might be outside of the facilitator's personal aesthetic. Further, facilitators are responsible for ensuring that storytellers think about how the media will affect the story they want to tell, asking questions when needed to encourage the storyteller to probe deeper into considerations of their audience and distribution methods.

Considerations for Story-sharing

As storytellers begin to complete drafts of their narratives, be they scripts, rough cuts, etc., it is important to consider how the sharing of such stories will affect the storyteller and participants within the workshop space. Ensuring that the community guidelines created at the outset of the workshop are visible and intact can help ensure participants feel able to take safe risks and share their personal narratives with others. Ensuring that the right witnesses are in the room to support storytellers and ensuring a structured feedback system can enhance the protection of the participants.

Story circles are the most common peer-feedback approach in digital storytelling workshops. Lambert credits the process behind the story circle to theatre artist John O'Neal, and suggests that the structure behind how the story circle operates today is due to the work of Amy Hill who joined StoryCenter in the early 2000s. Hill provided an ethics-based approach to story circle facilitation that ensured the safety and emotional wellbeing of participants (Lambert, "Zoom Interview").

Story circles "advance the development of story from concept/first draft to next iteration," "establish community among workshop participants," and allow the facilitator to "assess relative preparedness-readiness of all participants" (Kershaw, "The Story Circle"). During the story circle, the facilitator is responsible for presenting and maintaining the group guidelines and managing participants, time, and the flow of conversation to ensure that the focus of the conversation is on the story, that neutral questions and suggestions are given, and that each person has an appropriate amount of time to speak.

Determining the balance to ensure participants feel safe in sharing their stories is important for facilitators in co-creative media. Daniela Gachago and Pam Sykes caution that facilitators should be careful when opening the floor for storytellers to share their experiences, especially when those experiences position the tellers in vulnerable situations. In their essay, "Navigating Ethical Boundaries When Adopting Digital Storytelling in Higher Education," the authors question the ethics of producing digital stories in classroom settings where educators may meet challenging and difficult narratives. Gachago and Sykes create an auto-ethnographic account where they assess the ethical dilemmas they faced while working with populations affected by apartheid in South Africa. Gachago acknowledges a major tension of the project is "holding the line between therapy and pedagogical intervention" (97). To combat this tension, they implement various kinds of student support: Inviting peer counselors into the sessions; explaining the role of "discomfort" in the storytelling process, thereby providing practical expectations of the process; and identifying "at risk" students (97). Many story-sharing spaces may make participants feel too vulnerable to narrate the stories they want or to do so in the ways that they want. On the other hand, Gachago suggests that the digital storytelling "process" might "[take] over," enabling participants to "share much more than actually planned" (Gachago and Sykes 96). Setting the tone for balance, thanking participants for sharing their truths, and offering resources can go a long way to ensure the protection of participants.

Amy Hill additionally argues that facilitators need to be prepared to address the wellbeing of those depicted in the digital story. She recounts a project in which a participant told a story in a story circle about the impact of HIV and AIDS on his family. While he did not name specific people, the other storytellers decided that audience members from the local area would be able to identify the people about whom he spoke, and therefore cautioned him against making the digital story. This example depicts a moment where the other storytellers in the room took responsibility for assessing the needs of those depicted in the narrative. In the earlier *I Am UCF* example, project facilitators took responsibility to protect the identity of the friends of the storyteller from potential backsplash of their implied drinking. As we can see from these examples, helping participants tell stories only they can tell additionally means having them consider their responsibility to others in their lives.

Developing a Critical Feedback Structure

Digital storytelling should be understood as its own unique art genre. As such, it is important for the facilitator to understand how feedback affects the artistic creation process. The digital storytelling workshop process includes peer feedback, especially during the process of story circles. Over several years as a theatre teaching artist and digital storytelling facilitator, I've developed a critical feedback structure based on the work of dancer Liz Lerman, who coincidentally has worked in the performing arts world with StoryCenter's Joe Lambert. Lambert met Liz Lerman in the Alliance for Cultural Democracy, a network of progressive artists and in 1986 he became part of the formation of the National Performance Network out of Dance Theatre Workshop in New York, in which Lerman was also involved ("Personal Interview" n.p.). Lambert has also cited Lerman's work with the Dance Exchange as a successful community-arts program that digital storytelling practices can look to for inspiration ("Where It all Started," 84). While I learned about Lerman's structure independent from digital storytelling, Lambert's confidence in Lerman's work bolstered my use of it within digital storytelling programs.

Lerman's Critical Response Process focuses on helping artists in creative situations develop a dialogue about their work to invite feedback that will enable the artist to continue to grow their project. According to Lerman, the process "interrupts authority that is built on. Prestige, status, professional position, or hierarchy" (Lerman and Borstel, *Critique is Creative* 93), making it a supportive and successful tool for the response-able facilitator. Lerman describes the Process as "a multi-step, group system for giving and receiving useful feedback on creative processes and artistic works-in-progress" ("Liz Lerman"). Lerman's process is based on the same principles as response-ability: Giving space for a person to respond after feedback has been given. Lerman wanted to give power back to the artist in constructive conversations, rather than enabling their silence. In considering her own experiences in dance, Lerman and Borstel write,

> I had a sense that there was a supposedly mature way to hear comments of others: Keeping silent, writing private letters in my mind but

never sending them, and, if something really stung, letting time heal the wounds. To respond in this 'mature' way to criticism meant quietly taking it, rather than attempting to engage in a dialogue, since to respond at all was somehow deemed either defensive or a violation of an unspoken boundary.

(Liz Lerman's Critical Response Process 1)

In my experience, using the Critical Response Process within co-creative spaces, participants gain the ability to think more critically and thoughtfully about their own works and the works of others in a way that dismantles the need to feed the artist's ego. It provides a way for artists themselves to see their work through the eyes of observers and makes room for them to consider new ideas, questions, opinions, and suggestions about their work. Ensuring the creator maintains a sense of ownership even in collaborative processes is part of how we create response-ability within the digital storytelling workshop. Acknowledging how the personal becomes and is informed by the public can also help storytellers understand their ability to respond to peer review as they desire. Like the story circle, the Critical Response Process is best conducted in a circle. The circle provides a way for everyone within the workshop to see each other clearly and eliminates some of the hierarchy within the learning space. The work presented to the circle does not have to be complete. In fact, I would recommend undertaking the Critical Response Process multiple times throughout the digital storytelling residency. A dialogue can take place at every instance a new draft is produced as well as for draft(s) of the written script, the storyboard, and the draft(s) of the video.

There are three roles within the dialogue process: Artist (the one presenting their work), facilitator (the one guiding the conversation), and responders (the remaining participants). The roles will shift slightly as each responder will take a turn as the presenting artist. The artist's role in the Process is to present their work to the responders – in the case of a digital storytelling residency, the responders are the other workshop participants not currently presenting their work. Responders provide valuable information to the artist to help them understand what is resonating for them within the artist's work. Finally, there is the role of facilitator. Lerman and Borstel write, "The facilitator assumes a variety of functions: coach, translator, and traffic cop" (*Liz Lerman's Critical Response Process* 8). The facilitator ensures that all four steps of the Process are completed, ensuring that the group guidelines remain in effect, and guiding the course of the dialogue. Whether or not the facilitator participates in the dialogue as a responder is up to the digital storytelling facilitators. It can be beneficial to give space for peers to discuss work with the artist without the facilitator's input, and if this is the approach taken, be sure to leave time for the facilitator to provide feedback with the artist at a later time.

There are four steps to the Critical Response Process which take place immediately following the sharing of a work. These steps are meant to guide the responders to engage with the art itself, rather than with the artist's feelings (ibid. 10). That is, rather than having responders talk about the things they liked or disliked, they are encouraged to think more strategically about the work of art. This enables responders to focus on that which they observe and infer from a work, rather than focusing on their judgment (*I like this. I don't like that*). Lerman and Borstel write,

> When we start by naming the fact that the work has meaning at all, and offer options for responding to that meaning, we broaden the lens by which responders can experience and comment .... The whole dialogue becomes less about individual psychology and more about the power of art.
>
> (ibid.)

While personal narratives are inherently *personal*, by limiting the scope to the art, we further enable response-ability within the dialogue space, removing perceived personal affronts often associated with critique and giving space for the artist to respond within a need to defend themselves as a person. Limitations can be put in place that help peer reviewers consider the technical aspect of the art as opposed to questioning or criticizing ideas, perspectives, or experiences put forth within the work. I often start by asking participants to simply state what they saw or heard in the work. From there, I have them identify what these observations help them infer as an audience member. This is not always an easy task. Too often, our brains move too quickly for us to consciously dissect the things we see and hear and how we infer meaning from them, opting instead for quick judgments of work. By asking reviewers first to consider their base observation (*I saw a picture of a frog and I heard the word frog several times*) and second to consider what they infer (*I think this is a story about a frog*) we move away from any preconceived feelings about the subject into an objective analysis of the work. Meaning can then be layered into these objective observations through *Statements of Meaning*.

Lerman and Borstel write, "meaning is at the heart of an artist's work, and to start with meaning is to begin with the essence of the artistic act" (ibid. 19). In this first step, the facilitator elicits responses from the responders about the artist's work they have just experienced. Ask the responders what was meaningful to them about the work they witnessed. Lerman and Borstel also suggest using the following adjectives in place of meaningful: Stimulating, surprising, evocative, memorable, touching, challenging, compelling, delightful, different, and unique (ibid.).

The second step of the process is *Artist as Questioner*. During this step, the artist is able to ask questions of the responders. This phase of the process should be treated as an "act of clarifying" (ibid. 20). Lerman and Borstel suggest that artists avoid both the narrowest ("Should I have my arms up or down in the final image?") and broadest questions ("What did you think?")

in this stage as these questions, especially when used without the assistance of specific questions, can "limit the potential" of the feedback the author receives. In some cases, I have had to work with young artists to understand the types of questions that can be asked at this stage and which kinds of questions would provide the most support and guidance as they continue revising their work. Lerman and Borstel suggest artists consider the following when beginning to create a list of questions:

> Where am I in the process of developing the work? Working from the base of information I've heard in step one, where would I like to expand or focus the response? Do I want an overall gauge of the work's effectiveness, or focused guidance about particular challenges?
>
> (ibid.)

Guidance on specific challenges such as the use of images, color palette, tone of language, or flow, can be highly beneficial to storytellers during peer feedback. However, if storytellers cannot name any specific challenges, I often remind storytellers that audience reception to their work is a place of meaning-making and suggest they ask questions that evaluate how the assets included in their digital stories help their peers make meaning of their work. For example, I might suggest storytellers gauge their audience's end response to their work to see if it matches what they had in mind.

The third step in the process is *Neutral Questions from Responders*. Here is the opportunity for the responders to gain clarification from the artist. During this step, it is important for the responders to limit bias in their questioning, so that response-ability is maintained throughout the dialogue. Neutral questions are a way to remove bias from questions asked to the artist. Perhaps the best way to understand the difference between a neutral and biased question is to see how the questions change when rewritten. Lerman and Borstel use the example, "It's too long," as the opinion or critique from the responder. Questions can still have traces of this bias by couching the opinion inside of the question. For instance, asking, "Why are your pieces always so long?" contains the opinion within the question. To make this question neutral, Lerman and Borstel suggest reframing the question to either "'What were you trying to accomplish in the final section?' or 'Tell me the most important ideas you want us to get and where is that happening in this piece?'" (ibid.). Neutral questions can be tricky for people to develop on their own, especially if they are not in the habit of giving feedback in this way. Yet, they remain a significant part of the Critical Response Process experience. As Lerman and Borstel explain, "the actual process of trying to form opinions into neutral questions enables the responder to recognize and acknowledge the personal values at play. Often these are the very questions that the artist needs to hear" (ibid. 21). Lerman and Borstel suggest that the facilitator remains an active part of step three so that the questions in this phase remain neutral. To help participants through this step, they recommend the facilitator practices forming neutral questions with responders before this piece of the process begins.

Using neutral questions to provide feedback helps keep personal defensiveness away by focusing the dialogue on the work itself rather than on the artist or the artist's personal connection to the work. It allows response-ability for the artist rather than shutting down their ability to respond or forcing their response into a defensive rhetoric. Helping the artist enter a place of reflexivity is key to this step and to inviting response-ability to allow the artist to come to their own conclusions and advances within their art. Lerman's reasoning behind using neutral questions stems directly from an experience working with a famous director on a new dance piece. After showing the director her choreography a few times, the director included a suggestion in their critique – to include a ball of string in the dance as a way to make the theme and metaphors of the dance more tangible. The edit stuck and Lerman performed the piece to much acclaim. Lerman writes,

> People loved it. Critics loved it. And what they loved about it was the very thing she had fixed. I always felt that I should put an asterisk in the program and explain that the device that made it work was not my idea.
> (ibid. 46)

This sense of reduced ownership impacted Lerman's experience of performing this dance as well as her experience of accepting acclaim after the piece was performed. In her mind, a series of questions could have been more beneficial in helping her determine her own best practice for strengthening the dance, thus allowing Lerman to solve her own problem rather than having it solved by an outside force.

The final step of the process is *Permissioned Opinions*. Where the first three steps curb the sharing of opinions, step four invites them, as long as they are couched in a certain rhetorical practice. Before offering their opinion, "responders first name the topic of the opinion and ask the artist for permission to state it" (ibid. 22). In a digital storytelling workshop, this could look like a responder telling the artist: *I have an opinion about the use of photographs. Would you be interested in hearing it?* The artist can decide whether or not they would like to hear the feedback on this subject from the responder. Again, this step allows for response-ability, as it allows the artist to say yes or no before hearing a suggestion, rather than having a suggestion given when it isn't desired. Lerman and Borstel write that while there may be times when the artist declines to hear responders' opinions, in most cases the artist will say yes. In my own experience, storytellers have always been willing to listen to their peer's reflections. The rhetorical practice of allowing the storyteller to confirm their desire to hear feedback before it is given is a way to remind participants that they hold power within the digital storytelling workshop.

The facilitator should be actively involved in processes designed to provide feedback to artists although I often wait for other participants to speak first in every stage. I end each storyteller's review with a summary of observations from the dialogue and an open invitation for the storyteller to speak with me at a later time about specific concerns or for further guidance on how to create the changes they wish to make. In all of this work, as facilitators we should remember that we may be positioned, or at the very least perceived to be positioned, as an expert in the room. Therefore, during feedback it is especially important that we consider how our communicative interactions with participants will affect their narratives' development. I am continually asking myself: How can I provide feedback in supportive ways that lead participants to further their narrative? And where should we draw boundaries on influencing the direction of the narrative and visual composition of a digital story?

While Lerman's framework can be a powerful and beneficial tool for participants, it should be structured with care. Lerman's structure was designed with artists in mind. In my experience, storytellers sometimes have difficulty formulating questions of their own to ask during the *Artist as Questioner* segment. I have found this is especially true when working with young people. Having a list of open-ended prompt questions such as, "With what feelings does this piece leave you?;" "What moments are most impactful?;" "What moments need clarification," or "What areas would you like to see, know, or hear more about?" can aid in this process. Open-ended questions are helpful for understanding larger patterns within the work; however, closed-ended questions about a specific moment like a visual, line, or effect, can also be helpful for the storyteller to hear.

Another practice I utilize when storytellers struggle to identify their own questions is to gain neutral observations from the circle about what they saw and heard during the viewing. It is important in this first stage that they just answer with literalness, that is, the things they saw or heard. For instance, if you are reading this page, you might literally see letters, words, and the colors black and white. There should be no inference or judgment in this stage. This works well to get storytellers to identify what is most obvious or memorable from the circle. From there you can ask responders what the work or their list of observations reminds them of or what inferences or conclusions they draw. You might even do a third round of questions on how the audience feels about these things. This process can help storytellers decide if their piece is speaking to the audience in the way they intend.

Another concern might be that when an audience member wants to give a *permissioned opinion*, permission may be denied by the storyteller for any reason. This could create discomfort or animosity if the storyteller is denying that question based on previous experiences or preconceived notions about a person. It will be important to handle such group dynamics with care and response-ability. Creating a sense of safety amongst participants, as described above, can aid in building trust between participants and encourage comradery and sharing, hopefully eliminating any reason for the storyteller to deny permission to a responder. Many times, I ask the artist if they would be willing to hear feedback or opinions from the group, as a way to grant permission to anyone who wants to speak about the piece, instead of giving permission individually. Or if I have responders ask for permission in a way that previews what they are going to present: "I have an opinion about the visuals/audio/story arc/etc., would you like to hear it?" This helps ease the tension if a storyteller denies permission, by suggesting that the denial could come from storyteller's thoughts on the subject matter rather than on the person. I also encourage language in this stage that promotes respect to the storyteller as the artist of their own work. For example, I encourage responders to begin their opinions with "I wonder."

As you can see, the Critical Response Process, as is, may not be right for every group a facilitator will work with. It is therefore important not to treat this process as precious. There are alternative ways to host feedback circles or to modify this one. As I suggested, I sometimes make use of a different tactic in *Artist as Questioner* phase before returning to the framework. I would encourage you to work through the process to determine what parts are most helpful and useful for the storytellers with whom you work. As a tool for interrupting inherent or interpreted authority, the Critical Response Process invites response-ability and care, "calling on us to filter out the arrogance, cruelty, and authority from our giving structures, as well as to be honest" with our responses (Lerman and Borstel, *Critique is Caring* 149).

Considerations for Story Distribution

Responsible facilitation of co-creative media projects like digital storytelling should include ways that engage everyday storytellers in their own relationship building and dissemination processes. Rice and Mündle argue that the responsibility of facilitators follows them into all spaces of dissemination, even as they become listeners to the stories after the facilitation is complete. They write,

> How this responsibility is articulated varies in each context and require multiple kinds of listening — from holding participants' individual journeys in voicing particular experiences; to thinking about the institutional and political listening necessary as these stories are 'loosed' into the world (King, 2003, p. 10); to considering the implications of the stories being taken up in policy conversations. In all cases, our responsibility (as facilitators, as researchers, as artists, as neoliberal subjects) extends beyond the individual storytellers and acknowledges our complicity with the various systems that collude to produce us and inevitably structure our interactions and patterns of speaking and listening.
> (144)

Dissemination practices have traditionally fallen to the facilitators and facilitating institutions. This not only disengages participants from the critical ability to respond to their digital audiences, but it also removes them from the practice of navigating digital social networks. Storytellers should be engaged with the dissemination practices of their personal stories. Facilitators should include storytellers in the critical questions they consider when preparing for project and story dissemination:

> Which stories should or should not be made public through websites or DVDs? Does the project research team have the responsibility or the right to set parameters around what personal narratives can be created in these workshops? What message, or narrative, do these types of digital stories tell about the community in which they were created? Do they further perpetuate stereotypes? Or give voice to silenced peoples and issues? Is it justified to consciously leave out stories that have the potential to be 'used against' the community? Will some stories contribute to collective misunderstandings?
> (Cunsolo Willox et al. 140–141)

One way to navigate the political questions Cunsolo Willox et al. describe above is to share the responsibility of dissemination with the storytellers. Margaret Anne Clarke, creator of Brazil's *Um Milhão de Histórias de Vida de Jovens* digital storytelling project, feels the best way to ensure agency in participation during all phases of the storytelling process, from story workshopping to story dissemination, is to put the youth participants in charge of the entire process (151). The project is perhaps most unique in that where most digital storytelling projects have the facilitators disseminate the created stories, *Um Milhão de Histórias de Vida de Jovens* allows the young participants to choose where, how, and when they share their stories. In order for the digital storytelling methodology to promote voice and agency, it should not only instruct on the structures of narrative composition, but also teach methods of dissemination as Clarke's project does. Additionally, longevity was a foundational aspect of the project as Clarke wanted to create the ability to continue without the constant oversight of her team of facilitators. For this reason, she extended the workshop process beyond the traditional story creation component to include training so the participants could learn to be facilitators themselves and thereby learn to sustain and expand the process by facilitating their own story circles and digital storytelling creation processes (150).

Beyond involving them in how stories are disseminated, facilitators should give participants the ability to choose whether or not to disseminate their digital stories in live and digital public and private screenings. It is possible some participants may come to a digital storytelling workshop without the desire for their work to move forward outside of the workshop space. That is, they might participate in the work for their own sake rather than for the ability to share their story broadly in a digital landscape. This should be the right of the participant – to decide where, when, and how to share their story. If projects are designed with the specific purpose of creating stories for public dissemination, this should be made clear to participants from the beginning, and storytellers should still retain the right to ultimately choose whether or not their stories are made public. Participants should not feel pressured to sign release forms for the facilitator and/or the hosting institution allowing for the reproduction and dissemination of their stories and should further retain the right to alter their decision at a later date. If a storyteller chooses to remove her story from a digital collection, she should do so with the understanding that digitally disseminated works may have unintended second-lives that are beyond their control and the control of the hosting institution. For example, if the digital story has been downloaded from the Internet it may be used at a later date by the downloader. Also, if the digital story has been distributed in a hard copy format such as a DVD, then a storyteller would not be able to revoke the inclusion of her story on previously-published materials. Amy Hill suggests one way for a facilitator to make these points clear to storytellers is to share and discuss a consent and have a formal agreement (a document signed by the participants) at the beginning of the workshop (27).

Further, we should consider who owns these narratives and retains the rights to these narratives after they are produced to ensure that a framework of response-able facilitation continues into the dissemination of stories. In her article about intellectual property in digital storytelling, Christina Spurgeon writes,

> co-creative media activities are usually contingent upon the voluntary participation of storytellers. They are also usually facilitated by highly skilled digital media artists and practitioners who are personally committed to user-led (as distinct from user-generated) creative practice and seek creative excellence, often in difficult circumstances that offer uncertain economic rewards. Practitioner concern for the integrity of co-creative media practice is often expressed as a normative commitment to user/creator 'ownership' of the creative process (Lambert 2013, p. 191), if not the creative outputs.
>
> (120)

For Spurgeon, at question here is the resulting narrative produced in a digital storytelling workshop. Spurgeon found that "quite often there is direct alignment between the ethic of storyteller ownership that underpins the CDS [Center for Digital Storytelling] method and actual IP [Intellectual Property] arrangements, but this is by no means always the case" (122). This sentiment is in line with the findings of a survey of co-creative media practices in Australia (a study of more than just digital storytelling practices as discussed in this book) in which Spurgeon participated from 2010 to 2014.

Spurgeon et al. found that dissemination practices ranged from providing participants with the full rights of their created works to hosting and/or partnering institutions and organizations controlling some rights over the participants' created works, but that the largest arrangement between organizations and storytellers is to use Creative Commons licensing "to establish non-exclusive rights" (47). Spurgeon notes that the use of Creative Commons has many reasons, but are primarily twofold: (1) "Pre-existing licences provide an 'off the shelf' solution for under-resourced practitioners and has some capacity for easy adaptation to suit specific circumstances of a given project or production;" and (2) it "provides a pedagogic strategy for helping storytellers to better understand when it is legal for them to make use of other people's work (including other works also licensed under Creative Commons)" (qtd. in Spurgeon et al. 47–48).

Yet Spurgeon is careful to say that such licensing tactics are best practices (Spurgeon 131). She points to the fact that dissemination practices in digital storytelling still discount the participant in many ways:

> Co-creative media practitioners appear to have been sensitised to debates within the communities of practice and further afield about the status of end-user labour and its potential for commercial exploitation. The work of balancing these divergent interests in ownership usually falls to the facilitator and commences in the design phase of projects. Indeed, the variety of IP [Intellectual Property] management strategies used in co-creative media practice is framed here as a user-led contribution of co-creative media to more open systems of media and cultural production. It is explained as a demonstration of the problem-solving capacity of co-creative media practitioner and their wider communities of practice, necessitated by the collaborative character and complex practical politics of co-creative media.
>
> (131)

Here, Spurgeon acknowledges the ways in which digital storytelling dissemination practices remain potentially manipulative to workshop participants. Decisions about how and where the stories will be disseminated are often in place before the workshop even begins. Spurgeon suggests this is facilitator-driven, but I would posit that it is likely driven by the hosting and/or funding organizations who have hired that facilitator. Implied here, then, is that the participants are removed from this key conversation about what happens to their work after it is created. While many practices have in place – and should have in place – protocols for allowing a storyteller to remove their narrative from distribution, it is possible that the pressures of the workshop and, as Spurgeon contends, the presented *benefits* of "the problem-solving capacity of co-creative media" to expand the reach of that storyteller may push storytellers into dissemination practices they don't fully comprehend.

In a workshop with the Métis people of Fishing Lake, Yvonne Poitras Pratt faced similar debates about responsible dissemination of digital stories the participants created. In her book, *Digital Storytelling in Indigenous Education: A Decolonizing Journey for a Métis Community*, she discusses her endeavors to allow the digital stories to "remain in the community's control," rather than in the hosting university's control (53). However, Poitras Pratt acknowledges that this approach has drawbacks. She writes, "I believe that what has been a limited form of sharing since the stories were created has meant the full potential of the digital stories has not been fully realized...the risks of not sharing far outweigh any costs of controlling access" (ibid.). The risk of not sharing the works created in this program meant that stories about the Métis were remaining hidden when they could be used to educate and enlighten others about the community. While Poitras Pratt only encourages sharing digital stories with the storyteller's permission, she has changed how she approaches the dissemination practices for this project and now encourages the storytellers to share their stories beyond their community so they can serve to help educate and decolonize (ibid. 90). For as Rice and Mündel write, "The act of making space for people to tell their own stories coupled with the translation of these stories into a widely shareable multimedia format has allowed renewed and varied engagements with systemic issues of racism, sexism, ableism, classism, and colonialism" (123). It is through the act of dissemination – be it on a large or small scale – that makes room for the political listening discussed in the previous chapter.

References

Alexandra, Darcy. "Are We Listening Yet?" *Participatory Visual and Digital Research in Action*, edited by Aline Gubrium, Krista Harper, and Marty Otañez, Taylor and Francis, 2015, pp. 41–55.

Alexandra, Darcy. "Implicating Practice: Engaged Scholarship Through Co-creative Media" *Digital Storytelling in Higher Education: International Perspectives*, edited by Grete Jamissen, Pip Hardy, Yngve Nordkvelle, and Heather Pleasants, Palgrave Macmillan, 2017, 335–354.

Clarke, Margaret Anne. "Developing Digital Storytelling in Brazil." *Story Circle: Digital Storytelling around the World*, edited by John Hartley, and Kelly McWilliam, Wiley-Blackwell, 2009, pp. 144–154.

Cunsolo Willox, Ashley, et al. "Storytelling in a Digital Age: Digital Storytelling as an Emerging Narrative Method for Preserving and Promoting Indigenous Oral Wisdom." *Qualitative Research*, vol. 13, no. 2, 2012, pp. 127–147.

D., G. "My Favorite Murder Date." *YouTube*, uploaded by I Am UCF, 27 April 2017, www.youtube.com/watch?v=FHueLQnn9EY.

Eckles, Kathy. "Facilitating Reflective Structured Dialogue." presentation, Essential Partners, virtual, December 12, 2020.

Freeman, Emily, and Amanda Hill. "When One Door Shuts, Another Door Opens: A Dialogue on a New Residency with Homeless Youth." *InciteInsight*, vol. 3, no. 4, 2011, pp. 19–22.

Gachago, Daniela, and Pam Sykes. "Navigating Ethical Boundaries When Adopting Digital Storytelling in Higher Education." *Digital Storytelling in Higher Education: International Perspectives*, edited by Grete Jamissen, Pip Hardy, Yngve Nordkvelle, and Heather Pleasants, Palgrave Macmillan, 2017, pp. 91–105.

Hill, Amy. "Digital Storytelling and the Politics of Doing Good: Exploring the Ethics of Bringing Personal Narratives into Public Spheres." *Community-Based Multiliteracies and Digital Media Projects: Questioning Assumptions and Exploring Realities*, edited by Heather M. Pleasants, and Dana E. Salter, Peter Lang, 2014, pp. 21–43.

Kershaw, Rob. "Story Circles." presentation, Center for Digital Storytelling, virtual, February 2014.

Kershaw, Rob. "The Story Circle." presentation, Center for Digital Storytelling, virtual, January 10, 2022.

Kothari, Uma. "Authority and Expertise: The Professionalisation of International Development and the Ordering of Dissent." *Antipode*, vol. 37, no. 3, 2005, pp. 425–446.

Lambert, Joe. "Where It All Started." *Story Circle: Digital Storytelling around the World*, edited by John Hartley, and Kelly McWilliam, Wiley-Blackwell, 2009, pp. 79–90.

Lambert, Joe. Personal Interview. 27 March 2022.

Lambert, Joe. Zoom Interview. 19 July 2022.

Lerman, Liz, and John Borstel. *Liz Lerman's Critical Response Process: A Method for Getting Useful Feedback on Anything You Make, From Dance to Dessert*. Dance Exchange, 2003.

Lerman, Liz, and John Borstel. *Critique is Creative: In Theory and Practice*. Wesleyan University Press, 2022.

"Liz Lerman's Critical Response Process." *Dance Exchange*, https://www.danceexchange.org/merchandise/p/critical-response-process. Accessed 26, July 2021.

McWilliam, Kelly. "Digital Storytelling as a 'Discursively Ordered Domain.'" *Digital Storytelling, Mediatized Stories: Self-Representations in New Media*, edited by Knut Lundby, Peter Lang, 2008, pp. 145–161.

Oliver, Kelly. *Witnessing: Beyond Recognition*. University of Minnesota Press, 2001.

Poitras Pratt, Yvonne. *Digital Storytelling in Indigenous Education: A Decolonizing Journey for a Métis Community*. Routledge, 2020.

Rice, Carla, and Ingrid Mündel. "Multimedia Storytelling Methodology: Notes on Access and Inclusion in Neoliberal Times," *Canadian Journal of Disability Studies*, vol. 8, no. 1, 2019, pp. 118–148.

Rice, Carla, et al. "Project Re•Vision: Disability at the Edges of Representation." *Disability & Society*, vol. 30, no. 4, 2015, pp. 513–527.

Spurgeon, Christina "The Ethics, Aesthetics and Practical Politic of Ownership in Co-Creative Media." *Digital Storytelling: Form and Content*, edited by Mark Dunford, and Tricia Jenkins, Palgrave Macmillan, 2017, pp. 119–135.

Spurgeon, Christina et al. *Community Uses of Co-Creative Media. Digital Storytelling and Co-Creative Media: The Role of Community Arts and Media in Propagating and Coordinating Population-Wide Creative Practice*. Queensland University of Technology, 2015.

8 Epilogue
Where Do We Go from Here?

An Ethical Framework for Facilitators

Digital storytelling work takes place within communities, schools, and other institutions that have specific needs and desires. Ultimately, we should understand that digital storytelling workshops are not single-purpose institutions. That is, they do not operate solely for the purposes of developing a series of personal video narratives. Rather, there is significant additional work at play within the workshop's infrastructure and framing. Care work is the effort facilitators should undertake to address these needs and desires. Without understanding these fundamental needs and desires of a community, narrative creation and video production cannot be adequately accomplished. This care work can and will look different depending on the community with which the facilitator works. It might look like ensuring the basic needs of people are met. In working with young people, I have often provided sandwiches, toiletries, shoes, and other supplies that they need to ensure they are able to focus and be productive. Care work may also look like ensuring higher needs are met, such as inclusion in programs and inclusion in workshop activities. In one workshop I had a student who struggled with writing. In order to allow him to complete the digital storytelling workshop, I worked with him one-on-one to write his script, allowing him to move on to the next stages of production ("Food for Thought"). Care work may also look like ensuring diversity within the workshop, in terms of who is physically invited into and present within the workshop space; in terms of whose voices are represented in examples, literature, and lessons; and in the myriad other ways to give space to often under-told narratives and under-represented voices.

Care will also look like ensuring that your story creation process values the cultural and traditional storywork and traditions of the community with whom you are working. Speaking in the context of legal systems, Larissa Behrent reminds us that Indigenous cultures often place a greater emphasis on oral traditions of storytelling, where Western cultures focus on the written word. For the digital storytelling facilitator, this might mean that focusing on a composition methodology that relies on the written scripting of a narrative may impact and alienate some participants. Again, if the facilitator is not of the same culture(s) as the participants, gaining significant contextualization, preferably from the work of and conversations with people who originate within the culture, including elders, scholars, and experts.

In 2011 Lucy Harding and Amy Hill developed "Guidelines for Ethical Practice" and the "Digital Storyteller's Bill of Rights" for the program "Silence Speaks." These documents are shared digitally at www.silencespeaks.org as well as in the Addendum of *Digital Storytelling: Capturing Lives, Creating Community* (Lambert and Hessler 204–211). The first document, "Guidelines for Ethical Practice," is dedicated to digital storytelling facilitators and details a tangible check-list of an ethics of responsibility that should drive participatory media practices. The core principles listed in this document include 1) ensure participants' well-being; 2) allow participants to make informed choices; 3) allow story ownership to reside with participants; 4) develop facilitation methods that meet the needs of the specific community of participants; and 5) practice responsible and ethical facilitation as a continued process. Harding and Hill then provide ethical considerations for the workshop. These include reflections on protection, communication, structures, and looking forward. They follow this section with a list of considerations for after a digital storytelling workshop has been completed. These reflections consider protection, ownership, and communications and transparency. The "Digital Storyteller's Bill of Rights" is designed to be shared with workshop participants. Many of the ideas that Harding and Hill develop in their "Guidelines" and "Bill of Rights," are echoed in this book, and I am heartened to know that in the primary text for those interested in digital storytelling, that there is a readily available list of considerations for how to be an ethical facilitator and what rights should be given to digital storytelling workshop participants. I would recommend these documents to anyone interested in more specific ways to act as a responsible facilitator.

I would additionally point readers to Verna J. Kirkness and Ray Barnhardt article, "First Nations and Higher Education: The Four R's – Respect, Relevance, Reciprocity, Responsibility." Kirkness and Barnhardt developed the "Four R's" to create a protocol for university researchers and educators to interact with First Nation peoples. The Four R's are designed to "reduce the cultural distance and the role dichotomy between the producers and the consumers of knowledge" (10). For digital storytelling facilitators, the Four R's can be used in terms of facilitation and also in reference to storywork. The first R, respect, involves witnessing and embracing "cultural knowledge, traditions and core values" (8). The second R, relevance, involves taking such traditional knowledge and values and positioning them as legitimate understandings alongside the facilitator's own traditional and cultural values (11). For example, digital storytelling facilitators can include examples of digital stories from Indigenous storymakers and storymakers from non-Western culture around the world when sharing previously-created narratives to inspire and support the participants in their workshops. The third R, reciprocity, comparable to the problems of expertise, is about "making teaching and learning two-way processes, in which the give-and-take between faculty and students opens up new levels of understanding for everyone" (13). The final R, responsibility, involves moving from a celebration of cultural and traditional knowledge, values, and experience, into a critical examination of how these interact with the institutions and structures of society, often those institutions and structures formed and aided by practices of colonization (15). I believe Kirkness and Barnhardt's ethical framework can and should be applied more broadly to include facilitators outside of the university who might also enter into communities of which they are outsiders and to cultures beyond First Nation peoples. Digital storytelling facilitators can employ the Four R's to encourage greater responsibility, witnessing, and care within their practices. Summarizing Kirkness and Barhardt for storywork, Archibald et al. write, "In this story research process the researcher must listen to Indigenous Peoples' stories with respect, develop story relationships in a responsible manner, treat story knowledge with reverence, and strengthen storied impact through reciprocity" (2). This framework will be additionally important for approaching the storywork of cultures other than the facilitator's own.

Responsible Facilitation: An Invitation for Reflection

Throughout this work, I place a lot of importance on protecting the storyteller and their narrative. It's a lot of responsibility. Part of the reason behind this is to respect and champion *this* narrative being told at *this* particular moment, knowing we are preserving a sense of truth contingent on the time and context in which it is being told. But the truth is, there is never just one story. There are only versions of stories created out of the unique perspective of the storyteller and the moment in which they are telling them. Overtime, stories will grow and shape-shift. They will be many things to many people, who will see the same story in many different ways. As storytellers, we are always contending with influences that shape us from the past, and the influences building any current moment we have to be ready to share a particular story. As facilitators, we have to be able to hold space for people who are telling stories for the first time, the last time, or some time in the middle. We have to be willing to meet people where they are at. To hold respect for *this* story right now and for the possibility that the storyteller will retell - through digital storytelling or otherwise – these stories that are so meaningful to them. As facilitators, we may never get another chance to sit with a particular storyteller and help them consider the story they are telling at that particular moment, and we should honor the deep integrity and intentionality with which we communicate and collaborate with these storytellers.

Facilitators should keep an eye toward consistent reflection in relationship to the specific project, institution, and participants and always be ready to address the "changing contexts" of these spaces and adapt as needed (Gachago and Sykes 104). Reflexivity should become a practice for all of us leading community projects. As Schutz and Gere observe in their observation of community tutoring, "the *talking about*, must map onto the *doing*, the activity of the service component" (132). While the authors here are discussing service-learning practices and discussion that happens in an academic classroom, the practice they describe is essentially one of reflexivity where the students are encouraged to think critically and intellectually about their role in these community projects. It is no longer an option to think about the narratives generated in digital storytelling workshops as solely personal; we should dissect the ways in which they are simultaneously public, and created under the guidance of the facilitator.

As facilitators we should constantly work to understand how our own story and sense of identity has been formed and how this might impact others in our workshops, as well as how the process of story and identity formation take place so as to better understand our participants. We should strive to understand how we are re-formed as individuals through collaborative compositional practices. We should engage in searching for the ways that the social and material world impact our individual and collective understandings of ourselves and each other. As digital storytelling facilitators, understanding how these interpretations take form will help to comprehend the ways in which participants make sense of themselves and write their personal narratives. Such an understanding will allow facilitators to better connect to and interact with workshop participants. It will help facilitators guide participants through the story creation process to consider how their actions, communication, and composition affect the telling of their narratives, and help create a path by which participants can determine the best practices for reaching the audience they want in the way that they want.

Reflective practices will help facilitators come to understand how the process of identity formation happen. Facilitators will be able to situate their own facilitation practices in relation to the socio-historic contexts that produced them and understand how such practices have evolved over time. In turn, an understanding of facilitation practices in this way will open itself to more reflection with which facilitators can engage and question. Reflection will allow facilitators to look closer and more objectively at their own practices so that they are able to engage in practices that might change, reconsider, and modify their practices for current and future workshops. Locating facilitator practices in such a way can encourage facilitators to broaden their view of what digital storytelling practices can and may otherwise look like as well as help facilitators comprehend and more deeply consider how social interactions are created, affect participant, and can be redeveloped.

The responsible facilitator is one who actively engages in their own self-reflection. And, in similar processes of understanding the self as interconnected into public spheres, we should recognize that self-reflection for responsible facilitators is also a social process since it will direct changes in social interaction. As I have suggested throughout this book, the work of the individual affects the public sphere, and thus the facilitator affects the dynamic, trajectory, and outcomes of the group as a whole. The extent to which a facilitator impacts the digital storytelling workshop is dependent on the individual facilitator. Self-reflection and a move toward embracing response-ability within the workshop setting can help diminish these affects and provide more agency and subjectivity to the participants.

Reflection of oneself within the digital story facilitation involves reflecting on all components of the practice, as I have tried to contend with in this book. Facilitators should reflect on the planning and organization of the project, the instructive components of the project, the collaborative components of the project, and the dissemination practices of the project. In their discussion of Participatory Action Research (PAR), Stephen Kemmis and Mervyn Wilkinson list they ways in which researchers should approach reflecting on their practices. PAR is an approach to research that highly values self-reflection and their list is useful for digital storytelling facilitators as well. They write,

> action researchers may want to become especially sensitive to the ways in which their particular practices involve
> a) acts of material, symbolic and social
>   - production
>   - communication
>   - social organisation;
> b) which shape and are shaped by social structures in
>   - the cultural
>   - the economic
>   - the political realms;
> c) which shape and are shaped by the social media of
>   - language/discourses
>   - work
>   - power;
> d) which largely shape, but can also be shaped by, participants' own knowledge, expressed in participants'
>   - understandings
>   - skills
>   - values, which, in turn, shape and are shaped by their
>
> acts of material, symbolic and social production, communication and social organisation ..., and so on.
>
> (25–26)

By examining these aspects of digital storytelling facilitator practices, we will necessarily consider how these components are interrelated and how their symbiotic resonance will shape a workshop setting and affect participants. It will also help facilitators contend with their own objective and subjective identity, that is, their identity as perceived by others and as perceived by themselves and how this will alter and affect diverse workshop settings or workshops that involve diverse participants.

Rather than merely engaging in a reflective practice at the end of each workshop, facilitators should engage in a more systematic approach to reflection that occurs throughout the workshop. Approaching self-reflection during the workshop will allow for facilitators to make changes to actions that can affect the outcomes of a current project as well as those of future projects. Reflecting upon how interactions within the workshop space shaped certain outcomes, the facilitator can work to reduce interactions that feel like they are not based in response-ability, interactions that might feel to participants unfounded, unjust, unproductive, and alienating and those that might limit and constrain the narrative the storyteller truly desires to tell. Reflection in this way requires a keen awareness of the participant, which might be conducted through watching body language and gestures and asking participants to reflect on the dialogues and conversations that happen within the workshop setting.

Embracing a critical reflection of oneself is not an easy or pleasant process for many. It involves actively examining the actions you took in a social setting, considering the outcomes of that action, and devising a new plan for future actions when needed. It can be difficult to look at the self critically as we often don't like to acknowledge when we have erred. Yet such self-reflection is necessary for the responsible facilitator because it allows for a process of self-investigation and self-growth that will impact and improve current and future facilitation practices.

Self-reflection is continual. As a process, it is repetitive in that it asks individuals to reflect on their actions, investigate outcomes, make changes, and re-evaluate outcomes. The process in cyclical and ongoing, and can be a lot of work, especially for those just beginning their reflective journey. As a facilitator continues to question and process their actions in a systematic way, the process will become engrained. Yet, the reflective process requires this work. It is an active process, a process of doing and a process of learning by doing.

Understanding My Position as a Facilitator and Storymaker

In order to firmly grasp their place within the power structures of the co-creative storymaking workshop, facilitators should consider "the matter of [their] stories, stories about where [they] stand in relation to the community where [they] do this work, in relation to its ... people, its institutions, its histories, and inequities" (Taub-Pervizpour 246). People, here, indicates both the workshop participants and the people within the larger community to which they belong. This book is in fact a reflection of my own practice as an artist, educator, and scholar who facilitates. As a facilitator, I continually work on my own facilitation practice through a process of reflection on and in action. From these reflections, I work to revise my own thinking and actions to continually better my facilitation and, I hope, the experience of my workshop participants. At the beginning of each new workshop, and to some extent on each day of the workshop, I need to establish my position in the room so that I can better understand how my personal identity and my identity as a facilitator has been formed and continues to form through the process of facilitation. As a facilitator, I should acknowledge that I have only worked in this field for a decade, and recognize that my approaches to storytelling and facilitation are not the only approaches. In fact, my approaches to both are unique to my artistic, scholarly, and educational background.

As a facilitator, I acknowledge that I enter into the storymaking spaces often with a particular agenda, objective, or goal in mind. At the very least, I am coming in knowing that I have been hired to do a job or am being funded by a larger institution. Typically, this means that I am contractually obligated to create and facilitate a digital storytelling workshop, which additionally means that they expect to see digital stories created by workshop participants as a return on their investment. This is further complicated by whatever time frame is imposed by the funding organization and any partner organizations who provide space, participants, or other resources. Often funding and partner organizations will have their own particular vision and goals for the projects that I am responsible for seeing through. I am also responsible for ensuring that the workshop space is set up in a way that embraces and activates individual values and voices; encourages productivity, respect, and engagement; and is safe for participants to make themselves vulnerable without fear of ramifications. Participant well-being and contentment is perhaps my utmost concern as I enter these spaces. I may also have personal objectives such as to gather certain kinds of stories or try new technologies or lesson ideas.

As a scholar of narrative, I am strongly enmeshed in the work of White, Western theorists and storytellers. Scholars such as Poitras Pratt examine the way colonization at the hands of White Westerners "disrupted the traditional [Indigenous] ways of story" (123). Poitras Pratt writes,

> for an Indigenous audience, the interpretation of the story is left with the listener such that they derive the meaning they need from the story at that moment in time. This approach is very different from a Western approach to story where the tale is more often than not dissected, fragmented, and analyzed for meaning. In the case of children's fables, it is even more common practice to neatly summarize the moral of the story in a closing passage.
>
> (ibid.)

In my own facilitation, I work to remain open to the storytelling instincts my participants bring to the workshop, as I find that their storywork is often based in the narrative traditions with which they are most familiar. This sometimes means that in order to act responsibly and with care to witness the narrative participants want to create, I have to fight against some of the narrative experiences based in Western traditions with which I've engaged. For me, then, part of being responsible is ever-expanding my own narrative horizons by reading, watching, and otherwise engaging with narratives from Indigenous peoples and cultures from around the world. While I have some background in engaging with these narratives, it does not compare with the extent to which I have been immersed in Western narrative traditions, and it is my responsibility to actively seek out storytelling methods that will push me to understand better how these cultures share their stories and the meanings they hope these stories pass forward. Archibald argues that it is not just about engaging with the stories, but also about removing my Western literary traditions and theories from my context as I engage with these stories to "find the theories embedded in [Indigenous] Stories" (16). These are things that I am actively working on so that I can be a more responsible facilitator in co-creative work.

Finding Closure

The digital storytelling work I highlight in this book is just one genre of a larger umbrella of co-creative media practices. I hope that the practices and theoretical considerations presented in this book for facilitators of digital storytelling workshops will have broader reach for readers looking to engage in a broad scope of co-creative media practices. Understanding how to undertake responsible facilitation can have a range of applications for other creative writing and narrative work that engage in the development of personal narratives as well as game production, geo-locative narrative-development, transmedia storytelling, augmented and virtual reality narratives, radio narratives, film, and applied theatre.

If we view a personal narrative as collaboratively created, we call into question the very notion of digital personal narratives like digital stories as "authentic," which has been widely declared based largely on their use of the author's own words, voice, archives, and personal narrative (Wu; Thumim; Hertzberg Kaare and Lundby; Helff and Woletz). In reconsidering the "authenticity" of the story in this way, in reading personal narratives as publicly created artifacts, do we "diminish" the perceived power and impact of the works? We might here use John Hartley's definition of "smiling" stories, or stories that reflect the personal aspect, and are "appropriated to signal non-threatening communicative intentions, which would likely be rejected if the tale were understood to be on behalf of industry or government" (Hartley "Smiling" 207). Everyday audiences may never give thoughtful consideration of the other voices that contribute to the telling of personal narratives; however, understanding this important aspect of how we tell personal narratives invites an ethics of responsibility that can inform not only the practices of the facilitator, the institution, and the other storytellers in the room, but also open a more practical and thorough approach for audiences to analyze the media they consume.

Digital storytelling is a co-creative, participatory media, and I recognize, as facilitator, that I have a role in the way participants tell their personal narratives. At every turning point, I ask that facilitators of co-creative media practices remain firmly rooted in an ethics of response-ability to guide their practices. This will involve significant self-reflection before, during, and after the digital storytelling workshop takes place. Reflection cannot merely take place at the end of the residency; we should begin to survey how our daily actions impact the address and response of our participants. Understanding the rhetorical moves we make in the storymaking space can engage us in a process of reflection that moves beyond the words we use to the underlying motives behind them. It is critical that we address our personal agendas when leading co-creative practices and align ourselves with facilitating institutions with agendas motivated by an ethics of responsibility. Prepare your participants for all potentialities when beginning a new project so that they understand the ways in which you are responsible to them and the ways in which they are responsible to you.

Approaching the co-creative practice of storymaking responsibly is important to ensure a future of media policy and practice. It is not just the responsibility of the facilitator, although they are a large component. We ultimately need to affect change on a grander scale. As we grow our digital platforms and become more and more inundated with digital data, we should commit to asking facilitating institutions and funders to participate in the witnessing of the diverse stories we assist in producing. We should ask that they have faith in the voices of these storytellers and their stories. And then we should take this further. Because it is not enough for the institutions and individuals to laud voice. We should ultimately affect policy change and the media in the hopes of creating new avenues of attention that will increase the value of diverse stories and storytellers using a variety of media platforms and production techniques.

Affecting large-scale change of this nature will be no easy task. We should be ready to start by changing our personal approach in the room. We can begin by approaching current and future residencies with an ethics of responsibility and undertaking reflection throughout our projects. We should allow ourselves to be vulnerable and honest, so that we may own our mistakes, learn from them, and move ever forward. Modeling personal reflection and ongoing improvement and unpacking our own agendas is the start.

References

Archibald, Jo-ann. *Indigenous Storywork: Educating the Heart, Mind, Body, and Spirit.* UBC Press, 2008.

Behrent, Larissa. "Decolonizing Institutions and Assertive Self-Determination: Implications for Legal Practice." *Decolonizing Research: Indigenous Storywork as Methodology*, edited by Jo-ann Archibal Q'um Q'um Xiiem, Jenny Bol Jun Lee-Morgan, and Jason De Santolo, ZedBooks, 2019, pp. 175–186.

Gachago, Daniela, and Pam Sykes. "Navigating Ethical Boundaries When Adopting Digital Storytelling in Higher Education." *Digital Storytelling in Higher Education: International Perspectives*, edited by Grete Jamissen, Pip Hardy, Yngve Nordkvelle, and Heather Pleasants, Palgrave Macmillan, 2017, pp. 91–105.

Hill, Amanda. *Power to the People: Responsible Facilitation in Collaborative Storytelling Practices.* 2018. University of Central Florida, PhD Dissertation.

Hill, Amanda. "Telling Stories to Narrate Futures." *IAFOR Journal of Psychology & the Behavioral Sciences*, vol. 5, no. SI, 2019, pp. 63–73.

Kemmis, Stephen, and Mervyn Wilkinson. "Participatory Action Research and the Study of Practice." *Action Research in Practice: Partnership for Social Justice in Education*, edited by Bill Atweh et al., Taylor Francis, 1998, 21–36.

Kirkness, Verna J., and Ray Barnhardt "First Nations and Higher Education: The Four R's: Respect, Relevance, Reciprocity, Responsibility." *Knowledge Across Cultures: A Contribution to Dialogue Among Civilizations*, edited by Ruth Hayoe, and J Pan, Comparative Education Research Centre, The University of Hong Kong, 2001.

Lambert, Joe, and H. Brooke Hessler. *Digital Storytelling: Digital Storytelling: Capturing Lives, Creating Community.* 5th ed., Routledge, 2018.

Poitras Pratt, Yvonne. *Digital Storytelling in Indigenous Education: A Decolonizing Journey for a Métis Community.* Routledge, 2020.

Schutz, Aaron, and Anne Ruggles Gere. "Service Learning and English Studies: Rethinking 'Public' Service." *College English*, vol. 60, no. 2, 1998, pp. 129–149.

Taub-Pervizpour, Lora, and Erin Drisbrow. "Digital Storytelling with Youth: Whose Agenda Is It?" *Story Circle: Digital Storytelling around the World*, edited by John Hartley, and Kelly McWilliam, Wiley–Blackwell, 2009, pp. 245–251.

Index

Note: Page numbers in *italics* indicate figures.

Abrams, L. 74
Ace Space Show 17
Alexandra, D. 103, 115–116, 128, 129
Alrutz, M. 35, 89
alternative media 99, 100
Archibald, J. 145, 150
Arendt, H. 49–51
artist + festival method 88–89
Atchley, D. 16–20, 22, 33
Atton, C. 90, 99, 100
audience as stakeholder: attention and listening 87–88; digital dissemination 91–94; live screenings 89–91; reception of personal narratives 78–83; spaces of encounters 88–94; storytelling as resource 83–87
augmented reality (AR) game 73–75
Australian Center for the Moving Image (ACMI) program 120
authentic identity narratives, creation of 53, 64–65
authenticity 48, 55, 121, 150; authentic identity narratives, creation of 64–65; co-created 63–64; contextualizing challenges to 65–68; creation of personal narratives 71–73; "Getting a Job at Nikki's Place" 73–76; guided, challenge of 70–71; implied, challenges of 68–70; role of 64
authorship 3, 11, 18–19; autobiographical 43–48; in construction of texts 35–37; multi-media, multi-modal 33
autobiographical storytelling 35, 71, 80; component of 44–45; feature of 43–44; memories of moments for 43–45; theme of 44; Western 44

Barnhardt, R. 144, 145
Bauman, R. 67
Bickford, S. 103
Borstel, J. 131–135
broadcasting model 88–89
Bruner, J. 43–44, 46–47
Buckingham, D. 65
Burgess, J. 1, 3, 51

Capture Wales project 55, 89, 92, 93
care 103, 119, 136, 145; caring relation 107; defined 107, 109; ethic of 106–110; witnessing and 107–108; as work 109, 143
Center for Digital Storytelling *see* StoryCenter
Changing Climate, Changing Health, Changing Stories project 95, 113
Clarke, M. A. 138
co-creative media 5, 86–87, 104, 106, 139; community uses of 140; digital storytelling as 48–49, 78, 96; facilitators in 129–130, 151; live screenings in 90; responsible facilitation of 137
collaborative dialogic creation process 128
colonization 85, 102, 113, 145, 149
communication 91, 104, 107, 121, 128, 150; interaction 103, 136; mediated 88; narrative 84, 86; patterns of 51; requirement of 76; verbal or nonverbal 121; voice in 105
Community Advisory Committee (CAC) 57–59
Couldry, N. 25–26, 84, 85, 87–88
Creative Commons licensing 140

154 Index

critical feedback structure, developing 131–137
Critical Response Process 131–132, 134, 137; *Artist as Questioner* phase 133–134, 136, 137; artist's role in 132–137; facilitator's role in 132–137; *Neutral Questions from Responders* phase 134–135; *Permissioned Opinions* phase 135–137; phases of 132–137; *Statements of Meaning* phase 133

Dance Exchange community-arts program 131
deepfake videos 72
deep listening 69
Defining Moment, A project 44
dialogue 11, 36, 70, 89–90, 104, 123; co-productive 102; impacts of 63; intersubjective 101, 107; process, roles within 132; response-ability and 107–108, 133, 134; students in 110; use of 107
digital dissemination 78, 83–85, 89, 91–94
Digital Faith Stories 54–56, 79, 115
digital literacy 99, 119, 129; of author 81–82; co-productive media practices and 110–111; and multimodality 33–35; in workshop space 82
digital manipulation 72
digital storytelling 12–13, 15–16, 150–151; audience and *see* audience as stakeholder; audio assets in 28, 31; audio layers of 26; authenticity 63–65; author's personal connection to 3–6; autobiographical 43–44; based co-creative practices, personal narratives in 71–73; challenge of guided authenticity in 70–71; challenges of implied authenticity in 68–70; as co-creative media 48–49; combination process 32–33; community-arts lens persists in 20–22, 131; construction process 32–33; defined 1; distribution methods of 88–89; duration of 15; elements of 80; emergence of 16–23; employing user-generated media 120–121; ethical framework for facilitators 143–145; ethics of producing in classroom 130; facilitators 2–3; facilitators as researchers in 113–115; film work and 16–20; Four R's 144–145; genre of 15–16, 23–27; "Getting a Job at Nikki's Place" case study 73–76; Healthy Young Peer Education case study 110–113; in Ireland 115–116; literacy and multimodality in 33–35; multimodal 25–26; narrative strategies of 79; oral storytelling and 34–35; platforms 1–2; political 51, 53; in practice 119–141; at present 23–25; principles of 8–11; reflection within facilitation 145–148; response-able facilitation and 6–7; role of institution in 54–56; situations to define and share 5; storyboarding of 28, 29–30; in theory 99–116; visual layers of 26; visuals in 31–32; "why tell" function of 46–48; workplace-based initiatives 56; workshop *see* space, workshop; StoryCenter; story circles; writing of 27
Disbrow, E. 90, 110–112
domain-specific knowledge, use of 99
Dreher, T. 88, 91
Dush, L. 56

Earnshaw, S. 25
Essential Partners 4, 124, 126
ethical collaboration 99–100; digital storytelling in Ireland case study 115–116; ethic of care 106–110; ethics of responsibility 100–104; facilitators as researchers 113–115; group guidelines 123–127; Healthy Young Peer Education case study 110–113; informed consent, considerations of preparation 121; response-able facilitation, framework of 119–121; responsibility and voice 104–106; space and place 121–123; story composition, considerations for 127–129; story distribution, considerations for 137–141; story-sharing, considerations for 129–137
ethic of care 106–110; defined 109
ethics of responsibility 100–104; faith and 101–102; listening and 100–104; subjectivity and 101; witnessing 100–102
expert-led media pedagogy 121

faith 102–103, 151; -based listening 119; Digital Faith Stories 54–56,

Index 155

79, 115; ethical responsibility and 101–102; positive narratives 56
feminist 50–51, 109, 113; *see also* women
film 16–20, 33–36, 74, 94, 150
Flynn, B. 75
Ford, S. 91
Freire, P. 67, 70

Gachago, D. 130
game 4, 73–75, 150; augmented reality play 73; loco-mobile 73; verbal 69; video 15, 44
"Getting a Job at Nikki's Place" case 73–76
Gilligan, C. 106–109
Goffman, E. 64
Gotschall, J. 45
Green, J. 91
Grrrl Zines A-Go-Go project 100
guided authenticity, challenge of 70–71

Hanisch, C. 50–51
Harden, F. 17
Harding, L. 144
Hartley, J. 16, 49, 54, 56, 68–69, 81, 88–89, 93, 110, 150
Healthy Young Peer Education (HYPE) 110–113
Hendry, P. 88, 101–102, 119
Herman, D. 34
Hessler, B. 31, 69
Hill, A. 56, 82, 95, 112, 126, 130–131, 139, 144
Hull, G. 32, 34
humor 127

I Am UCF project 44, 55, 94, 127, 131
implied authenticity, challenges of 68–70
Indigenous people 83–84, 113–114, 143–145, 149–150
Information Cultural Exchange (ICE) 91
institutions 23, 65, 70, 79, 82, 92, 120; community 90; facilitating and/or hosting 89; funding 56–57, 115, 121, 140, 149; hosting 56, 82, 86, 90–94, 115, 120–121, 139–140; LGBTQ+ 57–58; monetary exchange for 57; receiving recognition 57; role of 54–59
interdependency, meaning of 108
Ireland, digital storytelling in 115–116

Jackson, M. 49–52
Jenkins, H. 91

Kaare, B. H. 54–55, 66, 68
Kemmis, S. 3, 147
Kirkness, V. J. 144, 145
Klaus, E. 83
Kothari, K. 120
Kress, G. 34

Lambert, J. 8–9, 16, 20–25, 31, 68–69, 78–80, 105, 130, 131
Lanham, R. 87
Larson, R. 71–73
Laub, D. 100
Lerman, L. 131–136
LGBTQ+ narratives 57–58
Lincoln, Y. 85
listening 69–70, 76, 113; active 21; audience attention and 87–88, 103; deep 69; ethics of responsibility and 100–104; faith-based 119; institutional 137; meaning of 103; new intensities for 85; in online spaces 86; political 103–104, 116, 137, 141; voice and 103; *see also* audience as stakeholder
Lloyd, J. 88
loco-mobile game 73
Lonelygirl15 case 66
Lundby, K. 33–34, 54–55, 66, 68, 71
Lünenborg, M. 83

McWilliam, K. 49, 68–69, 120, 121
Meadows, D. 16, 35–36, 93
Meadows, S. 88
Métis community 141
migrants 115–116
minimal direct intervention 1, 37
Mitra, A. 85–87
Mullen, N. 22
Mündel, I. 137, 141

narrative voice 79–80, 104
National Performance Network out of Dance Theatre Workshop (New York) 131
Nelson, M. E. 32, 34
Next Exit (Atchley) 16–19
Noddings, N. 107–110

Obama, B. 84
Ochs, L. E. 70
O'Connell, P. 88

official voice 79–80
Oliver, K. 100–102, 106–108, 119
O'Neal, J. 21, 130
Ong, A. 53
oral history 73–74
oral storytelling 15, 65–67, 86; Atchley's digital storytelling practices and 19; Indigenous 114; literacy and multimodality in 33–35
Orlando Repertory Theatre (REP) 4
Orlando Union Rescue Mission project 81

Page, R. 66
Participatory Action Research (PAR) 147
performance of self 63, 64, 81
personal narratives 1, 6, 9–10, 15–16, 115, 127, 150–151; artistic 85; audience reception of 78–83; audio assets 28, 31; authenticity in 10, 63–76; author in 43; authorship in construction of texts 35–37; based co-creative practices 71–73; combination and construction 32–33; composing 50; as co-productive practice 48; defined 2; digital storytelling, emergence of 16–23; genre of digital storytelling 23–25; limitations 133; literacy and multimodality 33–35; political nature of 50–51; role of institution in 54; storyboarding 28, *29–30*; StoryCenter's training to create 23; story composition considerations 128; story-sharing considerations 129–130; visual elements 31–32; writing process 27
Poitras Pratt, Y. 141, 149
Poletti, A. 79, 80
political listening 103–104, 116, 137, 141
prescription, concept of 67, 70, 115

queer 57–59, 94, 113
Queering the Museum 57–59, 94

radio narratives 66–67, 93, 150
Raley, R. 90
Rappaport, J. 85–87
reciprocity 78, 144–145; caring relationship and 107; of identity formation 54
recognition 64–65, 113; as driving factor 106; giving voice 104; institutions aim to receiving 57; witness beyond 101
reflexivity 3, 10, 81, 135, 146
refugees 52
relevance, for digital storytelling facilitators 144
research questions, formation of 5
respecting, storytellers 21, 82, 125–126, 144–145
response-ability 6, 87–88, 101, 123; by active witnessing and faith-based listening 119; creating opportunity to enable 13; dialogue and 107–108, 133, 134; listening creating 103; of narrator 101; principles behind framework of 8–11; subjectivity in 101
response-able facilitation 13, 37, 126; digital storytelling and 6–7; framework of 6–8, 119–121, 139; goal of 6; tool for 131
responsibility: ethics of 100–104; and voice 104–106
Revealing Queer 94
Rice, C. 137, 141
Riessman, C. K. 71, 91
Robert, N. 57–59
Ross, L. 102
Russo, A. 55
Ryan, M.-L. 46–47

San Francisco Digital Media Center 15, 22
Saper, C. 17
screenings 88–89, 138; consensus zones in 90; end-of-workshop 5, 89; face-to-face 90; inclusion of videos in 94; live 89–91; of youth-created documentaries 90
self-reflection 146–148, 151
Skærbæk, E. 108
Smith, L. T. 83
space, workshop 2–4, 12, 57, 143, 148–149; considerations of 121–123; defined 122; digital literacy education in 82; of encounters 88–94; facilitators and participants in 63, 70–71; group guidelines in setup of 123–127; place, considerations of 122; political listening and 116; safe space, creating 123; story-sharing in 129

Space Atlas (Atchley) 17
Spurgeon, C. 24, 48, 129, 139–140
stakeholders 65, 71, 94–95, 112; and agents 48; audience as *see* audience as stakeholder; institutional 4, 9, 56, 59; organizational 110
Stewart, Cal case 66–67
storyboarding 16, 28, 31–32, 132; advanced template 30; basic template 29; creation of 27
StoryCenter 1–2, 4, 12, 16, 27, 34, 94; artist + festival model of 88–89; growth of 6; guidelines 125; motto of 69; offering consulting and workshops 23–24; participation of 57; story work, defined by 25; training to create personal narratives 15
story circles 16, 21–22, 37, 83, 91; defined 68; hosting 122; as peer-feedback approach 130, 131; self-making and being-made in 53; uses of 68–70
story composition 25, 143, 146; considerations for 127–129; as layering process 26, 28; multimodal 33–34; performance of self in 81; professional media and citizen 91
story dissemination 5, 36, 57–59, 114; considerations for 137–141; critical questions considering 138; digital 78, 83–85, 89, 91–94; digital media platforms for 87–88; facilitator influence on 94–96; public 139; ways of 95–96, 140; *see also* story distribution
story distribution 16, 82, 103, 121; artist + festival method 88–89; in *Capture Wales* archive 55; considerations for 137–141; digital 93–94, 139; distributed unevenly 86; in hard copy format 139; methods of 88–89, 96, 129
story-sharing 15–16, 20–21, 76, 80, 116, 127; components and themes for 75; considerations for 129–137; critical feedback structure, developing 131–137; digital stories 82–83, 89, 141; within digital storytelling platforms 57; facilitator influence on dissemination and 94–95; group 50–51; medium for 86–87; personal histories 58; private, personal experiences 51–53, 69, 79, 92; reciprocity in 78; situations to 5; steps to Critical Response Process 132–135; storyteller voice in 121; through collaborative process 64–65; from welsh citizens 93; "why tell" function and 46
storytelling: author in autobiographical 43–48; digital storytelling as co-creative media 48–49; immediate influences on storyteller 49; institution, role of 54–59; as political 49–53; as resource 83–87; "why tell" function of 46–48; *see also* digital storytelling; oral storytelling; personal narratives
story work 22, 25, 126, 138
Stumm, B. 53, 103–106
subjectivity 106–108, 147; of CAC's selection process 58; form of ethical responsibility 101; form of response-ability 101; inter-subjectivity 109; in relation to witnessing 101
Sykes, P. 130

Tacchi, J. 105–106
tactical media 57, 85–86, 90
tallstoreez productionz program 120
Taub-Pervizpour, L. 90, 110–112
Taylor, C. 64
tellability of story 46–47, 80
theatre programs 16–17, 123, 130–131, 150; applied practices 4; Orlando Repertory Theatre 4; radical 20
Traber, M. 100
trust 56, 66, 72, 101–102, 113, 136–137; *see also* faith
Tufte, E. 28, 33

Um Milhão de Histórias de Vida de Jovens project 138
user-generated media 120–121, 139

Vandendorpe, C. 36–37
van Zoonen, Liesbet 63–64
vernacular creativity 3, 17, 46, 51
video narratives 4, 76, 143
voice-over 27, 28, 31, 72, 74
voices 5, 21–23, 63, 108–109, 150–151; defined 105; female 109; giving 13, 48, 50, 104–106, 138;

listening, impact on 103; narrative 79–80, 104; official 79–80; ordinary 51; participants 3, 114; responsibility and 104–106; in story-sharing and storymaking spaces 121; of storyteller 6, 7, 11, 121; students 110–111, 114; writers' 10

Watkins, J. 55
White, H. 27
"why tell" function 46–48
Wilkinson, M. 3, 147
Willox, C. 80–81, 95, 113–114, 138
witnessing 68, 106–107, 127, 130, 145, 151; active 119; bearing 101, 104; beyond recognition 101; and caring 107–108; ethics of responsibility and 100–102; eyewitness 66, 100, 101; in relationship to other 101; of women 108–109

women 106; care work 106; personal is political 50–51; witnessing of 108–109

writing process 2, 36–37, 84, 150; autobiographical 44–45, 53; co-creative 11; concise 15; creative 3, 10–12, 25–27, 150; digital 36; facilitator-led 128; official voice for 79; spaces 1; *see also* personal narratives

Young, I. M. 51–52, 82

zine culture 99–100
zone of proximal development framework 110